Architectural Guide
Honolulu Oahu

Buildings in Hawaii's Capital

Architectural Guide
Honolulu Oahu

Buildings in Hawaii's Capital

Edited by Martin Despang with DeSoto Brown, William Chapman, and Don Hibbard

DOM
publishers

Contents

Buildings and Projects

Essays

Paradisal

Martin Despang

Honolulu? Hawaii? Architecture? You probably expected something about nature! That is how your author was initially introduced to DOM city guides through the edition about my hometown of Hanover, in which the author Professor Zvonko Turkali characterized his hometown of Hanover by its baroque garden and city forest. Honolulu, even more unsurprisingly, abounds in natural beauty, with the blue Pacific Ocean in front, lush green mountains behind, and palm-tree-dotted golden beaches in between. Situated on the opposite side of the world to Germany, Hawaii's most significant difference is its underlying climate. On one side of the world, the Despang Architekten contributions to DOM Hanover include the city's first post-fossil preschool – a tremendous, perhaps even overachieved effort to reach carbon neutrality while coping with freezing winters and increasingly frequent summer heatwaves. On the other side of the world in Honolulu – the most remote place from all other landmasses on Earth – the same bioclimatic result can be achieved with the most minimal effort using traditional methods by allowing the consistently cool wind to blow through shaded spaces during the day and night, year-round, to constantly provide comfortable temperatures. This idyllic place known as Hawaii is blessed not only with trade winds, but also with mostly moderate humidity – unlike most places in the muggy tropics. This makes it an architectural paradise, where no thermal breaks are needed, as indoor and outdoor spaces seamlessly blend and blur all year round. Honolulu, on the island of Oahu, became Hawaii's most recent capital in 1845. Geologically it was created by volcanos; mythologically it was created

by Pele, the goddess of volcanoes. She sculpted two mountain ranges: the Ko'olau and Waianae Mountains. Captain Cook's descendants created a concrete jungle in the little remaining space between the mountains and the sea. The initial Polynesians who discovered the islands were blessed with fertile volcanic soil that supported year-round food growing and lived an easy, breezy life in 'hales' – simple tectonic shelters using tree trunks for the structure and lashed on grass thatch as the roof – to protect themselves from sun and rain. Much later, haole missionaries in following told Hawaiians to overdress themselves and their buildings with 'muumuu' and imported their related 'styles' in clothing as well as buildings. The following colonizer was the United States. The ultimate act of incorporation – the annexation of Hawaii as the 50th state – was culturally questionable, yet architecturally, it was a highly progressive mid-century American treat, as mid-century modern masters ensured their buildings took full advantage of Hawaii's unique climate. This heyday of pioneering 'forgot' to take Hawaiians along and make them part of that architectural rat pack (including Americans Pete Wimberly and Edwin Bauer; Austrian Alfred Preis; Russian-born, Japan-raised Vladimir Ossipoff; and Takashi Anbe, born in Hawaii of Japanese descent). Since the Reagan era and continuing to the present day, it is too often the opposite: imported International Style glass high-rises artificially air conditioned using imported oil, with prices reaching record highs in the nation. Given where this author literally and figuratively comes from (Hanover), here in Honolulu he would have liked to skip all of the historicist

Natural and artifical volcanoes
Photo: Lenny Despang

Full Hawaii(an) compass, inspired by the Breakers Hotel entrance aerial photograph's compass

post-contact built environments, following the great raw model of Vladimir Belogolovsky with his recently released DOM Chicago guide, which covers buildings from 1978 onwards only. However, all of the authors decided to do this book together with equal contributions and collaboration; the hierarchy on the book's cover is purely due to compliance with the publisher's standards. Following fundamental discussions, the authors agreed to base the selection of the buildings on cultural and climatic appropriateness. So, the book is mainly made up of buildings that do the same as humans used to do here: stay out of the sun and rain and in the cooling trade winds. The 'colonial' buildings dominating the beginning of the book might not seem to fully fit these criteria, although they had to work without artificial air conditioning as it was not available. They introduced thermal mass stereotomics using stone and later concrete walls, which were foreign to the original, easy breezy tectonics that either had no walls or later used single wooden wall constructions like those of the efficient, effective plantation houses. Thermal mass is generally and traditionally avoided in the tropics, but when it is constantly cooled by the nearly continuously blowing breezes, it can keep buildings cool, which is how these early imported buildings managed to be somewhat comfortable.

The missionaries complained about rain leaking through the thatched roof, which was not absolutely watertight. This was of no relevance to the native Hawaiians. Native Hawaiians, unlike the missionaries overdressed 'stuff', wore minimal natural, handmade clothing that required little maintenance. While your author Martin does not excuse the climatic and therefore cultural inappropriateness of early missionary architecture, the author team decided that this historical information should not to be hidden from you, the reader, for 'ideological' reasons. The following generations of mid-century modernism, however, seem to have learned from the past and made up for the earlier missionary muumuu stle, creating buildings that were technologically Western but operationally and environmentally Hawaii(an); however, they were created primarily not for Hawaiians – and even less so by Hawaiians. Equally consequential to the cultural domination of the missionaries was the arrival of the combustion engine, which brought the most disastrous change to this paradise: enclosed fossil-fueled automobiles and architecture. Since the 1980s, this author has consequently observed an ongoing return to missionary-style architectural manners with commercially-, climatically-, and culturally-driven hermetic buildings using double-loaded corridors rather than the naturally ventilated

Simplified Hawaii(an) compass

circulation used previously, and little to no use of the lanai as the predominant outdoor form of living, which offered roofed protection from sun and rain and remained open to the trade winds. See the following essay by Curt, which describes in detail the current condition of buildings that attempt to fool you by using pseudo-Hawaiian décor and names. The essay was written in the 1990s in the midst of this ongoing dilemma, but your authors decided to republish it here unedited in its original form. So, you are spared from countless enclosed box-like buildings and instead presented with the synergy between the melding of the world's most stunning natural and built environments. Author DeSoto – the only one of Hawaiian decent – insisted that collaborators Rainer and Helena create the north arrow in the form of a 'Hawaii(an) compass' as north, south, east, and west are not sufficient for DeSoto for orientation, as his ancestors discovered the Hawaiian Islands only with the help of stars, birds, and wind. Thus, even on land, one continues to navigate using the natural environment: makai (the Pacific Ocean), mauka (the mountains), Diamond Head (volcano). The midday sun is the highest from the south and rises east and sets west, which for many locations in Honolulu is rising at mauka and setting at makai. The wind direction indicated on your Hawaii(an) compass is the predominant one from the northeast and the cooling trade wind effect, named after early maritime trading when sailing ships came straight down from the Pacific Northwest of the US. Occasionally, Kona winds come from the south to bring humid conditions and 'vog' – smog of volcanic particles from the Big Island and its active volcanoes. This can make it harder to breathe, but it is beautiful to see sunsets tinted in hazy orange. As with everything in Hawaii, all moments are part of its extraordinary and exhilarating beauty. If you get excited about a climate- and culture-compliant building that you read about, you will find a related QR code in the video archive in the appendix. This will guide you to another 30- to 45-minute YouTube video by ThinkTech Hawaii's 'human(e) architecture' with extended information about the building. So, in many ways, this guide aims to be like the work of local architect artist Kaili Chun. You can simply browse through it like lovely land art in a pretty picture book or go deeper into its complex constructive critique. Has reading and viewing this sparked even more curiosity about Hawaii beyond Honolulu? There are other islands with stellar examples of mid-century tropical modernism. Perhaps Natascha Meuser and Philipp Meuser, the founders of DOM publishers, will share more about them in the future.

The View from the Lanai

Curt Sandburn

Late last year, I gave a very bad review to a book called *Architecture in Hawaii* in the *Honolulu Weekly*. I was angry with its fawning praise of some of the most hated new buildings in the state. In retrospect, my anger at the book disturbed me and made me wonder: If all these buildings are so rotten, what buildings in Hawaii are good – and why? Then I read a column on the subject of Hawaiian architecture by Star-Bulletin editor, Bud Smyser. Smyser's premise: that Hawaiian architecture should recreate its past as the best solution to the recent spate of ugly buildings. He calls for a return to 'kamaaina' architecture, a synthetic blend of traditional Asian, Polynesian, and European elements, similar to the 'kamaaina' style developed by Hawaii's early twentieth century architects. That style is illustrated by such well-known landmarks as the Alexander & Baldwin building, the Honolulu Academy of Arts, Honolulu Hale, and several buildings on the Punahou School campus. Smyser lists a few recent buildings, including the

Hyatt Kauai, the new Halekulani Hotel, and the Koele Lodge and the Manele Bay hotels on Lanai, as 'outstanding' examples of kamaaina architecture, and as a promising direction for contemporary building design. Outstanding? The massive Hyatt Kauai is plopped on the Poipu sand dunes like the Honolulu Academy of Arts on steroids; and the Koele Lodge is a rich man's hunting lodge as envisioned by Walt Disney. They're both fake. And no, we don't need imitation Punahou Schools all over the place in order to have taste or make practical, responsible, and inspiring buildings. Derivative architecture, no matter how pretty or nostalgic, is a clumsy dead end. If all architects subscribed to the notion of 'kamaaina architecture' there would be no possibility of extraordinary, innovative buildings, just the tasteful 'look' of a thousand double-pitch roofs, all the way to the horizon – sort of like Mililani. If it's not the past, then what is Hawaiian architecture? What buildings are good in Hawaii? What works? To the original Hawaiians, the lanai was central to life. As Hawaiians used the word, lanai was the outdoor area near the cooking and sleeping hale, shaded by hau, kou, and milo trees, where everything happened except sleep. Graciousness and hospitality were outdoors. Today, the purest approximation of the Hawaiian lanai is the weekend blue-tarp encampments at beach parks everywhere. The blue-tarp roofs keep things cool when the sun's out and dry when it rains, but that's all. The trade winds blow right through. That simple 'No need!' ethic is evident in any number of local architectural forms today, most of them overlooked by Hawaii's status-conscious taste makers and architects: 1) ... the typical, unambitious, one-story, single-wall-construction Kailua/Kahala house, a series of small rooms built around a large, epicentric, indoor/outdoor lanai and set in a garden. These post-Second World War houses, considered (until recently) Hawaii's most desirable suburban housing stock, celebrate two things at once: the ritual of family interaction on the communal lanai and the beauty of nature just beyond the lanai. These are the houses being demolished in record numbers to make way for Oahu's grand, air-conditioned new lifestyle. 2) ... the cool, white concrete, high-rise 'lanai stacks' that dot Honolulu; for example, the Colony Surf on Kalakaua Avenue, Banyan Tree Plaza at Punahou and Beretania Streets, Uraku Tower on Kapiolani Boulevard, 500 University Avenue, and scores of buildings in Makiki, McCully, and Waikiki. These well-ventilated apartment buildings, condos and hotels, with their backs to the Koolaus, with open hallways and ocean-facing lanais for every unit, are cheap to build, honest, and functional. Neither arrogant nor mysterious, they've also become quite attractive, in that they have come to characterize sunny Honolulu more than any other building type, much like San Francisco's bay-windowed flats. An artful variation on the lanai stack is Skidmore Owings and Merrill's pristine, double-stacked Mauna Kea Beach Hotel

The view (writing) from the lanai (The Seashore's)

on the Big Island. Its low-rise atrium design has been widely copied, but its grace has never been matched. 3) ... in the work of Hawaii's greatest contemporary architect, Vladimir Ossipoff: Of note, the huge lanai-spaces of his handsome late 1960s renovation of Honolulu International Airport, since ruined by the addition of shops, and his many modernist houses. It was Ossipoff who first saw the connection between the lanai and classical modernist architecture. His masterpieces: the sublime Pacific Club and the practical Outrigger Canoe Club, both of which are intelligent and perfectly resolved meditations on the function – and form – of the lanai. There are hundreds of other examples, just look around at how the best buildings work: the State Capitol with its wide tiered lanais (where all the state's deal-making gets done), wrapped around the central atrium ... older elementary schools, virtually all lanai ... the storefronts in Kapahulu, Kaimuki, and Hilo with their thoughtful overhangs shading the sidewalk, creating a continuous lanai-

façade on the street. The function of the lanai is obvious: it promotes outdoor life; the form of the lanai is by definition horizontal: wider or longer – not taller. This horizontal-ness is so ingrained in Hawaii's buildings and way of life that soaring lobbies and grand, arching entrances, not to mention sleek 'look-at-me!' towers, seem out of place here and somehow pretentious. There is modesty in horizontal-ness; an openness, a deference to nature – and what should Hawaiian architecture be if not deferential to nature? For many years, Western builders merely attached the lanai, the outdoor space, to conventional buildings – with generally pleasing results. From the earliest improvements made to the traditional grass hale, wherein the roof was angled outward and extended to create a skirt sheltering a wrap-around porch (the historical basis for the double-slope 'Hawaiian' roofline), to plantation housing with its requisite front porches, to the broad verandahs of the old Haleiwa Hotel and the Moana Hotel, to the tiny, vestigial balconies

on downtown residential towers, the lanai has proved an essential element of island architecture. But it is only when the lanai becomes the central element of a building, when the building itself is a lanai or collection of lanais, that the building becomes Hawaiian. Mr. Smyser and the architectural establishment may think they're being responsible, or sensitive, when they copy Honolulu's grand old civic buildings to create an office park or a resort hotel, but the real challenge to architects is to create something new ... and functional and efficient and honest and beautiful. There is an alternative to getting stuck in the past, and it's called 'modernism'. It is practical, egalitarian, efficient, and it readily lends itself to the central Hawaiian living space: the lanai. High-rise or low-rise, public or private, the lanai works. No decoration, no pomposity, just functional space, outlining its volume in straight lines, sitting light on the land, drinking in the view, letting the trade winds blow right through the building.

Beach Pavilions

Curt Sanburn (2015; updated by Don Hibbard, 2025)

'They're simple little buildings, totally different from the mainland. They take advantage of the weather.' Honolulu architectural historian Don Hibbard makes this observation as we talk about Oahu's wonderful if troubled collection of beach park pavilions or 'comfort stations' or restrooms or toilets or whatever you call them. They're threatened by a lot of things – by rust and rot and vandals, but mostly by neglect. Times change, homelessness is a scourge and senseless vandalism is a plague, but so is the thoughtless bureaucratic urge to make it newer, safer, and easier to clean. People will always need to use the facilities (another euphemism), and it would be smart if we could somehow continue to offer ourselves – and the rent-a-car hordes – the unique cultural experience that is Honolulu's heritage of great beach pavilion design, for years to come. Primarily developed during the 1950s–1970s period, the pavilions, while following a basic pattern, present distinctive, individual design solutions, with a multitude of different architects having been commissioned to design them. Some beach pavilions are indelible in the local mind: the Waialae Beach Park pavilion, with its quatrefoil columns raising its pleated roof well above its toilet stalls and shower

Photo: Martin Despang

Makapuu Pavilion on the beach

rooms; or the stark, lava-rock fortress at Makapuu, whose ramparts hide an extraordinarily graffitied and stinky men's toilet and changing room – from which you might want to look up through the partially open roof to see the sky and the Koolau rampart looming overhead; or Kailua Beach's grand pavilion-in-a-parking lot, so busy and so used! Hibbard says his favorite beach pavilion is the rustic comfort station huddled under the kamani trees at Kahana Bay landing, operated by the state's parks division. A pile of big lava-rock boulders with massive log beams and open rafters, the building, designed in 1964 by architect Robert Law,

feels primal and so firmly rooted to the place that it will never leave. Law and his partner James Wilson also designed the Waikiki Shell, the state DOT building on Punchbowl Street, and two important churches: the Kalihi Union Church on North King and the Church of the Holy Nativity on Kalanianaole Highway in Aina Haina. Hibbard and I talk about restoration and maintenance issues. 'I'm surprised that most of them are graffiti free,' he says. 'Maybe people seem to respect them too much for that.' I casually toured about 20 of Oahu's pavilions in mid-April to see for myself how they're doing. Many were graffiti free, but not all. A few,

Photo: Martin Despang

Hawaii Kai pavilion

Waimanalo Beach pavilion

mostly along the heavily trafficked southeast coast, had lots of graffiti, including, in a neat, red-inked font, libelous charges of pederasty, pyromania, thievery, money laundering, and yakuza connections made against named individuals. 'NALO', someone else scrawled, big and bold. 'Leave the f...en toilet paper alone, dummiez,' read one stall, with its messy stack of tiny sheets purveyed from an improvised wood shelf screwed into the cinder-block. At Kokololio Beach Park in Hauula, someone jerry-rigged a cut-open plastic milk jug to dispense TP. Happily for everybody, I can report that most of our pavilions come furnished with some sort of toilet paper supply (but not all!), and I'll guess that women's toilets do better. Broken fixtures – sinks, drinking fountains, urinals, toilets – covered with black plastic garbage bags were not uncommon. Most faucets worked, but some did not or had broken drain pipes. Waimanalo Beach Park has two distinct pavilions serving it: a small concrete-block comfort station with a butterfly roof set under the ironwoods near the beach and parking lot, while the larger, older pavilion, erected in 1959 and designed by Denver-born architect Frank Slavsky, is set back from the beach in a large lawn adjacent to the play field. Its main feature is a grand, central A-frame roof that looks like a big, open-air hale or longhouse, except for the massive concrete trusses on boldly canted footings. The stained concrete flooring is shiny and cool; on the weekday that I visited, there were bicycles, carts,

backpacks, coolers, and other camping/living gear stashed here and there inside and outside the hale. Front-and-center is a plaque affixed to the massive lava-rock wall that closes off the hale's south end: 'Waimanalo Beach Park Pavilion,' it reads. 'Dedicated to Gabby "Pop" Pahinui, 22 April 1921 – 13 October 1980.' Maybe a dozen people loll about around the Waimanalo hale perimeter. They talk among themselves and give me the finger when I take a few pictures of the room. In a lava-rock and concrete-block men's room that has seen better days, some guy's personal articles spill out from under a stall door. The man inside makes some noises as I approach but doesn't come out. No TP in the stalls. The soigné Haleiwa Beach Park pavilion was likewise home to a small family of presumably homeless folks on the day I visited, with their belongings strewn about the north end of the elongated pavilion. The building, which is mostly a long, vineless pergola with toilets deftly fitted in, was designed in the 1930s, according to historian Hibbard, by New Mexico-native Harry Sims Bent, the architect for the Honolulu Board of Parks in the late 1930s. With its elegant elongations and simplified slot openings, the structure, Hibbard observes, recalls the deco-inflected walls and pergola at Mother Waldron Playground, or Ala Moana Beach Park's original gateways and bridges, or the walls at Kawananakoa Playground in Nuuanu, all of them designed by Bent. I visit Ewa Beach Park and discover an amazing modernist dream, full of culturally rich meaning and rational efficiency: a sweeping green lawn that leads to the beach and the huge, open-sided roof of a great abstracted gesture of a Hawaiian hale. Next to it, along the park's boundary, is a very long cream-colored and faintly gridded wall, about seven feet high and made of square cement blocks. The wall zig-zags at 90-degree angles by the freestanding hale then reaches out in a straight line all the way to the beach dune. The zig-zags ingeniously hide the completely roofless (this is Ewa Beach!) men's and women's changing areas and toilets on the inside, while the angles define the two shower areas. It's the most beautiful beach pavilion I've ever seen, and it's not in bad shape. Don Hibbard tells me it was designed by Potter & Potter architects back in 1956, during architectural modernism's first bloom across the nation. London-born Mark Potter, a direct descendant of the renowned London architect Christopher Wren, also designed Kilohana, the Wilcox mansion just outside Lihue, Kauai, and, later, the modernist State Archive building that glints from behind the banyan tree at Iolani Palace. Hibbard suspects Potter's son, Gordon Potter, had a hand in the pavilion. Many of the older pavilions, in the words of Jon Hennington, the former public information officer for the city's Department of Parks and Recreation, 'though they're beautiful, are conducive to vandalism and mis-use. They're closed off visually from the outside, so it's quite labor intensive to inspect and clean them. And once they reach a certain age, there are stains and odors you can't remove. That's why there's sometimes a perception that a facility hasn't been cleaned, when most of our facilities are cleaned multiple times a day.' The parks department, with an annual budget of $65 million, runs 65 beach parks out of a total of nearly 300 named parks on Oahu. The newest comfort station the city built is at Nani Kai Beach Park in Maili. Maintenance and vandalism concerns continue to exist at a number of the beach pavilions and public restrooms, with the destruction of the problem always an enticing 'solution'. A sad case in point was the demolition of the Frank Slavsky-designed pavilion at Waimanalo Beach Park in 2019, due to structural safety concerns, while the picturesque lava rock restrooms designed by Shizu Oka at Kamamalu Playground have been fenced off, depriving park users of the use of the facility, in an effort to address the urban nomads' use of the premises. Destruction of such aesthetically pleasing public amenities does not solve the 'homeless problem', but it does make the lives of all of us a little bit poorer.

Photo: Curt Sandburn

The richness of the former Waimanalo pavilion

Indigenous

DeSoto Brown

Today we expect construction materials to come from literally anywhere on the planet that we choose. We trust that not only will individuals and businesses provide these raw elements for us, but that modern transportation technology will deliver them to our selected site on schedule. Obviously such expectations have only been possible for a very short segment of the total span of human existence on Earth. In the past, only materials within a confined radius of any particular place were available, and ingenuity was required to work with them. This was especially true in cultures like that of the indigenous people of the Hawaiian Islands, who only had themselves to carry, pull, slide, or roll objects over distances, lacking both wheeled vehicles and large animals that might assist in labor. They furthermore had no metal for tools or fasteners like nails or screws. Yet they obviously created and inhabited structures of different kinds. The topographies and climates of Hawaii are extremely varied, and in fact it is one of the most diverse such places on Earth, with conditions ranging from alpine (with snow and ice) to rain forests and deserts. Obviously the materials available for construction would be correspondingly varied as well,

but the most common type of home structure would have been as follows. First, a low stone foundation would be constructed. Around this, upright, lightly finished house posts would be anchored into the ground, several feet deep. Then multiple thin members made of thin branches would be tied together horizontally all along the walls and roof beams, forming a framework. Onto this would then be lashed thatching that could be made from different plants, but most often a particular type of grass (pili) tied in numerous bundles. These would be positioned tightly together to form what then appeared to be a fairly solid, shaggy exterior surface. In the nineteenth century, this came to be called a 'grass house' by foreigners, with the Hawaiian term 'hale pili' having the same meaning. Traditionally, Hawaiians lived in clusters of different types of hale pili that would have had different uses. They rarely spent time indoors during the day, working outside in the usually warm and benign climate. What we would think of as a 'house' was normally used just for sleeping at night, on stacks of mats woven from different plants. The only indoor nighttime lighting was either from a small fire or dim 'candles' made of oily kukui nuts.

Photo: DeSoto Brown

The only surviving historic hale pili, now in Bishop Museum

When it got dark, you went to sleep pretty early. Hale pili had no windows, and the single doorway was small and low, requiring adults to stoop down or crawl through it. These were usually fitted with solid wood panels on the inside that could be pushed down to close them. Hawaiians continued to build and live in their traditional structures during the nineteenth century, but as outside influences continued to be introduced, mostly from the United States, they made use of new materials as well. Historic photographs show hale pili with full-sized manufactured wooden doors and glass windows by the late 1800s, incorporated into the grass walls and roofs of ancient times. But by about 1900, the hale pili was approaching extinction. After the Bernice P. Bishop Museum in Honolulu opened to the public in 1891, the awareness of the need to preserve physical artifacts of traditional Hawaiian culture was growing. This led to the search for an actual surviving hale pili made in the old style, and one was found in Milolii, Kauai, on private land. It was no longer inhabited, and the landowner donated it to the museum. It was dismantled, brought to Honolulu, and then reconstructed in the museum's Hawaiian Hall in 1902. Still standing there today, it is the only authentic surviving such structure in existence. It must be pointed out, however, that even with this provenance, the structure in Bishop Museum has undergone the same regular refurbishing and repairs that any

Hale pili model in Bishop Museum

hale pili would have experienced in ancient times. Primarily the grass thatching would have fallen apart through damage by sunlight and weather as well as wear caused by humans. The plant fibers used to make cordage that tied together the building's framework would themselves deteriorate, too. So, over time, the Bishop Museum's valued grass house has been re-thatched and re-lashed as well. Since the early twentieth century, traditional-style Hawaiian hale pili have been reconstructed numerous times for displays, props, educational uses, and photographic backdrops. These have ranged from being as close to authentic as possible to crude and inaccurate copies. And just like the originals, the succession of these replicas over time have succumbed to the forces of nature, just as their predecessors did. We can be grateful, however, that documentation of the true and historic techniques and materials exists, as well as the knowledge of how to use them, to preserve these forever.

Early European illustration, 1782

Nineteenth Century

1

Hawaiian Mission Houses

553 S King St
Honolulu, HI 96813
Various
1821–1832

001 B

The present site of the Mission Houses Museum was the original headquarters of the Sandwich Islands Mission. The first wave of Protestant missionaries and their families arrived on Hawaii Island in 1820; Hiram Bingham and his wife, Sybil Mosely Bingham, moved to Honolulu on Oahu shortly afterward, finding housing originally in a thatched hut provided by their patron, Queen Kaahumanu. The existing frame building, constructed with materials shipped via Cape Horn and supplemented by locally procured wood members and reused siding from another early Honolulu building, dates to 1821. This first mission house resembled vernacular buildings in New England, complete with an attached kitchen and full basement – both features discarded in later building practice in the islands. The roof also omitted overhanging eaves, following New England precedents, but not accounting for Hawaii's needs for shade. The building and site experienced several changes at an early stage. A prominent wall gable was added to the mauka (mountain) side in the 1820s; and in deference to the tropical climate, a balcony and porch was appended to the 'Ewa (west) end around 1841. In 1831, a larger coral block building, known as the Chamberlain House (after its first residents), was added adjacent to the original dwelling. This building housed the missionaries' agent and a warehouse for supplies arriving periodically from Boston. Other buildings, including an additional residence and several utilitarian structures, were also added in the early nineteenth century. Converted in 1851 to use as a private house and dormitory for Hawaiian students, the old mission station became the property of the Hawaiian Mission Children's Society in 1925. Repurposed as a museum, the property became the subject of a major restoration effort in 1935, under the supervision of noted Hawaii regionalist architect C. W. Dickey. Since that time the Mission Houses Historic Site and Museum has hosted a library and offices of the Hawaiian Historical Society. A recent addition to the site is a replica thatched house interpreting the first year of the missionaries' residence in Honolulu. *WC*

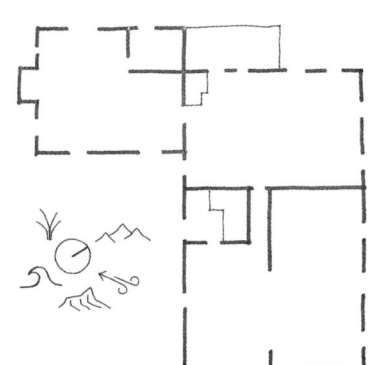

Photo: DeSoto Brown

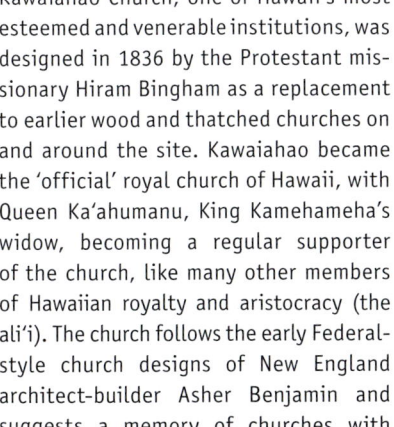

Kawaiahao Church

002 B

957 Punchbowl St
Honolulu, HI 96813
Hiram Bingham
1842

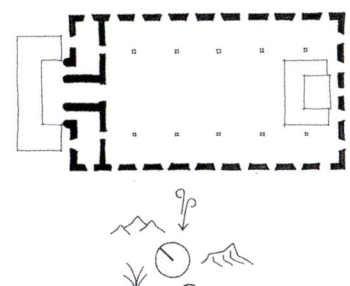

Kawaiahao Church, one of Hawaii's most esteemed and venerable institutions, was designed in 1836 by the Protestant missionary Hiram Bingham as a replacement to earlier wood and thatched churches on and around the site. Kawaiahao became the 'official' royal church of Hawaii, with Queen Kaʻahumanu, King Kamehameha's widow, becoming a regular supporter of the church, like many other members of Hawaiian royalty and aristocracy (the aliʻi). The church follows the early Federal-style church designs of New England architect-builder Asher Benjamin and suggests a memory of churches with which Bingham was familiar in his youth. Utilizing local materials, significantly

some 14,000 cut coral blocks dredged off the nearby coast, the church represented the sustained effort of Native Hawaiian church members, who volunteered their time in the building's construction, for which the total budget was $20,000. Wood members were from local sources, the timber for the roof extracted from the mountains behind Waialua. Other elements such as windows and furnishings were made from imported materials. The original roofing shingles,

002 B

however, were locally fashioned and procured. Completed in 1842 and dedicated on 21 July before the gallery had been completed, the church regularly attracted congregations in the thousands in its early years. The original low church tower and spire housed Honolulu's first public clock, installed in 1850. The present church tower was completed in 1885. The church became the site of baptisms, coronations (or inaugurations), and funerals for several generations of Hawaiian ali'i; portraits of many of Hawaii's early rulers and family members are displayed in the gallery. The block-like sanctuary was subject to extensive repairs in 1928, 1965, and 1977, efforts resulting in the substitution of metal windows for the original wood windows and changes to the interior gallery spaces. (The original scored and parged stones were covered in cement in 1928 but stripped in 1966, changing the overall appearance of the exterior walls). A popular wedding venue for visitors to the islands, Kawaiahao Church has an active ministry and features services and choral events in the Hawaiian language. A cemetery adjacent to the church is the resting place of early Protestant missionaries and their families; a second section was reserved for Native Hawaiian members of the congregation. In addition to the church, the site includes a well, gateways, and a surrounding coral block wall. The church property also features an 1835-period adobe schoolhouse, designed by the late nineteenth-century teacher Amos Starr Cooke. The

Gothic-style Royal Mausoleum, erected in 1876, is a memorial to the popular King Lunaliho. It was designed by Robert Lishman, then Hawaii's superintendent of public works. *WC*

Melcher's Building ↗

003 B

51 Merchant St
Honolulu, HI 96813
Unknown
1854

Built in 1854, toward the end of the reign of King Kamehameha III, this simple Greek Revival-style commercial structure at 51 Merchant Street exemplifies the earliest period of Western construction in Honolulu. It now stands out as the oldest surviving commercial building in the city. Constructed of coral block excavated from the nearby harbor area, with an outer coating of lime plaster, the property resembled shops and warehouses in New England towns such as Nantucket and New Bedford, both important homes of the Yankee whaling fleet. The building was originally home to the firm of Gustav Melcher and Gustav Reiners. The shop featured koa wood shelves and glass cabinets. In 1867, it became the property of the firm's clerk F. A. Schaefer, who operated it for many years. Occupied early in the twentieth century by the Hawaii Dredging Co., the building's owners expanded the original four-bay-wide structure substantially in 1937. After being purchased by the City and County of Honolulu in 1960, it served as the city's prosecutors office. *WC*

Photo: Olivier Koning

Kamehameha V Post Office ↓   004 B

32 Merchant St
Honolulu, HI 96813
J. G. Osborne
1871

Started in 1870 and completed the following year, this distinctive legacy of the Kingdom of Hawaii employed an innovative construction system of precast concrete blocks, reinforced by iron bars. Then experimental in Europe and not yet applied in the US, this system led to the construction of several other concrete structures in Hawaii over the next several years. The principal concession to Hawaii's climate was the two story gallery spanning the structure's makai (ocean) side. In 1987, the American Society of Civil Engineers designated the then century-old structure a National Historic Civil Engineering Landmark. The Kingdom of Hawaii instituted a postal system in 1851, issuing 5 and 13 cent stamps for letters and a 2 cent stamp for papers. Operated as a private concession for many years, the postal service expanded its work in the 1860s. David Kalakaua, later Hawaii's monarch, ran the service from 1862 to 1865. A. P. Brickwood became the

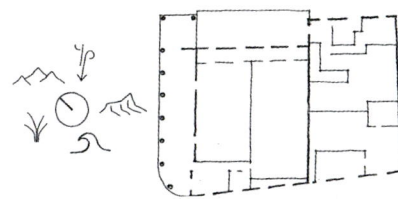

Photo: DeSoto Brown

postmaster in 1865, doing much to improve the system and pressing for a new building. King Kamehameha V laid the cornerstone for the edifice on 2 March 1870, and the building opened for business on 22 March 1871. J.G. Osborne, an 'experienced brickmaker' from Yorkshire, England, was the designer and contractor. He completed the job for $18,362.94. The Kingdom of Hawaii originally used the building for a variety of official purposes. However, in 1894, the Postal Department of the newly designated Republic of Hawaii took possession of the whole building. In the nineteenth century, there were separate windows on the lanai for Hawaiians, Japanese, and Portuguese. There was also a window for 'ladies' and one for stamp sales. In 1900, the old Post Office became a unit of the US Postal System. In 1922, operations moved to the new Federal Post Office near the palace. For several years, the building became the Territorial Tax Office and later the overflow quarters for the District Court. In 1993, the city renovated the building for use by the Kumu Kahua Theatre and as offices for the State Foundation on Culture and the Arts. *WC*

Aliiolani Hale

417 S King St
Honolulu, HI 96813
Thomas Rowe
1874

Originally planned as the royal palace, Aliiolani Hale is one of the defining elements of the Honolulu Capitol District. With its four-story clock tower, deeply rusticated walls and decorative paired columns, the Aliiolani Hale Hale serves as the backdrop for one of Hawaii's most revered art works, T.R. Gould's 18-foot bronze statue of King Kamehameha the Great. The sculpture is one of the most visited attractions in Honolulu. Utilizing a new structural system of reinforced concrete blocks, the neoclassical building historically housed governmental offices of the Kingdom of Hawaii and the courts. Conceived during the reign of Kamehameha V (who died shortly after laying the cornerstone on 19 February 1872), the impressive

five-section structure was completed by Australian (originally British) architect Thomas Rowe in 1874. The building closely resembles Palladian-style complexes in Great Britain, notably the Queen's Palace at Greenwich, designed by English architect Inigo Jones in the early seventeenth century. Until 1893, the building held most of the executive departments of the Hawaiian government, including the Hawaiian National Museum, which had a home there from the time of the building's completion. In 1911, the structure was gutted and extensively renovated to provide for additional space for offices and the courts. Aliiolani Hale has been the site of many of Hawaii's famous political and social events. In 1931, the famous Massey court proceedings took place within its walls. With the courts still facing a space shortage, a new wing was added to the building in the 1940s. The wing closely resembles the original

core building. In 1978 Architects-Hawaii Ltd., one of the state's leading architectural firms, undertook the rehabilitation and restoration of the structure. It now houses Hawaii Supreme Court offices and the Judiciary History Center. In 2005, archaeologists identified the location of the original time capsule placed at the cornerstone in 1872. The capsule contained photographs of royal personages, postage stamps, newspapers, a calendar, and books. In 2010, the building stood in for Iolani Palace on CBS's rebooted television series *Hawaii Five-0*. The site's statue of Kamehameha I depicts Hawaii's unifying king in the guise of a classical hero. The statue was commissioned by King Kalākaua's adviser Walter Murray Gibson to commemorate the hundredth anniversary of Captain James Cook's arrival in the Hawaiian Islands. Created in Florence and cast in Paris, the original statue sank off the Falkland Islands, requiring the making of a new version, which was installed in 1883, five years too late for the anniversary. In the meantime, the original statue was salvaged by fisherman and ended up in Honolulu, where it was relayed to the island of Hawaii to be erected near Kamehameha I's birthplace in North Kohala. *WC*

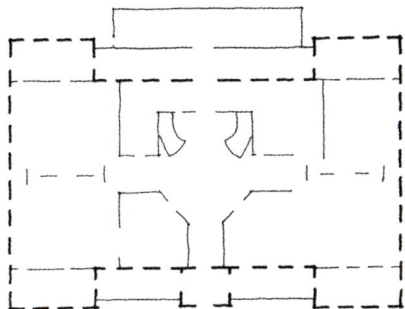

1

Photo: Bishop Museum, 1940

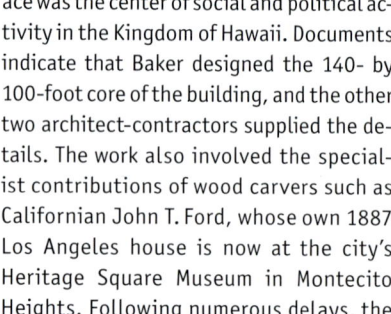

Iolani Palace

364 S King St,
Honolulu, HI 96813
Thomas J. Baker, Charles J. Wall,
Isaac Moore
1879–1882

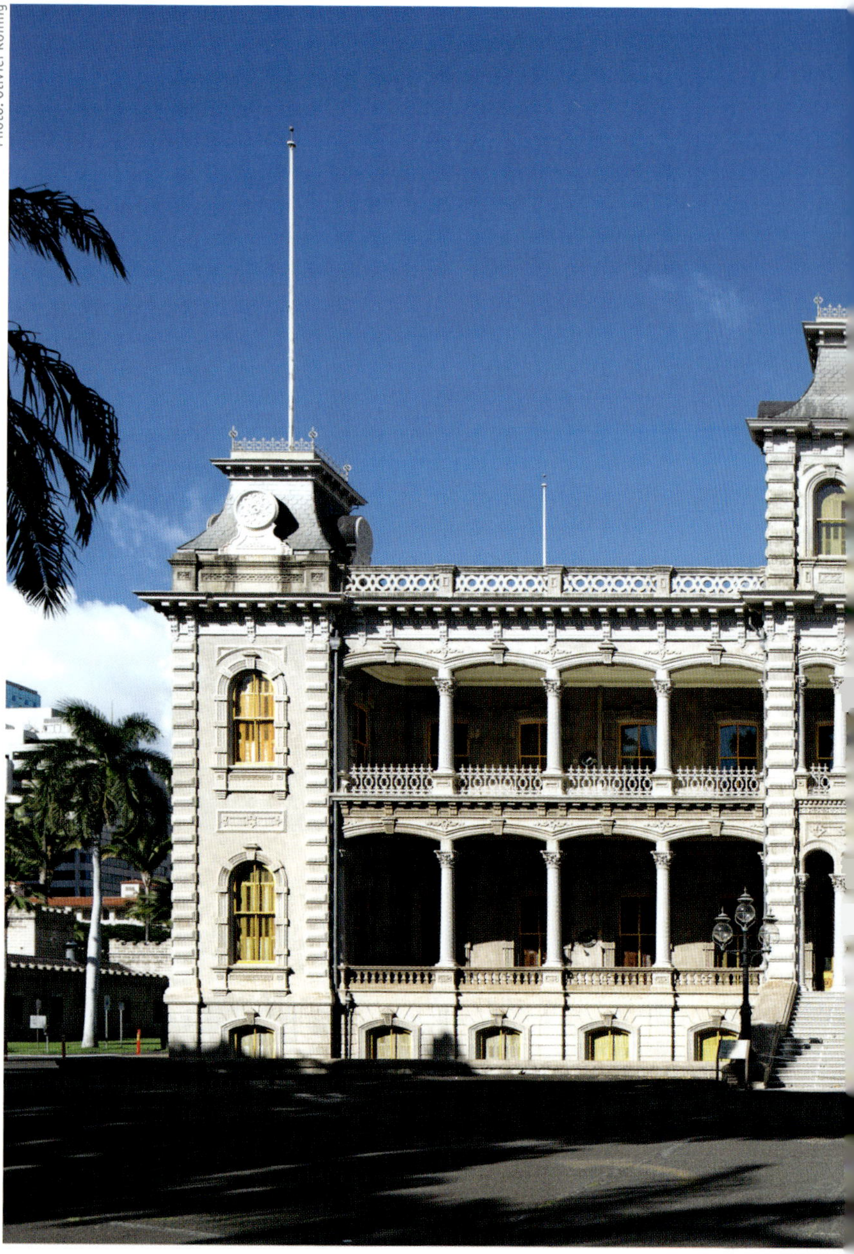

006 B

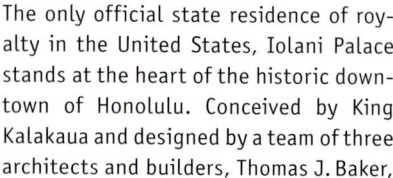

The only official state residence of royalty in the United States, Iolani Palace stands at the heart of the historic downtown of Honolulu. Conceived by King Kalakaua and designed by a team of three architects and builders, Thomas J. Baker, Charles J. Wall, and Isaac Moore, the palace was the center of social and political activity in the Kingdom of Hawaii. Documents indicate that Baker designed the 140- by 100-foot core of the building, and the other two architect-contractors supplied the details. The work also involved the specialist contributions of wood carvers such as Californian John T. Ford, whose own 1887 Los Angeles house is now at the city's Heritage Square Museum in Montecito Heights. Following numerous delays, the cornerstone for King Kalākaua's palace

was laid on 31 December 1879; it was completed in November 1882. The construction material is stucco-covered brick, with wood – both Douglas Fir and koa – used for floors, windows, and trim as well as the impressive central koa staircase leading from the main entry to the king and queen's living quarters above. The high basement follows the English convention, with a full height lightwell and additional wall space under the main floor. The cost of the building was $340,000, a large sum at the time. The style can be classified as Second Empire, though it was uniquely described as American Florentine Revival by Geoffrey Fairfax, architect for the 1970s restoration. Key features include the mansard-roofed corner towers, the open verandahs (lanai), and the rusticated quoins and other trim. Ornamental plaster distinguishes the interior spaces, which are distinctive as well for their draperies, fitted rugs, and unique features such as both electric and gas lighting and the first telephone in the islands. The palace remained the official

Photo: Kikuyo Hibbard

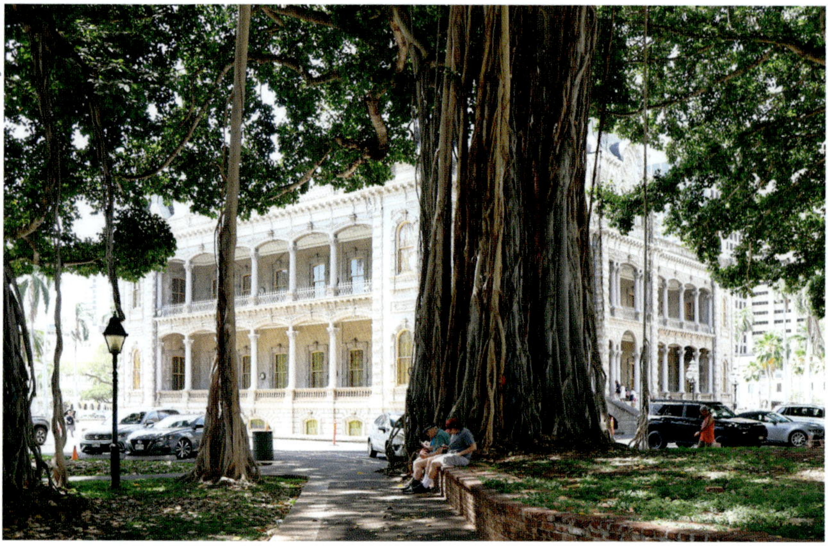

residence of the Hawaiian monarch until the 1893 overthrow of the Hawaiian kingdom by a mostly Euro-American faction. After the suppression of a counter revolution in 1895, Queen Liliuokalani was confined to a bedroom on the second floor for nine months. The palace served as the 'Executive Building' of the Republic of Hawaii and later as both offices and the capitol under the Territory of Hawaii. Most palace furnishings were sold, and the interior plan was altered to meet the requirements of government offices. In the 1930s, the interior was more thoroughly remodeled, using steel and reinforced concrete. During the Second World War, the palace served as the offices of the military governor. The first steps toward restoration came in the 1960s following the construction of a new state capitol, located to the north (mauka side). Designated a National Historic Landmark in 1962, the palace became the subject of a multi-year restoration initiated by the Junior League of Honolulu. In 1966, the Friends of Iolani Palace assumed control of the property, developing it as a museum. In addition to the main palace, the grounds of the palace area include a coronation pavilion constructed in 1880 for David Kalākaua's ceremony. This segmental dome-roofed structure was subsequently altered in the 1920s through the addition of a concrete base and has since served as the bandstand for the Royal Hawaiian band. The 1871 'Iolani

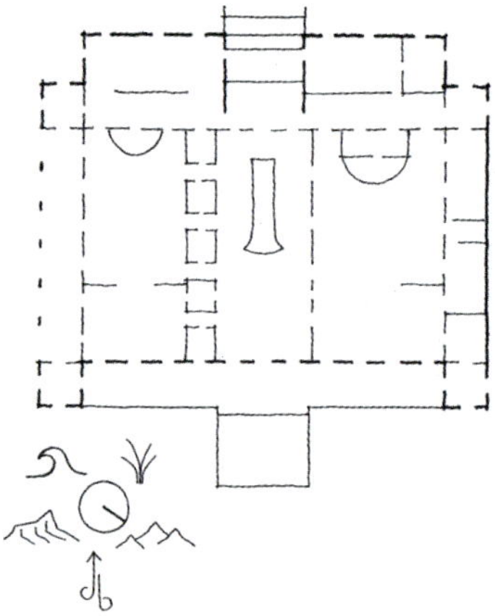

Barracks, now located to the northwest and formerly the home of the Royal Guard, was dismantled and moved to its present site at the time of the place's restoration, from its original location on Beretania Street. Other features of the palace grounds include the 1906 Archives Building, a neoclassical structure at the northeast corner of the lot, and an International-style State Archives building located nearby, added in 1953. The site also includes the archaeological remains of an early heiau (temple and possible cave site), still marked by a later burial mound. This area, at the southeast corner, was once the site of a Western-style tomb, though the remains of many of Hawaii's rulers were transferred to the Royal Mausoleum in the Nu'uanu Valley in 1865. The surrounding iron fence and gates installed in 1892 are also still visible at the site. *WC*

Queen Emma Summer Palace

007 B

2913 Pali Hwy
Honolulu, HI 96817
Attributed to Charles Vincent
1848

Hānaiakamalama, also called the Queen Emma Summer Palace, was the upland retreat of Queen Emma from 1857 to 1885 as well as the home of her husband Kamehameha IV and their son Prince Albert Edward before their early deaths. Built in 1848 from components shipped from Boston via Cape Horn, the property's first owner was John Lewis, a local entrepreneur and developer. The house is one of the finest examples of Greek Revival architecture in Hawaii, distinguished by the reeded columns of the front lanai, its open and large rooms, high ceilings, nearly floor-to-ceiling windows, and unique evidence of an early cloth fan or punkah. Queen Emma was gifted the house by her uncle, John Young II, the son of John Young, Senior, the well-known adviser to King Kamehameha I. Young had purchased the house in 1850 for $6,000. Emma added a shed-roofed addition to the rear in 1869 to receive the Duke of Edinburgh, who was visiting Hawaii as part of a Pacific Ocean tour. The Kingdom of Hawaii purchased the estate in 1885, intending it as a memorial to the one-time royal family. In 1911, the territorial government, which had inherited the property, began plans for a baseball park on the site. The Daughters of Hawaii, a local patriotic organization, soon afterward acquired the building and made it the centerpiece of their effort to commemorate the Hawaii of old. The house and grounds, now limited to a half-acre, are still maintained by the daughters and the site features furniture and decorative objects from the time of Queen Emma's residency. *WC*

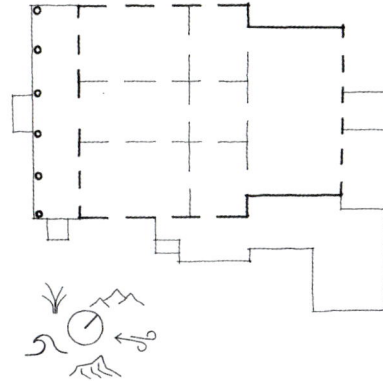

1

Photo: DeSoto Brown

008   Bishop Museum and Hall

Essay: Bluestone

Bishop Museum and Hall

1525 Bernice St
Honolulu, HI 96817
William F. Smith
1889

008 B

The Bishop Museum owes its origins to Honolulu businessman Charles Reed Bishop, who founded the Bishop Museum in 1889 as a memorial to his wife, the Princess Bernice Pauahi Bishop. Co-founder of what would become the First Hawaiian Bank, one of the Kingdom of Hawaii's first banking establishments, Bishop married the princess Bernice Pauahi Pākī, a descendent of the royal line of Kamehameha I. Her death in 1884 led Bishop to philanthropic efforts, including what would become Kamehameha School and the Bishop Museum, construction for which began in 1889. The first building is still at the center of the original complex. This is a Romanesque-Revival (Richardsonian Romanesque) rock-faced structure housing a one-story exhibit room, intended primarily to contain Hawaiian heirlooms inherited by his wife, and a two-story exhibit tower to its right. Designed by Boston-born, San Francisco-based William F. Smith and constructed from basalt quarried nearby, the structure also served as a picture gallery for the princess' and his collections of landscapes, still-life images, and portraits. This first building was augmented in 1892 by a substantial two-story addition, originally called Polynesian Hall (now Pacific Hall). This was completed in a similar style by the same San Francisco architect, William F. Smith. In 1898, Bishop funded a second addition to the original museum building, to be called Hawaiian Hall. Started in 1899 (marked by an inscribed cornice with that date) and completed in 1903, Hawaiian Hall was another product of William F. Smith's design and a substantial addition to the original two sections. Fully three-stories in elevation, the structure featured a large, central open area surrounded by three galleries. Supports for the galleries were paired iron posts with foliated capitals; lighting was by skylights, later darkened to cut back on heat gain and potential damage to the collections from the sun's ultraviolet rays. At the time of Hawaiian Hall's completion, the Polynesian Commercial Advertiser called the complex 'the noblest buildings of Honolulu'. The museum and the new school for Hawaiian boys were closely aligned. A classroom and auditorium were completed in 1891, originally to be called Memorial Hall. This was also designed by William F. Smith and is in the same style as the Bishop Museum complex. Renamed at the time of completion as Bishop Hall, the impressive Romanesque Revival (or Richardsonian) edifice was two stories high; the massive building also featured a bell-cast, circular tower at one corner and an impressive auditorium on the upper floor. Notable features included the cast

Photo: DeSoto Brown

concrete capitals designed by sculptor Allen Hutchinson and supporting the ground floor lanai. The building would remain the core of the school until 1940 when the school's operations – by then incorporating a preparatory school and a girls' school – moved to the new campus on Kapālama Heights. The museum itself went through several changes in the twentieth century. In 1909 work began on a new wing later to be named Pākī Hall in honor of Princess Pauahi's father, High Chief Abner Pākī. Originally planned as a basaltic stone building to match its neighbors, the new laboratory facility would be one of the first reinforced concrete buildings in what was then the Territory of Hawaii. Other additions followed. Konia (Kōnia) Hall, completed in 1926, was constructed expressly for the storage of the museum's many artifacts and other collections. Envisioned to serve as additional storage and office space for mostly natural history materials, Konia Hall was named for Princess Pauahi's mother Laura Kōnia. In the post-Second World War period, the museum's successive directors – with an eye toward changing perceptions of the role of museums, its role as the State of Hawaii's official natural history museum, and the public's interest – built a new astronomy center and a large structure for the museum's many natural history specimens. Designed by the firm of Merrill, Simms, and Roehrig and opened on 11 December 1961 as the Kilolani Planetarium (now the Jhamandas Watumull Planetarium), the facility features a 70-seat auditorium and an attached two-story observatory. An exhibition area, originally a children's museum, was added to this complex in 1971. In 1964, the museum added a four-story reinforced concrete structure at the 'rear' of the museum's campus and connecting to Pākī Hall at all four levels. Employing stylized figures derived from ancient Hawaiian petroglyphs as decorative screens, the new Pauahi Hall would house the entomology and botany collections. Subsequent additions to the Bishop Museum campus include the Castle Memorial Building officially opened in 1990. Designed by Architects Hawaii to house more popular exhibitions, the structure attempted (without complete success) to blend with the earlier structures. Finally, in 2003, the museum added the Richard T. Mamiya Science Adventure Center, designed by ZGF Architects and opened to provide an array of interactive exhibits focused on marine science, volcanology, and related sciences. In 2009, the museum reopened the late nineteenth-century Hawaiian Hall, following a $16 million restoration by Mason Architects and the redesign of its exhibitions. Pacific Hall, formally Polynesian Hall, experienced the same renewal in 2014, with Mason Architects supervising the architectural work and Ralph Applebaum & Associates redesigning the exhibits as they did at Hawaiian Hall. *WC*

Bluestone

Don Hibbard

Bluestone is a very dense, hard, unvesiculated volcanic stone, which results from the slow cooling of lava, allowing almost all the air in the stone to dissipate. The conditions needed to obtain such a result require a lava flow or pool that is at least 20 feet in depth. The earliest known Western architectural use of the stone in Hawaii occurred in 1890 with the construction of the Bishop Museum. This was followed a year later in 1891 with the building of Kamehameha School for Boys next to the museum, and then by the Masonic Hall of 1892 (no longer extant). All three of these buildings displayed a Romanesque Revival style, with the first two designed by William F. Smith of San Francisco and the third by Clinton Briggs Ripley of Honolulu. The Romanesque Revival arrived in the islands with the Bishop Museum, just as the style was falling into decline on the mainland. It remained the go-to style in Honolulu throughout the 1890s, following the overthrow of the monarchy, with Pauahi Hall (1895) on the campus of today's Punahou School, Bishop Estate Building on Merchant Street (1896), and Irwin Block (1896) on Nuuanu Avenue being rendered in the style. Both the Bishop Estate Building and the Irwin Block are noteworthy for their upper story stone work. The cast iron pilaster adjoining the Bishop Estate Building is a remnant of the Campbell Building (1883), which shared a common wall with the Bishop Estate Building until 1965 when it was demolished. In addition to the above mentioned buildings, a number of no longer extant Romanesque Revival style, bluestone buildings exerted the style's presence upon the city. These included the Von Holt Block (1894), Love Building (1896), Waverly Block (1896), and Central Fire Station (1897). Again, Ripley and one of his partners, either Arthur Reynolds or C. W. Dickey, had a hand in all of the projects mentioned. The style well reflected a desire for stability during this period of great uncertainty when Hawaii was under the rule of the provisional government and then the Republic. With its heavy

Cooke Hall (originally Cooke Library), Punahou School

masonry construction, squat round arches, deep set openings, and rough-hewn stones, architectural historian Alan Gowans observed that these sturdy buildings, 'seemed to stand for and from eternity' and 'brought to mind and eye an impression of solidity, an attitude of stability, a mood of security'. In addition to the numerous buildings rendered in the Romanesque style, a pair of no longer extant bluestone Gothic Revival churches – the Central Union Church (1889), designed by Oakland architect George Boardwell, and the Bernice Pauahi Bishop Memorial Chapel (1897) designed by Ripley & Dickey – made bold

Bishop Estate Building

McCandless Building

Photo: Bishop Museum, 1900

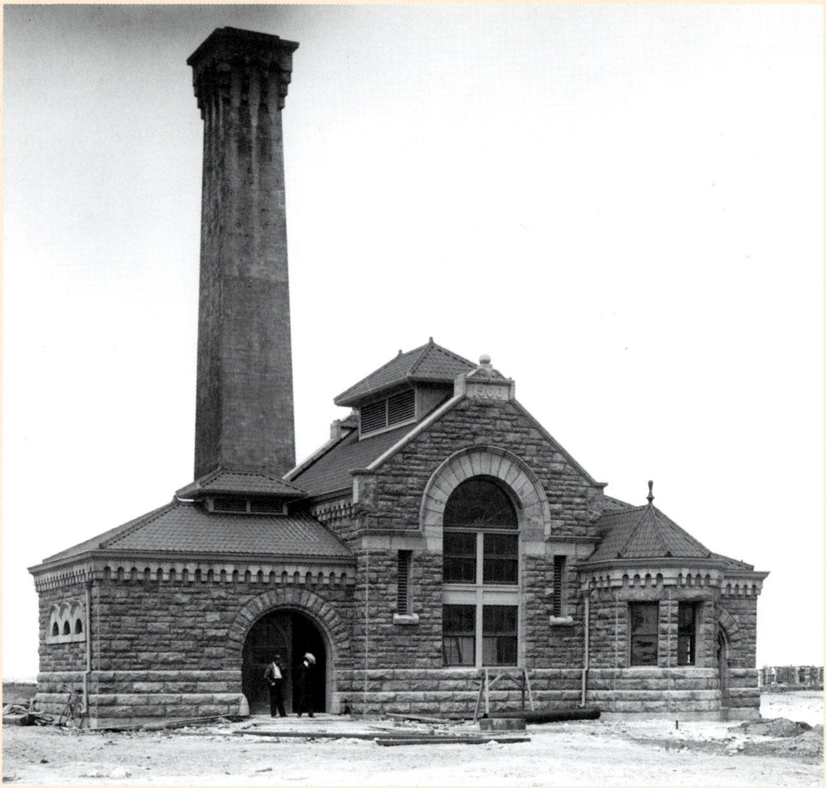

Kakaako Pumping Station

ecclesiastical statements. With the annexation of Hawaii by the United States in 1898, the Romanesque Revival fell out of favor in Hawaii; however, a scattering of bluestone buildings continued to be built, but they were no longer adorned with Romanesque associations. Examples of such buildings included the Model Progress Block (1898) at Fort and Beretania Streets and the Podmore

Photo: DeSoto Brown

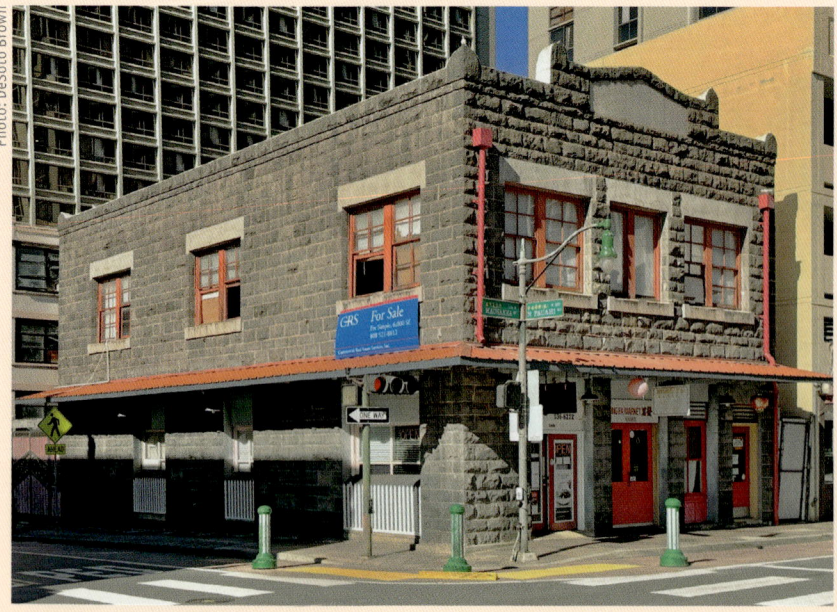

T. Sumida Building

Building (1902) at Alakea and Merchant Streets, both of which are devoid of any stylistic signifiers. The former was designed by Ripley & Dickey, while the latter was designed and constructed by Lee Wai. In addition, Oliver Traphagan designed both the three-story, bluestone Hackfeld Building (1902; no longer extant) in a Renaissance Revival style, and the more modest and eclectic Sewer Pumping Station (1900) on Ala Moana Boulevard, while H. L. Kerr designed the Renaissance Revival McCandless Building (1906) at King and Bethel Streets and the neoclassical revival Cooke Hall (1909) on the campus of what is now Punahou School, all of which reaffirmed Hawaii's new colonial status. Cooke Hall was the last major building to be constructed using bluestone; however, in Chinatown the use of the material continued into the teens in several small commercial buildings, including the single story Saiji Kimura liquor warehouse (1905) on Nuuanu Avenue, the T. Sumida Building (1909; with a second story added in 1916) at Maunakea and Pauahi Streets and the Fishel Block (1914) on Beretania Street. All of these solid buildings featured distinctive parapets, as did the earlier bluestone Winston (1901) and Armstrong Blocks (1905) along King Street, both of which are also in Chinatown. Bluestone also was used in a few residences around Honolulu, with two examples still standing: the late Queen Anne revival-style Alfred Hocking residence (1904) on Nehoa Street and the Tudor revival style C. M. Cooke residence (1912) on Manoa Road. The latter was designed by Emory & Webb, while the former was designed by Dickey & Newcomb. Dickey & Newcomb also designed the bluestone Wailuku Elementary school (1904) on Maui, a rare manifestation of the stone beyond Oahu. In addition to bluestone's use in buildings, it was also used for at least more than a dozen years as a street curb material throughout the city, with government specifications, found in the newspapers between 1913 and 1927, calling for the use of lava rock. A rare building material, in that it did not have to be imported to Hawaii, bluestone was used over a period of 25 or so years before disappearing from the local architectural scene. Its use was predicated not on any intention to celebrate a sense of place, but rather to convey an air of substantiality. The mere use of the material made an imposing statement regardless of the scale of the building. Even to this day, the bluestone buildings standout as distinctive elements in Honolulu's streetscape, expressing a sense of permanency rooted in their island origins.

Irwin Block

3

Moana Hotel

2365 Kalākaua Ave
Honolulu, HI 96815
Oliver G. Traphagen
1901

009 C

The Moana Hotel, completed in 1901, opened at a time when most visitors to Honolulu occupied rooms in the downtown area. The hotel, with its impressive two-story Ionic-columned porte-cochère, presented visitors to Hawaii with the familiar manifestation of the City Beautiful movement that had dominated the United States' public architecture since 1892. Adapting what the architect Oliver G. Traphagen called America's 'Colonial Style', the luxury hotel was designed to meet the needs of Hawaii's climatic needs, including large and door openings, a deep verandah or lanai, and a generous roof overhang to protect the exterior walls and openings from both sun and rain. Traphagen declared the hotel was 'designed for Honolulu alone. It was difficult to adhere to any strict method of architecture for such a climate and there is no hotel on the face of the Earth which is similar in outline'. Developed by wealthy Honolulu landowner Walter Chamberlain Peacock to establish a fine resort in the previously relatively quiet Waikiki area of Honolulu, the Moana Hotel was incorporated as the Moana Hotel Company in 1896. The Moana officially opened on 11 March 1901. Its first guests were a group of Shriners, who paid $1.50 per night for their rooms. The Moana represented the height of luxury. Some of the 75 guest rooms had telephones and private bathrooms (unusual at the time), and the hotel featured a billiard room, saloon, main parlor, reception area, and library. Peacock provided the resort with the first electric-powered elevator in the islands. Peacock's endeavor was unsuccessful, however, and he sold the hotel to Alexander Young, a prominent Honolulu hotelier, in 1905.

Following Young's death in 1910, a company called the Territorial Hotel Company operated the hotel. Despite its inauspicious beginnings, the Moana grew along with the popularity of Hawaiian tourism. To meet the need, the hotel was expanded in 1918, with concrete wings added to the wood-framed center section. The wings more than doubled the size of the hotel. The company's owners also created the banyan court, which served as a center for outdoor dining. In 1925 the Matson Navigation Company and the sugar factors Castel & Cooke bought a controlling interest in the hotel, placing it under their multi-property entity Hawaii Properties Ltd. This dissolved in 1941 and the Matson Company became the sole owners. Up to this point the Moana remained a popular venue for Hawaii's wealthier residents and a magnet for visitors. Over the years, guests would include the Duke of Windsor, Agatha Christie, Amelia Earhart, Joe DiMaggio, Walter Chrysler, Frank Sinatra, Lucille Ball, Boris Karloff, and Loretta Young. Despite its reputation for celebrity visitors and the popular radio broadcast *Hawaii Calls*, begun in 1935, the hotel's fortunes declined, especially in the post-Second World War period. Ill-conceived renovations completely masked the hotel's once grand spaces, and following the purchase of the property by Kenji Osano and his Kyo-Ya Company in 1963, plans were afoot to demolish the grand old structure. The presence of the Surfrider Hotel in 1952 and the Sheraton Moana in 1969, however, saved the old Moana, providing an opportunity for consolidation of the properties. In 1989, the owners, in cooperation with Sheraton Hotels and Resorts, undertook a $50 million renovation of the premises, a project initiated by preservation architect Virginia Murison. The Ionic-columned porte-cochère was reconstructed at this time, the lobby was rehabilitated, and the intricate exterior woodwork restored, including the front lanai's round-arched openings and fleur-de-lis ornament. The fourth floor's observatory lanai also was returned, creating a distinctive public space with its round-arched arcade and balustrade. *WC*

Oahu Market ↑

010 B

145 N King St
Honolulu, HI 96817
Unknown
1904

Built in 1904 by Anin 'Tuck' Young, a Chinese entrepreneur, the Oahu Market is located at North King and Kekaulike Streets. Owned by the Young family for 80 years, it was sold in 1984 to the Oahu Market Corporation, founded by 24 of the market's tenants with the support of the Historic Hawaii Foundation. The market still operates from its original building, which is constructed of bricks and coral blocks, with a stone foundation and a wooden roof. The interior is divided into stalls that open to the interior passageway or to the street, as they have since 1904. The market is distinguished by the red sign on its roof, the red roof lining, and by red awnings hanging from the edge of the ceiling. When it was first built, the Oahu Market rivaled a government-owned public market located on Alakea Street. The public market was primarily occupied by Caucasian storeowners, whereas the Oahu Market provided spaces for Asian shopkeepers. The Oahu Market provided an alternative place for the local community to buy fresh meat and vegetables. *WC*

St. Peter's Episcopal

1317 Queen Emma St
Honolulu, HI 96813
William O. Phillips
1914

011 B

The story of St. Peter's Episcopal Church stretches back to the late nineteenth century and the founding of nearby St. Andrews Cathedral. Kamehameha IV and his queen Emma were attracted to the Anglican Church and were christened by Bishop Thomas Nettleship Staley during his visit in 1862. King Kamehameha died the following year on St. Andrew's Day, leading his brother King Kamehameha V to dedicate a proposed pro-cathedral to the saint. In 1885, Queen Emma donated land for a second church designed to serve the growing Chinese population in the islands. The Chinese Anglican community, many converted by Christian missionaries in China, had begun services in a shop in Oahu, afterward attending services on the grounds of St. Andrews. By 1912 they had sufficient funding to take advantage of Queen Emma's gift and build their own church. This, like the by then cathedral, was in the Gothic Revival style, constructed of rendered masonry with details such as a crenelated entry, pointed windows, label lintels, and an asymmetrical façade with a bell tower at the north (mauka) end. It was completed in 1914 and has served the Chinese and other immigrant communities since that time. The name consciously calls attention to the relationship between Andrew and Peter, brothers among the original apostles. *WC*

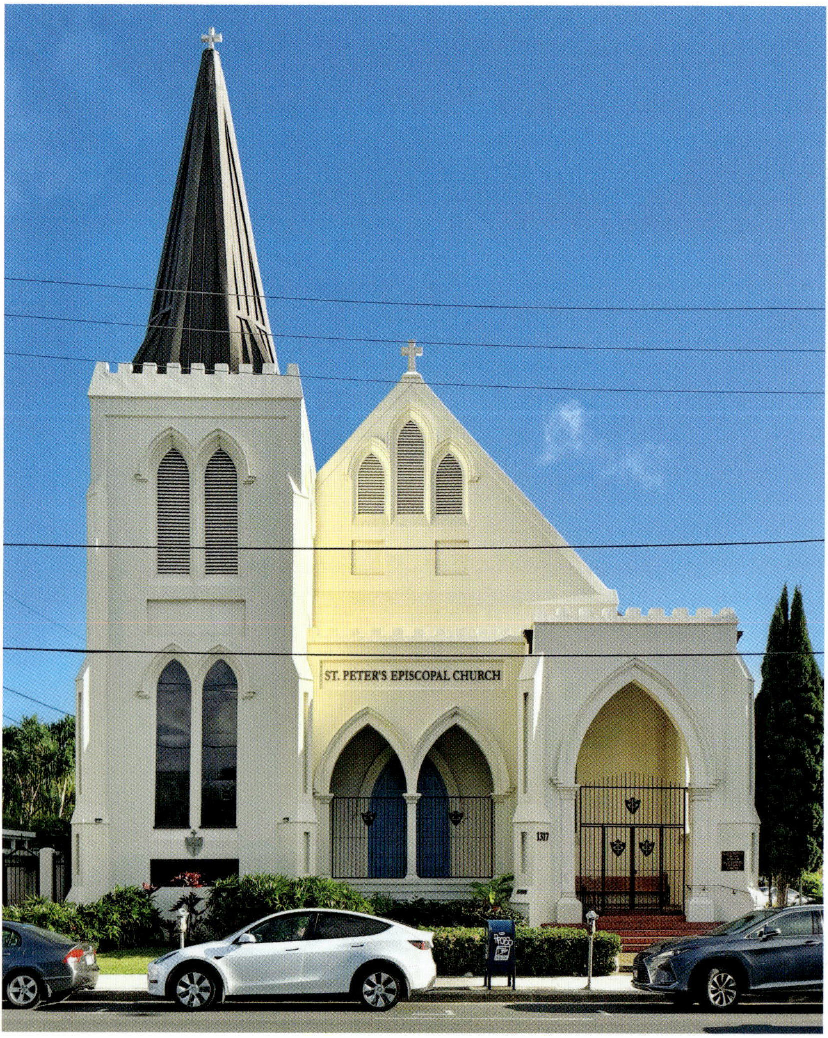

ST. PETER'S EPISCOPAL CHURCH

1317

Hawaii Theatre

1130 Bethel St,
Honolulu, HI 96813
Emory and Webb
1922

Photo: Martin Despang

3

The Hawaii Theatre was the crown jewel of the Consolidated Amusement Company when it was constructed in 1922. Honolulu-based architects Walter Emory and Marshall-Webb were the architects for the 1,760 seat Beaux Arts-style structure, which displays elements of Byzantine, Moorish, neoclassical, and art deco architecture, as well. The main façade consists of three two-story arched openings on the Bethel (Diamond Head) side. These are flanked by Corinthian order pilasters rising through two floors. A full entablature featuring combined modillions and dentils spans the building's top. A fly loft is at the rear. The interior featured (and features) Corinthian columns, a gilded dome, statuary, carpets, silk hangings, and a Lionel Walden-designed mural above the proscenium. The original curtain, proudly labeled 'asbestos', was replaced by a new curtain with the word Hawaii substituting. The interior includes an orchestra and a single balcony with two rows of loge seating surmounted by additional balcony seating. Two private boxes flank the stage. The original furnishings were a combination of cane, wood, and metal. The loge seating included free-standing cane and rattan chairs. The theatre was designed for both films

and Vaudeville shows. There was an orchestra and a Robert Morton pipe organ to accompany the silent movies originally shown. In 1938, following a transition to 'talkies', the original bulb-lit rectangular canopy was replaced by an art deco marque featuring a credit board and neon lighting. Environmentally, the theatre followed innovations introduced in the late nineteen century in New York, Chicago, and other larger cities to include a system of fans blowing over ice to lower the interior temperature. While the exact first use of dry ice is difficult to pinpoint, its use became common in the 1920s and 1930s, with dry ice being commercially available around 1924; so, it is likely that the Hawaii Theatre at least began with regular ice. The vents for the cooling system are still visible. The theatre continued as Honolulu's premier movie palace until new venues opened in the 1930s, including Waikiki Theatre on Kalakaua Avenue in Waikiki. By the 1960s, the Hawaii Theatre was in decline, a condition aggravated in the 1970s as entertainment shifted away from movie houses to televisions and mall-based cinemas. Closing in 1984, the theatre's future was secured by a non-profit organization formed just two years later. This Hawaii Theatre Center group spearheaded an extensive renovation of the interior, which followed in 1994, undertaken by Hardy Holzman Pfeiffer of New York. The theatre reopened in 1996, though exterior renovations continued through 2005. The large marquee from 1938, which had deteriorated and been removed, was replicated and installed, featuring new electronic display panels. *WC*

Photo: Olivier Koning

Hawaii State Library ↑↓

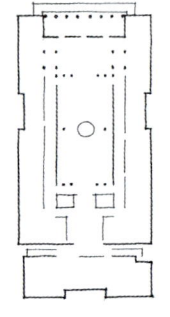

478 S King St
Honolulu, HI 96813
Henry Whitfield, C. W. Dickey,
Aotani & Associates
1913, 1929, 1992

013 B

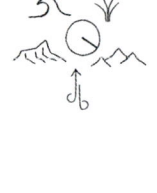

One of the many municipal and state libraries financed by the Carnegie Foundation, the neoclassical and Mediterranean Revival-style structure was designed by Andrew Carnegie's brother-in-law Henry D. Whitfield with the help of local architect H. L. Kerr. The original construction cost, provided directly by Carnegie, was $100,000. The local community raised another $27,000 for books and furnishings. Ground-breaking took place in 1911 and the imposing mixed neoclassical and Mediterranean Renaissance Revival-style edifice opened in 1913. Among the building's features are murals depicting Hawaiian legends by artist Juliette May Fraser in the Edna Allyn Children's Room, a mosaic in the courtyard of ocean currents by Hiroki Morinoue, and Barbara Hepworth's cast bronze statutes called *Parent I and Young Girl* at the building's entrance. The building was expanded in 1927 by local architect C. W. Dickey; a further extension took place in 1991, designed by Aotani and Associates Inc. Whitfield would also design the US Post Office and Courthouse in Hilo, completed in 1915. *WC*

Honpa Hongwanji →

1727 Pali Hwy
Honolulu, HI 96813
Emory & Webb and Kenji Onodera
1918 (1954)

014 B

For the Honpa Hongwanji Temple, the architects Emory & Webb (Walter Emory and Marshall Webb) turned to India and the origins of Buddhism for their inspiration. Bishop Yemyo Imamura wanted the building to embody a modern image for Hawaii's principal Buddhist sect, yet retain the stability of a form based on tradition and that would be identified with religion. Built in 1918, the original 80-by-120-foot temple was remodeled and enlarged by architect Kenji Onodera in 1954 to its present 137-by-144 footprint, while retaining the spirit of the original design. The two-story re-inforced-concrete building features a social hall on the ground floor and a temple on the second. The centered Tuscan-columned portico, inset balustraded porch, frieze, open parapet, and central dome date from 1918. The original three-bay porch was expanded to five bays in 1954, and the end towers, which framed the original composition, have become projecting wings ornamented with screens decorated with a repeating wisteria crest. The stepped spires of the wings emulate the termini of the earlier towers. As a result of Bishop Imamura's initiatives,

Buddhist temples became places for worship and preaching, as was the practice in Christian churches. This innovation became popular throughout the islands as well as in Japan. After the Second World War, 74 per cent of Buddhist temples constructed in Hawaii followed this prototype. The temple's more recent annex was designed by Arthur A. Kohara. *WC*

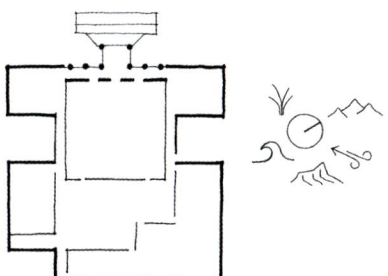

3

First Church of Christ Science

1508 Punahou St
Honolulu, HI 96822
Hart Wood
1923

This picturesque sanctuary, designed by regionalist architect Hart Wood, sits on a spacious lawn shaded by large, spreading monkeypod trees. Occupying a lot once adjacent to the Walter and Mary Emma Dillingham Frear estate and garden (now occupied by the 1967 Arcadia Retirement Residence), the distinctly 'Hawaiian Style' church, with its coursed lava-rock walls and steep, shingled gable roof with wide overhanging eaves, is one of the great examples of regionalist architecture in the islands. Completed in 1923, the church was one of several essays in regional contextualism by Hart Wood – another notable example is the Albert Spencer Wilcox Library in Lihue, Kauai, of 1924 – and represents his and his contemporaries' efforts to create a cohesive architectural vocabulary for what was then the Territory of Hawaii. One of Wood's innovations was to introduce side lanai to allow circulation, ventilation, and vistas of the grounds, a device emulated by Ralph Adams Cram at the nearby Central Union Church. The modified Tudor-style entrance and spire point to the church's connection to other church sanctuaries, whereas the rough coursed walls seem to speak to the Hawaii of ancient times. Inside, the simple, high volume with dramatic exposed trusses tie the sanctuary to longstanding Tudor Revival and Arts and Crafts designs, as does the ornate altar screen. *WC*

Photo: Lijin Zhao

Aloha Tower ↓
155 Ala Moana Blvd
Honolulu, HI 96813
Arthur L. Reynolds
1926

016 B

At one time the tallest building in Honolulu, the ten-story Aloha Tower originally served as both a lighthouse and a grand symbol of arrival in Honolulu Harbor. Conceived as early as 1920, the tower was completed in 1926 to a design by noted architect Arthur L. Reynolds. An Englishman by birth, Reynolds came to the islands in 1891 following work in Chicago and San Francisco. He subsequently practiced both in Hawaii and California, designing in a wide range of period revival styles. Reynolds unfortunately died of a stroke shortly before the completion of the tower project. The total cost of the tower was $160,000. The structure, which contained the offices of the Honolulu Port Authority, is 184 feet tall surmounted in turn by a 40-foot masthead. Stylistically, the structure incorporates aspects of Renaissance Revival, Second Empire, and art deco decorative details. Clocks occupy the four faces of the upper part of the tower. Following the attack on Pearl Harbor in December 1941, Aloha Tower was occupied by the US Coast Guard and repainted in a camouflage pattern. In 1981, the tower and the area around it became part of a redevelopment plan, spearheaded by the Hawaii State Department of Business, Economic Development, and Tourism. The result was the creation of the Aloha Tower Marketplace, a project undertaken by Aotani and Associates with D'Agostino and Izzo Quirk architects. Inspired by the hotels of the 1930s, the urban marketplace consists of four large two-story pavilions decorated with stucco walls and other features evocative of Hawaii's regionalist architecture of the early to mid-twentieth century. Boston architect Bruce D'Agostino had worked with Benjamin Thompson and Associates on the Faneuil Hall Marketplace in Boston, and his project echoed many of the innovations introduced there. Unfortunately, the festival marketplace enjoyed only partial success. The site is now leased to Hawaii Pacific University for offices, classrooms, and housing. *WC*

Central Union Church →
1660 S Beretania St
Honolulu, HI 96826
Ralph Adams Cram
1925

017 C

Built in 1925 as a tribute to the early New England missionaries – ancestors of many in the congregation – Central Union Church pairs with Kawaiahao Church as the architectural expression of the Protestant, largely Congregationalist presence in Hawaii. The architect was Ralph Adams Cram of the Massachusetts firm of Cram and Fergusson (formerly Cram Goodhue and Fergusson), a noted exponent of Gothic Revival and designer of the Gothic-style buildings at West Point in addition to many other commissions. Cram took his lead from the congregation, which wished to recall its roots in New Haven, home of the Yale Divinity School and the beginnings of the historic mission to Hawaii. The origins of Central Union Church go back to 1832 when the Oahu Bethel Church was formed. Primarily

serving seaman in port, the membership of the Bethel Church extended to outsiders as well as newly arrived foreigners. With the increase in the number of sailors in the city, Honolulu residents formed the Second Foreign Church in 1853 for their own use. This became the Fort Street Church in 1856. After the Chinatown fire of 1886, which consumed Bethel Church, the Fort Street and Bethel congregations united and constructed a first Central Union Church at the corner of Beretania and Richards Streets. This church remained on the site until 1922 when the changing character of the building's surroundings led to the congregations' decision to build a new church farther from downtown. (The late nineteenth-century church became an automobile dealership shortly afterward and was eventually demolished for the new Capitol prior to its construction in 1966). Sitting on an expansive eight-acre lot that recalls New Haven's central green, this superb Georgian Revival church closely reflects designs set out in James Gibbs' 1728 *Book of Architecture*. Gibbs was the first architect to gracefully combine the medieval church tower with the classical portico and was indirectly the progenitor of countless churches throughout the world. Although the Central Union Church followed this model, there were distinctly local features as well. The basalt stone for the building was procured from the quarry in Moili'ili, the site of the University of Hawaii's lower campus and parking structure. The interior's 12 Corinthian columns substitute pineapple and palm leaves for acanthus. Most important, five sets of French doors on each side wall open the nave and its high, barrel-vaulted ceiling to the outdoors. Round-arched second-story windows and recessed clerestory windows further contribute to the interior's light and airy atmosphere. *WC*

Royal Hawaiian Hotel

2259 Kalākaua Ave
Honolulu, HI 96815
Warren & Wetmore
1927

018 C

The Royal Hawaiian Hotel, sometimes referred to as the 'Pink Palace of the Pacific' was built in 1927 by the Matson Navigation Company to provide luxury accommodations for its passengers and to encourage visitors to Hawaii. The architects were the New York firm of Warren and Wetmore, renowned for Grand Central Station in New York, Steinway Hall, also in New York, the Newport County Club in Rhode Island, the New York Yacht Club, and many other works. Up until that time most of the large hotels were in downtown Honolulu; only the 1901 Moana occupied an important site in Waikiki. The Territorial Hotel Company owned most of the hotels, and Matson wanted to break into the business. Partnering with one of the 'big five' sugar factors, Castle & Cooke, the Matson bought out the Territorial Hotel Company, demolishing one of their Waikiki hotels to make way for their new luxury resort hotel. The design matched the times, reflecting the nation's infatuation with Spanish colonial architecture. Warren and Wetmore's design built on earlier efforts on the West Coast, notably the Panama-California Exposition in San Diego of a decade before. Specific influences were Spanish missions, notably San Xavier del Bac in Tucson, Arizona, which provided prototypes for the hotel's two towers. Ground-breaking took place in 1925; the hotel opened in February 1927 with a black-tie event attended by 1,200 guests. The total cost of construction was $4 million, an astronomical sum at the time. The hotel offered a truly luxury vacation. The rooms were large and airy and there were promenades and lanai

Photo: Curt Sandburn

Photo: Martin Despang

to suit every time of day and every weather condition. Hotel guests could bathe in the ocean and play golf at the associated Waialae Golf Course. Situated on land owned by the Bishop Estate (now Kamehameha Schools) the hotel required an annual lease for the land, which was historically the site of Kamehameha's early palace and the area's sacred grove of coconut palms. Decorative features included the bamboo awnings over the windows and the use of pink (or coral) on the exterior and throughout the interior, including bed sheets and towels. (The pink color may derive from mansions in Lisbon, Portugal, which were painted this color; the color combination of pink with blue-green trim was admired by Matson's director William Roth, who saw it used at the home of his friends Kimo and Sarah Wilder in Honolulu. The Spanish and/or Moroccan style architecture possibly also reflects the popularity of these exotic locations in Hollywood films of the time, notably Rudolf Valentino's *The Sheik*, and its sequels, which were released in the late 1920s. The bellmen and elevator operators wore a combination of Arabic and Chinese costumes.) Due to the Depression, the grand hotel fell on hard times in the 1930s. With the outbreak of the war in 1941, the US Navy signed a lease for the use of the Royal Hawaiian as a Rest-and-Relaxation (R&R) Center. Submariners received special privileges to stay there, bunking four or six to

a room. The hotel bar, which occupied the Diamond Head end of the waterfront lanai, was a popular watering hole for military personnel, as well. Recovering in the post-war era – including a major repair and restoration project carried out in 1947 – Matson sold the hotel to ITT Sheraton in 1959. Sheraton added an additional wing and restored some of the hotel's earlier splendor. In 1974, the Japanese businessmen and brothers Kenji Osano and Masakuni Osano purchased the Royal Hawaiian Hotel. They formed Kyo-Ya Company Ltd. to manage this and other holdings. In 2008, the company embarked upon a multimillion-dollar renovation project to bring the hotel into the twenty-first century. Fortunately, a proposal to reorient the entrance to the mauka (north) side was vetoed at the last minute. *WC*

3

Photo: DeSoto Brown, ca. 1930

Halekulani Hotel

2199 Kālia Rd
Honolulu, HI 96815
C. W. Dickey
1927–1932

019 C

The Halekulani Hotel, one of Honolulu's premier hostelries, balances the past and the present in a strikingly unified composition. The site of Earl Derr Biggers' hit 1919 novel *The House Without a Key* – still the name of the terrace-side restaurant today and the origin story for the popular detective Charlie Chan, himself based on real-life Honolulu detective Chang Apana – the Halekulani exudes luxury and good taste. Originally a two-story house converted to hotel use, the Halekulani expanded in 1917 under the proprietorship of Clifford and Juliet Kimball to become a luxury destination. In 1932, the hotel grew again when the first modest house with its five bungalows was replaced with a distinctive Hawaii Regionalist main building. This was designed by Hawaii's preeminent architect and the doyen of the style, C. W. Dickey, who employed his double pitched, bell-cast room to good results. Other buildings filled out the

Photo: Don Hibbard

site, including additional wings and more private bungalows. These, too, featured the so-called 'Dickey Roof' and other signature island elements such as lava rock and open lanai. The Halekulani continued in operation, still attracting celebrities and other discerning visitors following the end of the Kimbell era in 1962. In 1981, the hotel was purchased by the Japanese firm Mitsui Fudosan, now the Honolulu-based Halekulani Corporation, and was subject to a massive renovation and rebuilding effort. The managing firm selected the firm of Killingsworth and Associates, which, in collaboration with chief executive Shuhei Okuda settled on a respectful post-modernist design that retained the main building and introduced three towers of differing heights that respected the original character of the resort. Carrying out the work for Killingsworth was Ron Lindgren, who also designed the Kapalua Bay Hotel on Maui, The hotel's three towers contain 456 rooms, each with sliding louvered doors and generous lanai. In a carefully considered composition, the towers step down to the ocean and define two courtyards by their E-shaped plan. The courtyards magnify the sense of openness created by the porte-cochère and lobby. A gatehouse within the walls of the complex features a waterfall, a thunbergia-festooned pergola, bubbling tiled fountains, and planter beds. A pair of red Indian marble sculptures of mahiole (feathered helmets for ali'i) by Chuck Watson guard the entrance. Finishes include polished travertine floors and the exposed concrete structural frame. The

original main building of 1932 is at the far end of the courtyard. Although remodeled, it retains the spirit of Dickey's original design through its 'lava rock' accents, hala motif railings, and its double-pitched hipped roof. The second courtyard features a swimming pool of glass tiles that creates a cattleya orchid pattern on the bottom. Killingsworth and Associates, the Long Beach, California, architectural firm headed by Edward Killingsworth, designed several hotels in Hawaii, including the Kahala Hilton, Waikiki Parc, and Ihilani on Oahu, and the Mauna Lani Bay Hotel on the island of Hawaii. The firm also designed the Phoenician Hotel in Arizona and Hilton Hotels in Bali, Jakarta, Malaysia, Saudi Arabia, Borneo, and Korea. *WC*

Honolulu Academy of Arts ↑ 020 B

900 S Beretania St
Honolulu, HI 96814
Bertram Goodhue
1927

One of Honolulu's great buildings, the Honolulu Museum of Art (formerly the Honolulu Academy of Arts) is a bold example of Hawaii Regionalism of the 1920s through 1930s, displaying many of the key elements of that style and utilizing local materials in a creative way. It is also a masterwork in adapting architecture to climate, celebrating Hawaii's ideal weather through its open courtyards and formerly open gallery spaces. Architecturally, the block-size building blends the cultures of Asia, the Middle East, and Europe in a single sweeping

structure fronted by downtown's most expansive designed landscape, Thomas Square. Designed by the well-known East Coast architect Bertram Goodhue in a version of the Spanish Colonial Revival style, combined with references to Chinese buildings and Spain's Alhambra, the Honolulu Museum of Art also embodies the ideals of Hawaii as a 'Crossroads of the Pacific'. Constructed of coral blocks, sandstone shipped from Molaka'i, and paving stones retrieved from Chinatown's streets, the structure tells the story of Hawaii's connection to Asia – the granite pavers were once ballast from ships involved in the early nineteenth-century sandalwood trade and the art itself is reflective of Hawaii's mixed cultures and outreach to the Pacific and Asia. The museum was founded in 1927 by Anna Rice Cooke, a descendant of Protestant missionaries and a passionate supporter of the arts. To further her aim of art education she donated her former house site on Beretania Street for the new museum, working directly with Goodhue on the design. Cooke's vision was first entertained in 1922, when she and her daughter Alice (then Mrs. Philp Spalding) and her daughter-in-law began a catalog of Mrs. Cooke's own collection. It was Mrs. Cooke's idea to make the museum a multicultural institution and to honor Hawaii's unique environment as part of the design. Goodhue, formerly of the firm of Cram, Goodhue and Fergusson, managed the firm's New York office until 1913 when he left to run his own practice. He collaborated closely with Mrs. Cooke, acceding to many of her suggestions. One was to employ

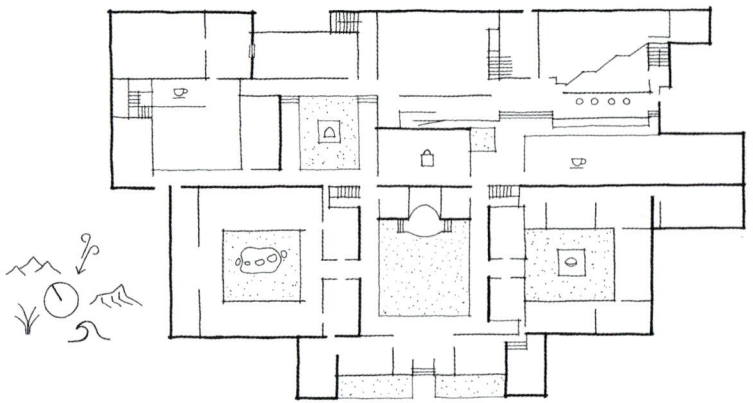

a double-pitched roof, by the late 1920s a signature of the Regionalist movement, and to eliminate a pagoda-like tower in the Chinese courtyard, which Mrs. Cooke found superfluous. Goodhue had been the supervising architect for the 1915 Panama-California Exposition in San Diego, where he had experimented with versions of the Spanish Colonial Revival style. He also designed the Nebraska State Capitol, which employed an unusual mixture of Byzantine, Assyrian, Gothic, classical and art deco styles in its realization. Unfortunately, Goodhue died before the completion of the Honolulu Academy project, and the museum was completed by New York architect Hardie Phillip. Subject to repairs and new facilities such as a library, a giftshop, and a café, the museum was relatively unaltered until 1998 when its board agreed to a large new addition on the mauka (mountain or north) side. Containing two floors of additional gallery space and offices above, the addition was designed by Honolulu architect John Hara and relates stylistically to the historic complex. This addition also features a set of large ceramic pillars created by internationally recognized ceramicist Jun Kaneko. Since 1990, the museum has maintained an art school, known as the Honolulu Museum of Art School (previously the Honolulu Academy Arts School), which is located just makai of the museum. The school occupies a one-time schoolhouse called Lineakoa School, built in 1908, and constructed of boldly rusticated concrete blocks – an innovative building system of the period. The art school closed in 2021 for extensive repairs, which are now complete. *WC*

![building photograph]

YWCA

1040 Richards St
Honolulu, HI 96813
Julia Morgan
1927

021 B

The YWCA Building at 1040 Richards Street, Honolulu, Hawaii, known as the Richards Street Y and now Laniākea, was designed by San Francisco architect Julia Morgan, who considered it one of her favorite projects. The style is Mediterranean Renaissance Revival, suggestive of palazzi in cities such as Genoa, Italy. The main façade, facing Diamond Head, divides into five units: a central pavilion and two connectors and two terminating blocks, very much in the tradition of the École des Beaux-Arts, of which Morgan was a graduate. The central block features a broken segmental pediment over the entry, Corinthian pilasters and half columns, a balustrade – repeated elsewhere on the building – a wrought iron balcony, stacked quoins, and decorative console brackets. Morgan's 1927 building was very much in the spirit of the Mediterranean and Spanish Colonial Revival architecture then favored in the Territory of Hawaii for its compatibility with the local climate. Meaning 'open skies' or 'wide horizons' in the Hawaiian language, the compound's name suits its open plan and generous use of courtyard spaces. Composed of two large sections, connected by a two-story loggia, the main building is three stories high and has a frontage of over 160 feet. The second section, at the rear, has a two-story elevation and raised basement area. The mauka side of the courtyard space features a swimming pool and fountain flanked by classical pilasters topped with urns. The rear of the property contains the Elizabeth Fuller Memorial Hall, a spacious meeting room and auditorium. Hawaii's YWCA movement dates back to 1900 and the patronage of several socially prominent women. Fundraising for a new building began in February

she was already the architect of several YWCAs in California and was the principal architect for Mills College in Oakland, which had its own connection to Hawaii through Susan Mills, a former teacher at Oahu College (now Punahou School) and wife of Cyrus Mills, the school's one-time president. Work on the building began in March 1926. The property was a portion of the Laniakea Tract from the Allen Estate, which had been purchased by the YWCA in 1924 for $238,566. Morgan had been in Hawaii in the past, including designing a women's residence called Fernhurst, also for the YWCA, and a columbarium in Hilo. She managed the work on the Richards Street YWCA from California, corresponding through her project manager Edward Hussey. Noted local designer Catherine Jones Richards (later Thompson) did the landscape plan. *WC*

3

1925; within ten days the goal of $350,00 was surpassed by $1,500. Grace Channon, the secretary of the local organization, traveled to California to select the architect. Julia Morgan, known for her design of William Randolph Hearst's eccentric estate San Simeon, was an ideal choice;

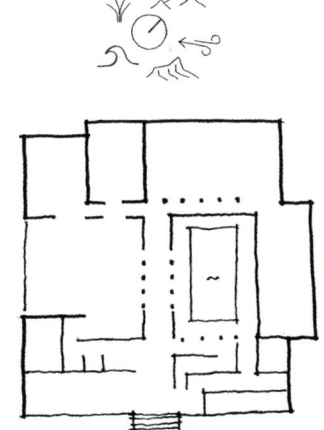

War Memorial Natatorium

2815 Kalākaua Ave
Honolulu, HI 96815
Lewis P. Hobart
1927 (2000)

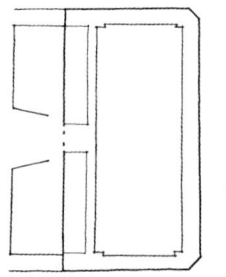

The Waikiki Natatorium War Memorial's large saltwater swimming pool and grandstand, which date from 1927, collectively remain one of Hawaii's most threatened architectural and historical sites. The pool served Hawaii's newfound international reputation for competitive swimming and is a memorial to Hawaii residents who lost their lives in the First World War. Designed by Beaux-Arts architect Lewis P. Hobart, the memorial is associated with Olympic swimmer and celebrity Duke Paoa Kahinu Mokoe Hulikohola Kahanamoku – the 'Ambassador of Aloha' – as well as fellow Olympians Buster Crabbe and Johnny Weissmuller. It was listed on the National Register in 1980 after closing in 1967. Despite the efforts of preservation advocate Nancy Bannock and others to save the unique site as a branch of the Swimming Hall of Fame and an attempt in 1999–2002 to repair the crumbling structure, the Natatorium entered a new period of indeterminacy in 2004 when the then mayor put a stop to funding. It now sits awaiting a now projected infusion of an estimated US$25.6 million needed for its stabilization and restoration. The Natatorium's origins lie with the effort of the Daughters and Sons of Hawaiian Warriors' 1918 proposal to erect a memorial to the approximately 10,000 men from Hawaii who served in the First World War. A committee that included several figures active in the city's civic life convened a public meeting to discuss possibilities, the result being the formation of a subcommittee to oversee the design and placement of a memorial. The subcommittee recommended the purchase of land on Waikiki Beach and the creation of a 'Memorial Park'. A second committee was then formed to review designs for the actual memorial. By 1920, plans had evolved to make this both a monument to fallen military personnel and a saltwater swimming pool 'of Olympic proportions'. An ensuing commission appointed to pick a winning design and headed by Louis Christian Mullgardt, a Fellow of the AIA, chose the proposal submitted by Lewis P. Hobart of San Francisco. Hobart was trained in the Beaux Arts tradition and had studied at the American Academy in Rome and in Paris. His work spanned civic and domestic commissions, including the Academy of Sciences buildings in Golden Gate Park. His plan for Waikiki featured a 100-by-40-meter pool, a masonry set of bleachers, and an entrance gate, embellished with a classical arch and four stone eagles. *WC*

Photo: DeSoto Brown, ca. 1930

Alexander & Baldwin

822 Bishop St
Honolulu, HI 96813
Dickey & Wood
1929

023 B

The Alexander & Baldwin (A&B) building is considered one of Honolulu's architectural masterpieces. Listed in both the state and national registers, the A&B building incorporates several design motifs reflective of the company's history and source of wealth: sugar cane reeded columns, bas relief cattle heads. It also includes Chinese ornamentation and mosaics illustrating nautical scenes from Hawaii. Clad in architectural terra cotta, the building was designed by the team of C. W. Dickey and Hart Wood. A&B followed the standard for other buildings on Bishop Street, including the headquarters of the Castle & Cooke, Bishop Bank (now First Hawaiian Bank), and the Alexander Hotel. The building also introduced new standards of detailing and design to downtown Honolulu. It remains a company headquarters and cherished Honolulu landmark. Alexander & Baldwin was among the largest and most successful of the Big Five of the Territorial Period in Hawaii. Founded by the sons of early Protestant missionaries, the partnership was founded in 1870 as a sugar plantation operation in Maui. The firm eventually expanded into cattle ranching and railroads and later pineapples. In 1900 the partnership became Alexander & Baldwin, Ltd. By 1905, A&B owned plantations throughout Maui as well as on Kaua'i. In 1908, the company also purchased part of the Matson Navigation Company. The new building on Bishop Street would serve as an advertisement for the firm's success and provide office space for its many clerks and other personnel. With the A&B building, the architects' aim was to 'produce a building suitable to the climate, environment, history, and geographical position of Hawaii'. The completed structure of the building was also innovative in several ways, including the steel structural skeleton, the introduction of a logia on the fourth floor, and the planned setback, filled with tropical trees and vegetation (including mature coconut palms) by landscape architect Richard C. Tongg. Its double-pitched (bell-cast) roof recalled early buildings of the Kingdom Period and helped sustain a precedent that came to define the 'Hawaiian Style' architecture of the Territorial Period. Both architects agreed upon the application of Chinese motifs throughout the building. These include circular symbols of good fortune on the portico's ceiling and travertine door frames, images of bats (fu, also a representation of fortune), and the Chinese symbol for longevity (shou) on the column capitals. Other motifs include relief panels of Hawaiian fish, buffalo heads, and Chinese cherubs. Another innovation was the two-story interior lobby space. Unfortunately, this building was remodeled with the insertion of a floor to create more space for users. However, the black Belgian marble and travertine floor remains as do the murals above. *WC*

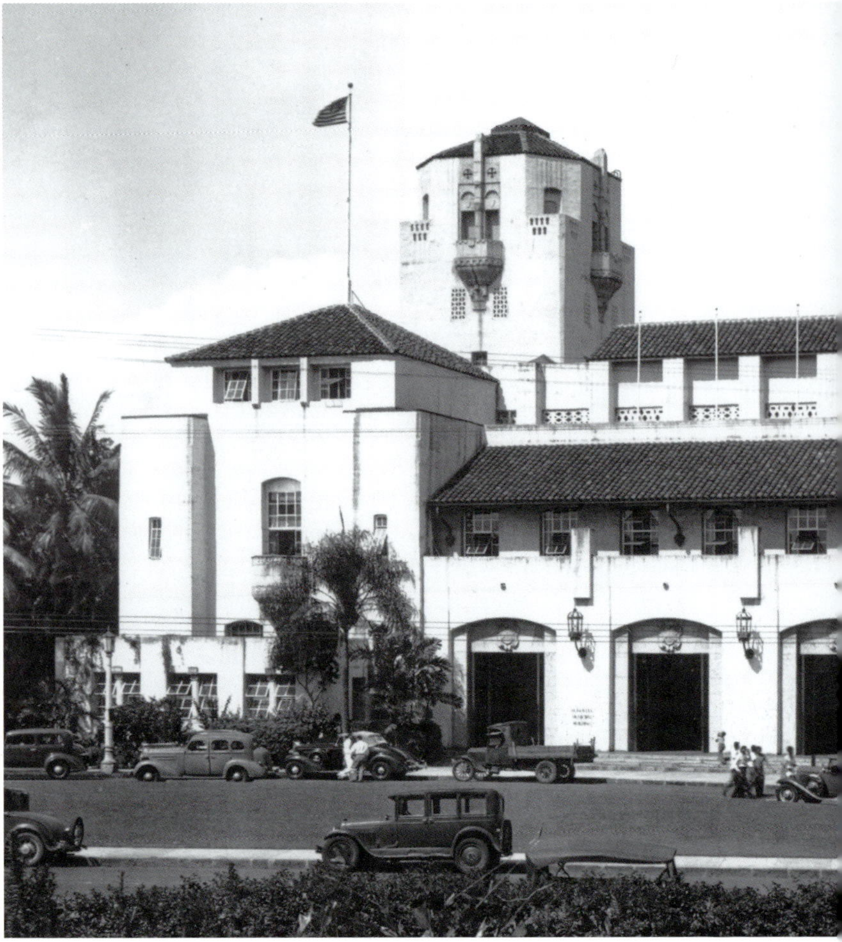

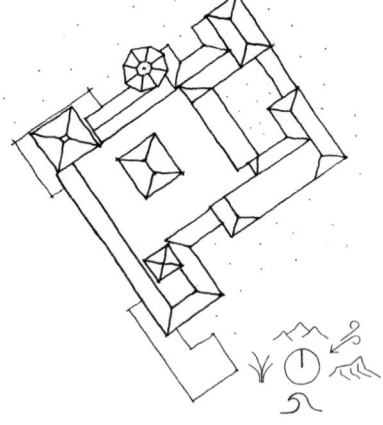

Honolulu Hale

024 B

530 S King St
Honolulu, HI 96813
Robert Miller, Guy Rothwell,
Dickey & Wood
1929

Another of Hawaii's impressive Spanish Colonial Revival buildings, Honolulu Hale is the composite creation of three well-known Hawaii architects, C. W. Dickey, Hart Wood, and Robert G. Miller, together with the larger firm of Rothwell, Kangeter & Lester. The city hall complex combines elements of Spanish Colonial and Islamic styles reflective of the preferred architectural design in Hawaii during the 1920s and 1930s. The structure includes an octagonal tower and an open courtyard space (with retractable roof). It remains a place of considerable civic pride and the location of many public events. The first city hall for Honolulu, also known as Honolulu Hale, was on Merchant Street. It served nearly all the functions of government, including the Kingdom of Hawaii's Custom House, the Treasury Department, the Department of Education, and the Departments of Interior and Foreign Affairs. In 1905,

3

under the Territory of Hawaii, the government moved the city's services into a building on King Street. Two years later, the existing County of Oahu and Board of Supervisors for the city combined to establish the City and County of Honolulu. With several false starts, the City Council finally agreed upon a new City Hall to be built at the corner of King and Punchbowl Streets, on a lot acquired for $245,791. With many of the city's merchants surprised by the move away from downtown, the mayor, Charles Arnold, defended the choice as enhancing the beauty of nearby Iolani Palace. The architects ascribed the design to a range of architectural styles. The interior courtyard was modeled after the Bargello in Florence. Other features recalled Spanish architecture of the Alhambra in Granada and public buildings in Seville. The architects, who assumed the collective name of Allied Architects, completed their designs in 1927. The city awarded the contract to Walker & Olund, Ltd. The project was completed in 450 days, following the construction firm's initial bid of $714,120. The contractor hired Einar Peterson to paint frescoes for the interior; Mario Valdastri installed the intricate stonework. The building officially opened on 17 December 1929. Landscaping, designed by Richard Tongg, was an afterthought and did not begin until 1930. The City Hall, soon named Honolulu Hale, required an extension in 1951. This new addition followed the design of the original and consisted of two three-story wings built on the mauka (north) side of the original structure. Later additions include the introduction of a driveway on the King Street side and a fountain, dating to 1967. The City Hall's earlier parking area was eliminated by Mayor Frank Fasi in 1978, creating the present park-like space around the building. *WC*

US Post Office, Custom and Court House

025 B

335 Merchant St
Honolulu, HI96813
York & Sawyer
1919–1929

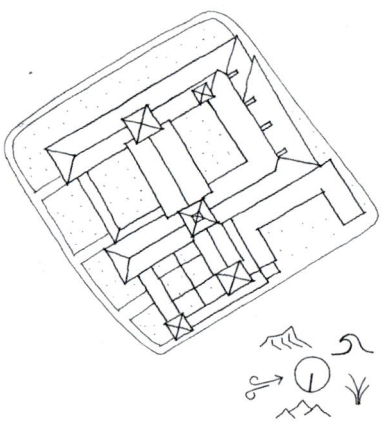

Designed by New York architects York and Sawyer, the United States Post Office and Customs House also served as the federal district court for much of the twentieth century. In 1977, many of the functions of the complex were transferred to a new federal building located on Punchbowl Street. First completed in 1922, the National Register-listed property adheres to the Spanish Colonial Revival style. This style, characterized by arched windows, broad overhanging eaves, a red tile roof, and a courtyard garden, came to typify official architecture in Hawaii in the Territorial Period. Today the building still houses the downtown post office and other state offices. The federal presence in the territory was slow to catch hold. With annexation in 1900, the new territorial government relied on existing buildings from the Kingdom Period for its many functions. The government chose the New York firm of York and Swayer. They were known for their classically inspired architecture in the Beaux Arts tradition. Among their buildings were the New York Historical Society on Central Park, the Federal Reserve Bank in the financial district, and the Herbert C. Hoover Building in Washington, D.C. One of their only buildings in an exotic style was the Edificio First National Bank of Boston in Buenos Aires, built in 1921, which in fact employed Spanish Colonial motifs. The architects began their design in 1918, with construction delayed until 1921 to 1922. The structure included a custom department, a post office (replacing the 1877 Kamehameha V post office on Merchant Street), and offices of various departments of the federal government. In 1929, the government authorized an expansion of the complex – a project completed in 1931. The Spanish Colonial Revival complex matched the nearby Honolulu Hale and the Hawaiian Electric Company building one block ewa (west), both completed in 1927. The Hawaiian Electric Company building was also designed by York and Sawyer. *WC*

Honolulu Advertiser Building 026 B

605 Kapiolani Blvd
Honolulu, HI 96813
Emory & Webb
1930

The former home of the *Honolulu Advertiser,* Hawaii's longest-running newspaper (1856–2010), the News Building is a combined neoclassical and Renaissance Revival-style structure with distinct nods to its Hawaiian setting. The recessed entrance's balustraded steps, round-arched central window, and two-story Ionic pilasters still provide a dynamic focal point and once anticipated an ornately decorated lobby beyond. Unfortunately, much of the interior was lost as part of an early twenty-first-century project that added 1,000 affordable housing units on the 3.7-acre site. The 1930 Beaux Arts structure, designed by architects Walter Emory and Marshall Webb, was put up for sale by Gannet Pacific Corp. in 2005, but an initial agreement for its purchase came only in 2010. That failing, the property lay dormant for a few years while it served as a soundstage for the television show *Hawaii Five-O*. In 2017, local housing developer Marshall Hung and the investment group Tradewind Capital Group Inc. purchased the property, subsequently constructing the twin-towered complex around and over the original structure, leaving the mauka and Ewa façades intact. *WC*

Photo: Don Hibbard

Ewa Plantation → 027 A

91 Park Row
Ewa Beach, HI 96706
Various
1890–1935

Ewa Plantation consists of the preserved remains of a one-time sugar plantation, consisting of offices, a community center, schools, society buildings, and housing for as many as 5,000 sugar workers and their dependents. Initiated by Scotch-Irish immigrant James Campbell, who bought the land for the plantation for $2.32 an acre in 1877, the 41,000-acre tract at Honouliuli had been considered suitable only for cattle grazing. Circumstances changed in 1879 when Campbell hired Englishman James Ashley to place an artesian well in the tract. Ashley struck water at 240 feet,

providing a source of water for irrigation for over 60 years. In 1889, Campbell leased his lands to Benjamin F. Dillingham for $50,000 a year; Dillingham, whose principal financial interest was in transporting sugar on his railways, in turn leased the property to W. R. Castle, who began sugar production. In 1890 the Ewa Plantation Company was founded. The first crop, resulting in 2,849 tons of sugar, was harvested in 1892. Under the management of W. J. Lowrie, Ewa was developed into the beginnings of a model plantation complex. Lowrie supervised the building of the original mill structures, an office, stables, blacksmith shop, barracks-like buildings for the 470 Chinese contract laborers and two small villages, known as camps, primarily for Japanese married workers and their families. Under Lowrie's successor George F. Renton, who took over as manager in 1899, the company expanded its housing and other facilities and moved to the forefront of sugar companies with the plantation's experimentation with the use fertilizers and new varieties of sugar cane. Renton's son George, Jr. expanded upon the company's tradition for innovation when he assumed control of operations in 1920. With the company showing a profit of $5,000,000 in 1921, the decision was made to make a substantial investment in plant improvements and housing. The historic community that remains today is primarily that created during George Renton, Jr.'s stewardship. In 1924 he reported that 337 laborers' cottages had

been remodeled, 20 skilled workers' houses were renovated, and 246 new cottages were built. Spread over 14 camps by the end of his time as manager in 1937, Ewa included probably the most advanced mill and processing plant in Hawaii, numerous supporting structures, a post office, company store, a large administration building, a recreation center, hospital, schools and modern, well-maintained houses for the company's employees. With its construction campaign of 1936, Ewa created what was on the surface an ideal – though strongly hierarchical – society. The houses constructed that year, designed by one of Honolulu's leading architects, Hart Wood, were equal to and even exceeded middle-class housing elsewhere in Hawaii. These feature double-pitched (bell-cast) roofs, exposed Douglas fir interiors, and inset lanai. Additional housing was added in the post-Second World War period, again resembling middle class residences elsewhere in Hawaii. With the end of sugar production and the decline of the community in the late twentieth century, Ewa Plantation became the property of the City and County of Honolulu, which began a long-term effort to preserve the character of the historic community. Called the Ewa Villages Revitalization Project, the priorities for the program were: 1) to preserve the historic character of the remaining plantation complex; 2) to provide housing for the approximately 1,100 residents; 3) to develop a water diversion program to remove the villages from the flood zone; and 4) to break even

financially. In addition to rehabilitation, the city's plan called for the construction of 1,500 infill units scattered among existing housing or in separate new villages. There was also a call to preserve the manager's residence and the company headquarters and to repurpose other buildings such as the original plant. Some of this ambitious plan was realized; other aspects were not. Nonetheless, the existing array of plantation buildings, ranging from simple 1920s and 1930s residences through larger houses once inhabited by overseers and accountants still provides a vivid sense of the plantation community during its peak period of operation. *WC*

Dillingham Transportation Building ↓

028 B

735 Bishop St
Honolulu, HI 96813
Lincoln Rogers
1930

Located at the foot of Bishop Street, the Dillingham Transportation Building is one of the last remaining palazzo-like business headquarters in downtown Honolulu. Once one of about ten large office complexes – only Castle and Cooke farther mauka on the same street rivals it – Dillingham Transportation is an elegant composition of cast stone, rough-textured stucco, and terracotta tiles, punctuated by an ornate arcaded entrance and both single and paired windows with conventional operable sashes. Adjacent to the harbor, the structure points to the Dillingham family's longstanding connection to transportation in the islands. Motifs include the street openings decorated with a twisted-rope pattern and large medallions featuring sailing and steam ships. The glazed bricks in the arcade area represent ship's compasses. Lincoln Rogers was a prolific New York and local architect, also noted for the design of the United Armed Services YMCA (originally the Army and Navy YMCA) on Hotel Street, a project completed in 1928. The Dillingham Transportation Building is a prime example of the kind of Mediterranean Revival or Italian Renaissance architecture that dominated large Hawaii buildings in the 1920s. Mediterranean and Spanish Mission architecture seemed tropical and appropriate to Hawaii's climate and the closest thing traditional European architecture had to offer Hawaii. Such buildings featured hipped roofs, arched arcades, ornately playful decorative motifs, and a sense of airiness despite their solidity and bulk. The entrance lobby and arcade provide a slight contrast to the tripartite main block. This features not only the nautical references but also elegant art deco-style light fixtures, burnished bronze elevator doors, and cast stone panels depicting Hawaiian flora and fauna. The decorative ceiling is the work of artist Einar Peterson. A separate owner's apartment pokes out from the roof of the central pavilion. The Dillingham Transportation Building shares arcade space with the nearby mirror-clad Pacific Guardian Building, whose street address is via the Dillingham Transportation Building's lobby. *WC*

Photo: Bishop Museum, 1930

C. Brewer Building

827 Fort Street Mall
Honolulu, HI 96813
Mayers, Murrey & Phillip
1931

More like a home than an office building, the C. Brewer & Co. exemplifies the 'Territorial Style' of architecture in Hawaii – a combination of Moorish, Mediterranean Revival, and Spanish Colonial Revival elements, which came to define high-end residential, commercial, and governmental projects during the 1920s and early 1930s. The building, with its high masonry walls, shaded garden areas, and two-story elevation, has the feeling of a private estate, expressing a sense of proprietorship and authority that C. Brewer & Co. clearly wished to convey in its Honolulu headquarters. Occupying a key corner in downtown Honolulu's commercial core, the C. Brewer & Co. building presents a strongly textured stucco surface toward both Queen and Fort Streets. A curved stucco-covered concrete and basalt (blue-stone) wall defines the corner of the site along the Queen and Fort Street intersection, lending it a sense of privacy and mystery. This rises about 7 feet above grade to envelop the two garden spaces – one toward Fort Street and one at the rear of the property – offering passersby views of the tops of hedges and groves of coconut and Palmyra palms within. In its organization, the building consists of the central block with two intersecting wings, one on the Queen Street side and another at the rear toward the Diamond Head direction. Two stories in height, the building has combined basalt and concrete walls, uniformly covered with a rough stucco coating identical to that used on the garden walls. The most prominent features are a belvedere over the Fort Street entrance, a longer second-story recess along the garden side of the Queen Street section, and a cantilevered balcony with cast and wrought iron rails, posts, and balusters extending the full length of the central block, again on the garden side. The cantilevered balcony links the building to the Monterey style, a sub-set of the Spanish Colonial Revival style originating in California and popular in many parts of the US at the time. There is also a covered lanai at the edge of the rear garden, forming a protected walkway on two sides of the open terrace area. Irregular lava rock (basaltic) slabs cover the open area; square mission tiles provide the flooring for the covered lanais. A red, barrel-tiled roof gives unity to the complex. The roof has the distinctive bell-cast (double-pitched) shape associated with what scholars now identify as a distinctive regional style in Hawaii. Although unifying, the roof has several distinct sections. These include the taller hipped roof form of the principal block together with a matching cross hip on the makai and Diamond

Photo: Bishop Museum, 1938

3

Head wings. Shed roofs cover the lanai in the rear garden area and an enclosed utilitarian space at the rear of the building. The history of the company stretches back to the mid-nineteenth century. Once located in the government-constructed Market House at the base of Nu'uanu Street, this smallest of the Big Five companies had completed a new two-story office building in 1899 on Queen Street, designed by architects and C. W. Dickey and Clinton Briggs Ripley. In 1921, the partners decided to gamble on a much larger site, purchasing a large lot at the corner of King and Richards Street. This plan fell through, however, and in 1928 the firm decided to build its headquarters near the center of Honolulu's commercial life at the intersection of Queen and Fort Streets. The company's newly elected President Richard A. Cooke took charge of the project beginning in 1930. With the concurrence of Philipp E. Spalding, his eventual successor and his brother-in-law, Cooke hired Hardie Phillip of Mayer, Murray and Phillip – Goodhue Associates' successor firm – to design the new building. The owners intended the building to stand for 'hundreds of years', according to a report in the *Honolulu Advertiser* in November 1930. Ben Hiyashi was the project's engineer. Local Japanese mason Edward K. Sugihara supervised the installation of 'thousands of blocks of natural stone'. The general contractor was Walker and Olund, Ltd. Contractors and Builders; the total contract was for $319,258. Reminiscent of some of the older private houses that once graced the port city's back streets, the new headquarters also encompassed a garden area. While supervised by Phillip, the actual design of placement and installation of the many tropical shrubs, vines, and trees was the responsibility of landscape architects Catherine Jones Richards and Robert Oliver Thompson. The C. Brewer Building opened on 5 November 1930, after a little over one year of work. There were periodic modifications of the interior, including a major renovation in 1956. The C. Brewer Building would serve as the company's headquarters until 1998 when the firm's management moved to Hilo. The property management firm American Land Company took over the building and initiated an extensive renovation of the interior and garden areas as well as repairs of the building's many bronze windows and other features – a project the Historic Hawaii Foundation recognized with a special award in 1998. Modified to suit its new tenants, the property served for several years as the administrative offices of the University of Phoenix, an internationally recognized center for non-traditional learning. The building now houses the statewide headquarters of the Hawaii Community Foundation, which moved into the building in 2010. *WC*

Photo: Bishop Museum, 1940

Harkness Nurses Home
 030 B

1301 Punchbowl St
Honolulu, HI 96813
C. W. Dickey
1932

Designed by well-known regionalist architect C. W. Dickey in 1932, this essay in combined Italian Renaissance and Spanish Mission Revival styles served originally as a nurses' home on the grounds of Queen's Hospital. Distinctive features include a red tile, a double-pitched hipped roof, and a central arcade defining the garden area. The asymmetrical plan provides a sense of balance, with the front-facing projection of the gable-roofed makai wing offsetting the square, slightly elevated mauka corner and its shorter, hipped-roof wing. Framed by the wings, the first-story Corinthian-columned arcade provides a backdrop for the generous lawn of the courtyard space. The arcade second-floor balconies and open third-floor corridor further break up the mass of the building, creating a sense of continuity between the garden and the building's structure. It is interesting that Dickey chose to cite the Italian Renaissance architect Filippo Brunelleschi in the courtyard area. The arcade suggests that of the Spedale degli Innocenti (Hospital of the Innocents or Foundling Hospital) in Florence, one of the Italian architect's first major projects. The projecting balcony of the mauka block also aligns with the Monterey style, a popular revival

movement associated with the settlement of California. The second-story belvedere over the arcade also hints back to an earlier time, its short columns and wide capitals suggestive of medieval architecture. The building was gifted by philanthropist Edward S. Harkness of New York City. It now functions as offices and laboratories, though its future is under threat by plans for the hospital's expansion. *WC*

Makiki Christian Church ↗
 031 B

829 Pensacola St
Honolulu, HI 96814
Hego Fuchino
1934 (1952)

An extraordinary monument off King Street and opposite McKinley High School, Makiki Christian Church brings a starting vision of late medieval Japan to Honolulu. Designed after the congregation's abandonment of an earlier church and location, Makiki Christian Church was the singular translation of a Japanese castle to a new religious purpose. The design began after the decision to move in 1927. The architect was Hego Fuchino, a combined architect and engineer architect who had studied civil engineering at the University of Hawaii following his arrival to the Territory of Hawaii as an older teenager. Before working on the Makiki Christian Church he had designed the Nippon Theatre and Kaimuki Playhouse and had renovated the Hawaii Shingon Mission. Many of his designs favored Japanese precedent, so

the Makiki Church was not out of character. The Makiki Church was a collaborator of Fuchino and the church's pastor, Takie Okumura. The pastor had begun his mission in 1903, following his separation from the Honolulu Japanese Christian Church (now the Nuuanu Congregationalist Church). This resulted in the creation of the Makiki Church, originally located on land donated by Honolulu businessman George Castle in 1905. The resulting church, constructed the following year, served its purpose well, but by the 1920s was showing its age. The present Makiki Church was meant to be its replacement. The new church's castle-like design was based on the Edo-period Kochi Castle in Kochi Prefecture, Japan – the place of Okumura's birth. The pastor intended it to signify the peace and security of his home, despite the evident military connotations. The construction is primarily wood. Built in 1931, the project was completed in time for its dedication on 6 November 1932. A dining hall and classroom building, designed by local Chinese architect Y. T. Car, were added in 1936 and the Christian Education Building followed in 1960. *WC*

Montague Hall ↓

1601 Punahou St
Honolulu, HI 96822
C. W. Dickey
1937

032 C

Described by the *Honolulu Advertiser* at the time of its opening as 'an idealized conception of modern Hawaiian' architecture, this music building combines the simplicity of the then-emerging modern movement with features of the Hawaiian style advocated by Dickey. With its plastered concrete walls, deep lanai, and clay tile, double pitched hipped roof, the building continued the forms previously established by Dickey and Goodhue Associates at Kamehameha School for Girls (1931). The L-shaped building's entry focuses on a 40-by-72-foot courtyard bounded by a mock orange hedge.

Photo: DeSoto Brown

The two-story main body of the building features deep inset lanai on each story and the graceful single-story recital hall wing opens to the courtyard thanks to its 72-foot long recessed loggia with three sets of double doors. The lanai and loggia feature sleek columns with inscribed astragals, and the building's beautiful acid stained concrete floors were the work of Robert Lammens. A prominent outdoor set of steps help frame the makai side of the courtyard and ascend to a second story roof terrace, which further emphasizes the open air character of the building. Stylized musical motifs in masonry screens remind people that Montague Hall houses Punahou's school of music. Named in honor of missionary wife Juliette Montague Cooke, who taught singing at Royal School in Honolulu during the 1840s and 1850s, the building holds an 80-seat recital hall, a large orchestra room and 13 sound-proofed studios, as well as administrative offices. In addition, the courtyard serves as a venue for outdoor evening performances. *WC*

Doris Duke Residence

4055 Pāpū Cir
Honolulu, HI 96816
Marion Simms Wyeth
1939

Known for its collection of Islamic objects and rooms, the Shangri La Museum of Islamic Art, Culture and Design occupies the former home of heiress and philanthropist Doris Duke. Designed in 1936 by architect Marion Simms Wyeth, the original estate property incorporated Duke's unparalleled collection of Islamic antiquities, including several entire rooms acquired during trips to the Near and Middle East. The present complex occupies a beach and rocky headland known as Black Point – at the time of construction a remote rural spot on the island of Oahu. Duke's plan called for cut coral rock from the bay, and workers moved volcanic rock around to create a slip for her then husband James Cromwell's yacht. As docents explain, Duke continually rearranged the

Photo: Olivier Koning

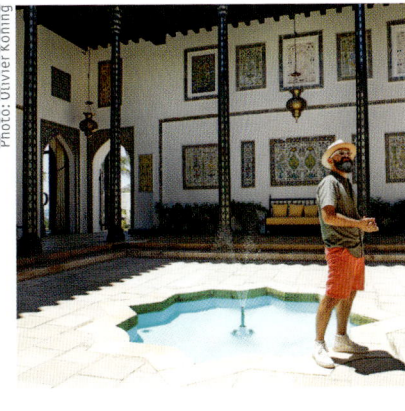

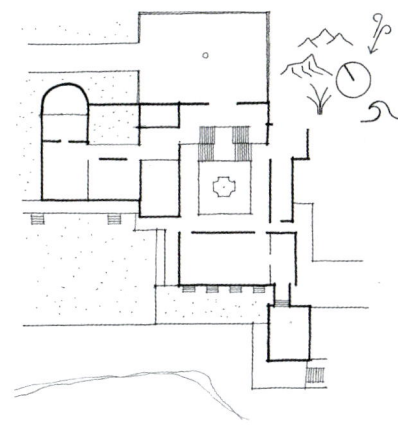

collections and often re-situated pieces and designs, including tile works from Isfahan and Turkey to create a total design environment. In all, the collection includes objects and rooms from Iran, Morocco, Spain, Syria, Egypt, and India. The house complex itself includes several conjoined rooms and pavilions. The seaside terrace and principal living area borrow directly from Persepolis, repeating the unique double capital motif common to Achaemenid architecture of 500 BCE. Duke's own bedroom features a marble bathroom based on Moghul designs. A 'playhouse' located at the head of a saltwater pool is a reduced-scale version of the fourteenth-century Chehel Sotoun in Isfahan. An extensive cascading garden is inspired by the Moghul Shalimar Gardens in Lahore, dating from 1641–1642. It is possible to visit the 4.9 acre house and grounds through the Honolulu Museum of Art, which partners with the Islamic museum. *WC*

Photo: Philipp Meuser

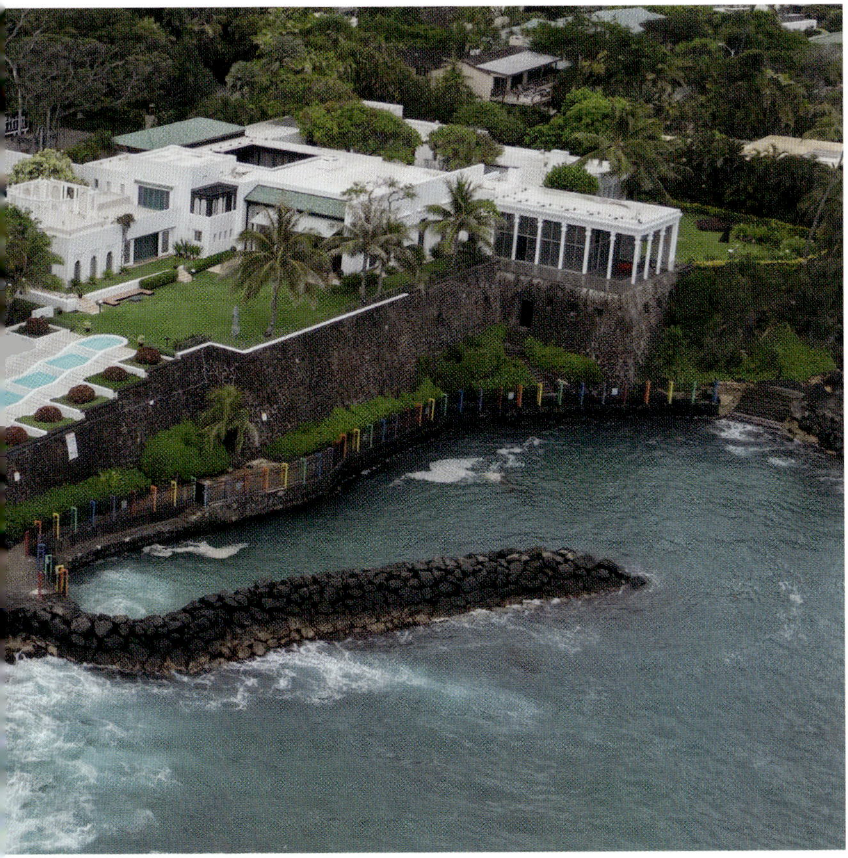

Photo: Bishop Museum, 1936

Church of the Crossroads ↑

034 C

1212 University Ave
Honolulu, HI 96826
Claude Stiehl
1934–1937

An early example of modern-style architecture in Hawaii, the church complex celebrates the splendid climate of Hawaii with its layout around a central courtyard. A covered colonnade, inspired by the Summer Palace outside Beijing and the Temple of Heaven in that city, connects the four buildings and provides respite from the heat of the sun and the frequent Manoa showers. The classroom and meeting hall draw on Japanese design and their large sliding windows allow breezes to circulate within. The compound presents a mix of traditions, including Hawaiian, Japanese, Chinese, and Western art deco, well reflecting that the church was Hawaii's earliest inter-racial congregation, having been formed in 1923 by students from Mid-Pacific Institute and McKinley High School. The art work of Honolulu artist Margarite Blasingame graces the Philippine apitong (mahogany) lectern and pulpit as well as appearing in the cast-stone panels framing the entrance to the church. The sensitivity to scale, detailing, and integration of art with architecture make the complex a distinctive statement on regional design in Hawaii during the 1930s. *DH*

Ala Moana Park
1201 Ala Moana Blvd
Honolulu, HI 96814
Harry Sims Bent
1937

035 B

One of the wiser expenditures of federal money, unskilled laborers paid by the New Deal's Federal Employment Relief Administration and Civil Works Administration programs converted a former garbage dump into a 76-acre public park. Ala Moana is one of the two principal parks in Honolulu, along with Kapiolani Park, and is the largest of four art deco-inspired parks designed by Harry Sims Bent during the 1930s. The others include Mother Waldron Park in Kakaako, Kawananakoa Play Ground in Nuuanu, and Haleiwa Beach Park. Laid out by landscape architects Catherine Jones Richards and Robert O. Thompson, the park retains its semicircular drive traversing the length of the park and lagoons at each end. The eastern lagoon, with its bordering coconut palms, was given a Hawaiian character, while the western body of water has a Japanese accent. The single mile of white sand beach was added in 1955, and the 36-acre Magic Island was constructed in 1962. The eastern entrance portals (1934), a whimsical equestrian bridge (1934) with round arches, the McCoy Pavilion (1937), and the Lawn Bowling Green (1939) are all the work of Bent. The McCoy Pavilion features an extraordinary Mughal-inspired banyan court, which drew its inspiration from a postcard of a Balinese garden with stone tree boxes adjacent to shaded reflection pools. With coral-stone pavers, mature Chinese banyan trees in elevated planters, and slightly below-grade concave and convex water elements, the enchanting banyan court is an idyllic world unto itself. Marble bas reliefs and slate opus sectiles by local artist Margarite Blasingame further adorn the space and celebrate traditional Hawaiian culture, as do a pair of murals by Robert Lee Eskridge in the entry pavilion. Across from the McCoy Pavilion, Bent bequeathed the city another unusual architectural experience: a meticulously crisp, clean-lined, art deco bowling green. The enclosed green provides an ordered, tranquil setting for a round of relaxing outdoor recreation beneath the trade-wind-cooled, blue sky. *DH, HM*

Wo Fat Restaurant ↓

103 N Hotel St
Honolulu, HI 96817
Y. T. Char
1938

036 B

An overt expression of the Chinese presence in Honolulu and in turn a celebration of Hawaii's multicultural population, this building is a rather rare example of an explicitly 'Chinese'-style building within Chinatown. With its corner, pagoda-like tower, this reinforced concrete framed building transmits a strong heritage statement, which is further augmented by a tile roof with upturned eaves and fretted transom windows. Originally designed with retail spaces on the ground floor and a restaurant on the upper stories, it is now undergoing an adaptive reuse to house a boutique hotel. Wo Fat was one of a number of Asian-style buildings designed by Y. T. Char. Other buildings include the Lau Yee Chai restaurant in Waikiki (1929; no longer extant), Chungshan Chinese Language School (1935; no longer extant), Korean Christian Church (1938; no longer extant), and Hilo's Chinese Christian Church (1937). Born in Waipahu in 1890, Char graduated from Mills Institute (later Mid-Pacific Institute) and then in 1915 from Cornell's school of architecture. *DH*

Photo: Olivier Koning

Photo: Don Hibbard

3

Seaside Apartments

037 C

440 Seaside Ave #910
Honolulu, HI 96815
Dahl & Conrad
1939

A rare surviving example of the garden court apartments that dotted Waikiki prior to the Second World War, the two-story brick Seaside Apartments focus on an enclosed, paved courtyard, to which a moon gate provides street access. Once accommodating ten apartments, the L-shaped building now houses a pair of restaurants. Its cantilevered second story lanai/corridor retains its original wrought iron railing rendered in a stylized foliage pattern. With its scale, original decorative motifs, and open air ambiance, the former apartments stand as a wistful reminder of a gentler time when the Royal Hawaiian Hotel was the tallest building in the area. *DH*

Photo: Don Hibbard

Photo: Don Hibbard

Church of Jesus Christ of Latter-Day Saints

1560 S Beretania St
Honolulu, HI 96826
Pope & Burton
1941

One of the earliest major buildings in Honolulu to be rendered in a modern style, this complex of five buildings spreads over a 4-acre parcel, with a lushly landscaped front terrace and two internal courtyards. Set back from the street, royal palms and a 100-foot-long reflecting pool define the main axis of the entrance terrace and recall the grand processional from the highway to the Latter-Day Saints temple in Laie. Folding doors and wood louvers open each of the buildings on three sides, and lanai, covered passageways, concrete grilles, and pergolas further accentuate the tabernacle's embrace of nature, making 'the outdoors a part of the harmony of the completed project'.

Architect Harold W. Burton informed reporters that the climate determined the design of the building and allowed the development of 'an intimate relation between the interiors of the building and the garden'. The 14-foot-high mosaic of Christ above the entrance portal contains over 100,000 Italian colored glass tesserae and was designed by Eugene Savage, a professor of painting at Yale University, who is best known in Hawaii for his paintings that graced the Matson Ocean Liner menus of the 1950s. *DH, RL*

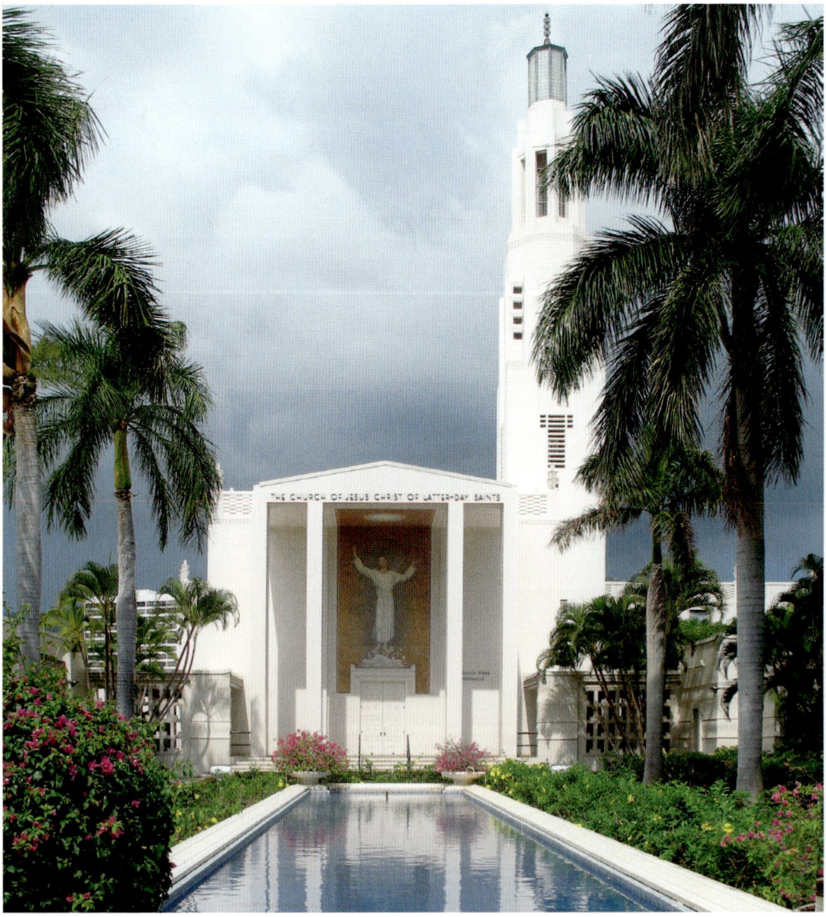

National Cemetery of the Pacific

039 B

2177 Puowaina Dr
Honolulu, HI 96813
Thompson & Thompson with
Weihe, Frick & Kruse and Theodore Vierra
1949

The National Memorial Cemetery of the Pacific is located within the crater of a 275,000 year old volcano, Puowaina, also known as Punchbowl, and occupies 30 of the 114.54 acres located on the floor and sides of the caldera. The verdant interior walls of the crater form an all-encompassing green backdrop for the cemetery, shielding any disturbing elements from the bordering areas of urban development, making Punchbowl a hallowed place removed from the exigencies of everyday life. An approximately 800-foot central boulevard is lined by Chinese banyan trees and provides the cemetery an east-west axis from which its symmetric plan radiates. Above the boulevard's western terminus, an imposing, semi-circular Pacific War Memorial serves as a focal point. Honoring the missing from the Second World War's Pacific theatre and the Korean and Vietnam wars, it was the first memorial erected on American soil by the American Battle Monuments Commission, with two other memorials later built in New York and San Francisco to honor those who perished during the Second World War in the waters of the western Atlantic and eastern Pacific oceans respectively. The center point of the memorial is dominated by a 33-foot statue of Columbia designed by sculptor E. Bruce Morse. Behind the statue is a small chapel with a groin vaulted ceiling. Accessed through openings on either side, the chapel has no doors and its stone side walls each feature a pair of round arched, 8' 9" bronze grilles adorned with gold, blue, and red glass cabochons that were made in Italy. The grilles look out on enclosed gardens and offer an open-air serenity. The curved arcades to either side of the chapel feature mosaics depicting the major battles of the Second World War in the Pacific and Korea. Two more recent pavilions, designed by Fung Architects, honor those who perished in the Vietnam conflict. *DH*

Photo: DeSoto Brown

3

4

Canlis Restaurant

2100 Kalākaua Ave
Honolulu, HI 96815
Wimberly & Cook
1954

040 C

In 1947, Peter Canlis opened his own new restaurant in Waikiki, having run the dining room of the Army-Navy YMCA in downtown Honolulu since 1941. He called his new place the Charcoal Broiler, which featured exhibition cooking on a custom copper grill in the dining room. This was successful but was forced to close when its building was demolished in 1953 for the construction of a new hotel. Canlis then thought about leaving Hawaii, but he did not, and instead signed a lease for another spot in Waikiki on the corner of Kalakaua Avenue and Kalaimoku Street. His architect friend Pete Wimberly designed an eye-catching new structure for his Canlis Charcoal Broiler on this site that took only three months to build, opening in March 1954. The new restaurant used a great deal of native lava rock and mortar for rough-textured walls that contrasted with shiny terrazzo floors. Sliding doors were copied from traditional Japanese shoji panels. The roof, sheathed with 10,000 pounds of copper, was fitted with a checkerboard of 15 square plexiglass skylights that provided sunlight for the ferns and orchids growing on the entry wall below. Here, water dripped down a tiled surface into a shallow decorative pool containing various ceramic fish sculptures. A 14-foot tiki-themed carving by sculptor Ed Brownlee hung on one rock wall of the bar. Carrying over from the previous restaurant was an even larger custom copper grill for the steaks that were a feature of the menu. Canlis was an upscale, high-end restaurant that carried on for decades. Eventually it passed into different ownerships, the last being a Japanese restaurant company that purchased it in 1987. Only two years later it closed forever. This notable mid-century structure, sadly, was demolished. *DB*

Waikikian Hotel

041 B

1811 Ala Moana Blvd
Honolulu, HI 96815
Wimberly & Cook
1956

Constructed on a narrow 2½-acre lot, the Waikikian Hotel combined some established elements of American motels with fantasy touches from Polynesia. Most of the business consisted of two two-story walk-up buildings containing hotel rooms with various tiki motifs, along with the then-popular sliding doors that copied traditional Japanese shoji panels. The structures faced each other, and in between were the 'Tiki Gardens' that contained 18 wooden carvings by sculptor Edward Brownlee among the lush foliage. While the exotic touches were special, the overall layout was like what could be found in many parts of the United States. The really unique part of the Waikikian was its lobby. This was an angled structure with a dramatically curvaceous and swooping roof that was described in the hotel's publicity as being a 'hyperbolic paraboloid'. The shape was chosen by architects Pete Wimberly and Howard Cook to attract attention, since just next door was the much larger and heavily publicized Hawaiian Village Hotel, developed by the ultra-wealthy Henry J. Kaiser. The highest points of the all-wooden roof were 42 feet high; it weighed 26 tons and rested mostly on just two concrete supports. When the supports for this structure were first removed, Wimberly supposedly stood in the center of the roof and jumped up and down to insure it would successfully remain standing. A six-floor addition to the Waikikian called the Tiki Tower opened in 1959. The Waikikian's dining room was the Tahitian Lanai, a restaurant built and owned by the local Spencecliff Restaurants chain. It was actively patronized by local residents in addition to the hotel's guests and remained popular until it closed in 1996. The hotel, in increasingly decrepit condition, was mostly demolished in 1997 and the property remained vacant for nine years until construction began on the Hilton Hawaiian Village Hotel's Grand Waikikian timeshare tower; this finally opened in 2008. *DB*

4

International Market Place

042 C

2330 Kalākaua Ave
Honolulu, HI 96815
Wimberly & Cook
1956

Photo: DeSoto Brown, ca. 1958

Don the Beachcomber began his career in Hollywood in the early 1930s, one of the creators of exotic cocktails and the tiki bar concept. After spending the Second World War in the US Army, he returned in 1945 to a business break-up in which his ex-wife took control of his restaurants and he was forced to move to Hawaii. In 1948 he opened a complex of three Polynesian-style structures in the heart of Waikiki, where he served his established Cantonese menu and well-known rum-based cocktails. The property, however, had a lease that would expire in 1956, which led Don to even bigger plans. Backed by two wealthy investors, Don signed a new lease for a larger site from the landowner and was then able to dream up a grander version of the South Seas fantasy that he had merchandized for years. This was the International Market Place. Working with architect Pete Wimberly, who was already established with projects that combined American mid-century idioms with Polynesian elements, a mixture of exotic structures comprised the Market Place when it opened in March 1957. Essentially just a shopping

Photo: DeSoto Brown, 1960

Photo: DeSoto Brown, 1964

Photo: DeSoto Brown, ca. 1960

center – a booming business model in the US in the 1950s – the International Market Place added an abundance of palms and other tropical vegetation, water features, open-air storefronts, and the attraction of free hula shows to pull in tourist customers from busy Kalakaua Avenue. Carved wooden sculptures by popular commercial artist Ed Brownlee highlighted the main entrance and smaller versions were dotted around in the shrubbery inside. Even the trash cans (re-used metal oil barrels) sported their own miniature thatched roofs. A notable addition to the Market Place's fantasy feeling was Don's treehouse, perched in the immense banyan tree just inside the entrance. Originally used as a private hideaway dining room for romantic couples who were provided with a gourmet dinner and

4

Photo: Olivier Koning

Photo: Daniel Luna

two bottles of champagne, the treehouse then passed through a variety of other uses including as a radio station broadcast studio and one of Don's business offices. Over the succeeding decades, the International Market Place continued to grow until it reached Kuhio Avenue on its inland boundary. More and more structures were added, increasingly disparate in appearance, along with hundreds of individual merchants using small kiosks and pushcarts. In 2013 the complex closed and was subsequently demolished in its entirety, retaining only the iconic banyan tree. Three years later the current International Market Place opened as an entirely new and coherent structure with an emphasis on upscale retail tenants. *DB*

La Mariana Sailing Club ↑

50 Sand Island Access Rd
Honolulu, HI 96819
Amalgamation
1957

043 **B**

Located in a truly unexpected industrial area, the charm of La Mariana is plainly evident to all who appreciate a true old-style tiki bar. The interior decor is a mix of carvings and other faux-Polynesian objects gathered from classic, now-vanished establishments in Honolulu – Trader Vic's, Don the Beachcomber, Kon-Tiki, the Waikikian Hotel, and the Tahitian Lanai. The late and beloved Nanette Nahinu came to Hawaii in the 1950s on a sailboat with her then-husband.

Living aboard their moored vessel, they got the idea to create a small marina for others like them. This they did, in Keehi Lagoon, and onshore they constructed the La Mariana Sailing Club that offered showers along with food and drink for their aquatic tenants. In the 1970s the club was evicted and moved with amazing rapidity to a site not far away after the debris of a junkyard was cleared away. And then, in the 1980s, members of the public discovered the restaurant and bar, which initially required patrons to sign up as members in order to dine. Nanette ran her establishment on her own for years, charming diners by circulating among the tables to chat in her genteel voice. And although she's been gone since 2011, the restaurant and bar are still going strong. Admittedly, the ramshackle surroundings may put some off, but for those who appreciate the tiki genre, La Mariana is the real deal and is justifiably treasured by its followers. *DB*

Honolulu Zoo Entry ↓

151 Kapahulu Ave
Honolulu, HI 96815
Alfred Preis
1963

044 C

The steep, shake-shingled declivities and intersecting angles of the zoo's former entrance pavilion's skewed butterfly roof establishes a strong visual dynamic, while its varied materials add texture and visual delight. A centered low-but-broad foyer-like lanai/breezeway offers an inviting, open-air hospitality, with the steps leading up to it framed by coral-sheathed planters, adding a light sense of formality. The mauka wing with its walls of painted concrete brick and extruded mortar joints once housed the zoo's administrative offices, while the coral-clad makai wing was originally open to the foyer and conceived to house educational displays. A gentle mini-masterpiece, it was restored by the city in 2022. *DH*

4

Photo: Olivier Koning

5

Gold Coast

Martin Despang

It is unimaginable today to propose confronting Honolulu's picture-postcard Diamond Head volcano with a cluster of high-rises. Alfred Preis must have foreseen the rising of artificial blue glass high-rise mountains in Kaka'ako and Midtown Ala Moana when he created the low-key original entrance of the zoo in front of Diamond Head (in 1962, the same year as his Arizona Memorial) soon after leaving his private practice to become an advocacy policy maker, among many

Photo: WATG

Pete Wimberly's 3019 Kalakaua Avenue

Lanai life

Photo: WATG

other activist activities, and prevented any clustering happening to Diamond Head. That was not necessary in the same way with the Gold Coast development, as the involved 'who's who' of island architects in their mid-century heydays still breathed the innocent zeitgeist of a time driven by cultural ambitions rather than today's predominant commercial ones. So, going by today's building height standard of 400 feet, these buildings are small, although for their time they were tall apartment towers with a specific role in this play of mid-century modern marvelousness: Jo Paul Rognstad with the most slender of his ziggurats, the 2947 Kalakaua Avenue's 1969 'Diamond Head Beach Hotel & Residences' and the 1968 stacked lanai '3056 Kalakaua'; Takashi Anbe's most flower-powered 1960 'Seabreeze Apartments' at 3065 Kalakaua Avenue; Alfred Yee as architect and engineer of 3015 Kalakaua Avenue's dramatic lava rock wall mousehole-entranced 1964 'Oceanside Manor'; Vladimir Ossipoff's 'bonsai Ilikai' 1957 'Diamond

5

Sans Souci lanai beach life

Photo: Docomomo

Vladimir Ossipoff's Diamond Head Apartments

Gold Coast's chain of pearls

Head Apartments' of 2969 Kalakaua Avenue; Pete Wimberley's 1960 slender slice '3019 Kalakaua Avenue'; Edwin Bauer with Hammarbarg & Fraser's 2999 Kalakaua Avenue's 1958 tropical Bauhausian 'The Tahitienne'; Johnson and Perkins 2987 Kalakaua Avenue's international tropical style 1954 George 'Dad' Center Condominiums; and 2943 Kalakaua Avenue's 1958 'Tropic Seas', to name but a few. The success of this tropical exotic enclave, besides the individual synergistic architectural excellence, seems to be the urbanist undogmatic virtuous mix of scale and scope with strategic high and low points, with the 1961 boomerangish in plan Hammarbarg & Herman 2877 Kalakaua Avenue 'Sans Souci' stacked lanai as the tallest and Vladimir Ossipoff and Pete Wimberley's 2909 Kalakaua Avenue 'Outrigger Canoe Club' of 1963 serving as the contrasting close-to-invisible piece. A most charming clique of literally and figuratively cool constructions of the heyday of mid-century modern Honolulu, the genetic code of which was unfortunately not able to be duplicated. Given the urbanistically and architecturally lifelessness and lovelessness of the ever-growing contemporary high-rise mountains, it seems about time to look back to the past to relearn from these raw models. The proof being that while it is no surprise that this neighborhood has been a celebrated part in the opening credits of the original *Hawaii Five-O* of 1968–1980, it makes it even more obvious that it was still present at the very beginning of its 2010–2020 reboot. Further in the reboot episodes, however, in contrast to the original series that often showed mid-century modern buildings from this Gold Coast, the more recent version presents predominantly anonymous glass boxes that serve as interchangeable palm-tree-decorated hermetic high-rise urban wallpaper. Leaving this architectural Gold Coast crew even more an evergreen.

5

Photo: Martin Despang

Ossipoff's star and Rognstad's ziggurat

5

Liljestrand Residence

3300 Tantalus Dr
Honolulu, HI 96822
Vladimir Ossipofft
1952

045 A

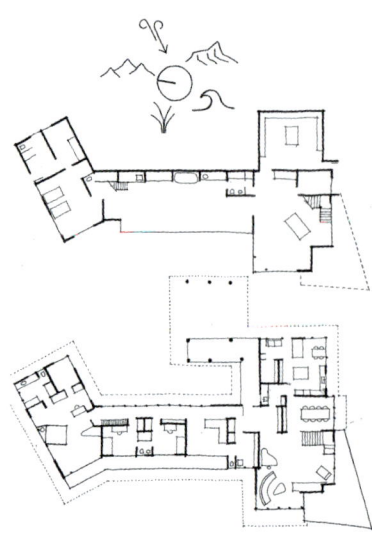

In the 1940s, Betty and Howard Liljestrand decided to buy land and build a house in Honolulu. They liked the cooler, wetter upper regions of the Koolau Mountains behind the city, and while hiking one day in 1946 they discovered a property for sale when they encountered the owner on his undeveloped land. With the land in their possession, the couple hired famed local architect Vladimir Ossipoff to design their

Photo: Olivier Koning

5

home. This was a lengthy process, lasting from 1948 to completion in 1952. The Liljestrands were exacting in their requirements, while Ossipoff was strongwilled but inventive. Endless discussions finally resulted in this masterpiece of mid-century Hawaiian architecture. The view of Honolulu some distance below, with the Pacific Ocean spreading endlessly into the distance, is a major part of the house's appeal. Its lower floor is made up of concrete blocks set into the sloping terrain, while the upstairs is wood. Unique built-in furniture and other custom pieces are found throughout. The stairs between the two levels are composed of floating polished wood treads that are seemingly suspended from narrow metal rods. Magnificently finished wooden surfaces form the floors, walls, and ceilings. An entire issue of the national *House Beautiful* magazine in 1958 was devoted to the Liljestrand House, recognizing its significance as embodying the ideals of American architecture of the time period. Today it is preserved in its original condition, hosting selected visitors for specific events. *DB*

Photo: Daniel Luna

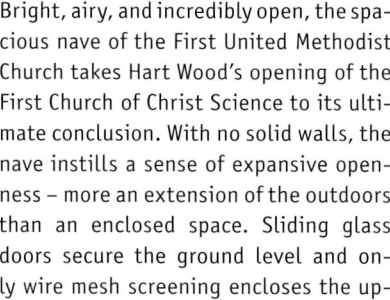

First United Methodist
046 B

1020 S Beretania St
Honolulu, HI 96814
Alfred Preis
1953

Photo: Olivier Koning

Bright, airy, and incredibly open, the spacious nave of the First United Methodist Church takes Hart Wood's opening of the First Church of Christ Science to its ultimate conclusion. With no solid walls, the nave instills a sense of expansive openness – more an extension of the outdoors than an enclosed space. Sliding glass doors secure the ground level and only wire mesh screening encloses the upper story. The church's solid end walls are characterized by a pair of rectangular slabs that convexly converge on a sliver of glass block, which at the altar end expands to form a luminous Latin cross. Constructed of lava rock embedded in concrete, a method Alfred Preis had previously employed at Laupahoehoe School on the island of Hawaii, the church presents a straightforward yet subtle and delightful composition. *DH*

Photo: Daniel Luna

Soto Zen Mission

047 B

1708 Nuuanu Ave
Honolulu, HI 986817
Fuchino & Katsuyoshi
1952

5

A 70-foot stainless steel, four-sided pyramidal tower rises above a composition that strikingly reinterprets traditional forms in a modern manner. Inspired by the Great Tower of Bodh Gaya Temple in Bihar, India – the site of Buddha's enlightenment – the tower serves as a focal point for a tour de force of Mughal-Western delight. Octagonal brick wings, elbow-bracketed columns, and cusped-arches mingle with sliding doors that open both sides of the nave to cantilevered lanai running down the sides of the building. A fine level of detail and craftsmanship is evident throughout the building, from the wood and glass-block wall of the foyer to the exterior brickwork of the wings. The magnificent 20-foot-high gold statue of the 11-faced Kannon dates from 1933, and the carving of the naijin's (chancel) elephant-head beam ends and the ramma (transoms) depicting the life of Buddha are of high quality. *DH, HM*

Breakers Hotel

250 Beach Walk
Honolulu, HI 96815
Edwin Bauer
1954

048 C

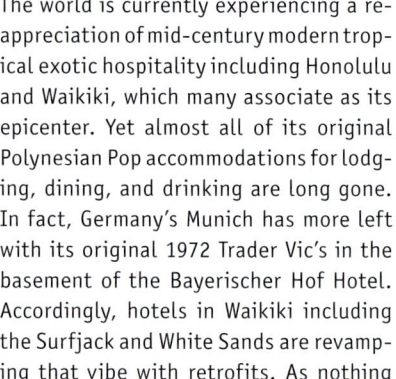

The world is currently experiencing a re-appreciation of mid-century modern tropical exotic hospitality including Honolulu and Waikiki, which many associate as its epicenter. Yet almost all of its original Polynesian Pop accommodations for lodging, dining, and drinking are long gone. In fact, Germany's Munich has more left with its original 1972 Trader Vic's in the basement of the Bayerischer Hof Hotel. Accordingly, hotels in Waikiki including the Surfjack and White Sands are revamping that vibe with retrofits. As nothing beats the original, this is it: The Breakers

Hotel, with its low-rise, double-pitched roof walk-ups around a central oval pool in a lush landscape, was created in the early prime time of Edwin Bauer's productivity and has miraculously remained in its absolute original condition over its 70 years of existence. Authentic not only in terms of its wooden anatomy from the structure to the jalousies, but also through to the interior appliances from a time when America was great, as it was manufactured with pride. The secret to this authenticity is loyalty to guests and staff, as many have been with the hotel since the beginning and passed on the tradition to following generations. Landscaper Usen Guzman has worked on the grounds since he was a little boy, with his father also gardening the property, and he continues to do so with loving care, nurturing bonsai pineapples in the

building's lanai hanging planters so that guests can pick them fresh for breakfast. The staff were kept through the Covid-19 pandemic by the generous, gracious care of the second owner: Japan's utmost tea ceremony masters who are immune to the temptations of capital concentration – having crept as close to it as next door due to the recently renamed former Trump Hotel high-rise. Having been with the Breakers since its beginning, manager Ethel Nada recalls Mr. Bauer contemplating that this project was one of, if not his best. He said it was certainly better than the building next door, which he designed a year later in 1955 as a slightly more modern version of it: the Hawaiiana Hotel. That hotel has not received the same high level of care. It has been through several remodels and rebrandings and deserves to be brought back to a similar original condition in the next remodel. The Breaker Hotel shows how that pays off, from the multigenerational loyalty of guests through to respect from Hollywood, with Cameron Crowe having Emma Stone and Bradley Cooper fall in love in the hotel and with it in his 2015 movie *Aloha*. Enjoy watching DeSoto Brown and the Breakers celebrating their 70th birthdays. *MD*

Farias Building

436 Ulunui Street
Kailua, HI 96734
Herbert Bayer
1955

A harmonious blend of contemporary design and island charm, the Farias Building stands as a mid-century modern delight in Kailua, with its dramatic fin-like concrete brick columns, a corbelled CMU bracket, and canted display windows. The windows not only proclaimed a break from tradition, but were also said to reduce glare. The front and rear lanai on the second story celebrate the ease of outdoor living in Hawaii, as does the perforated front wall of the stairway. The latter is an early example of a screen as a wall that allows the wind to blow through. The staggered laying of the concrete bricks to allow openings between the bricks may be viewed as a precursor of decorative breeze blocks, which became popular in Hawaii during the late 1950s and 1960s and continue to be in use to the present day. This open design provides ventilation, partial shading, privacy, and beauty, and instills a dynamic of solid and void, as well as light and shadow. *DH, DHa*

5

![Farias Building]

Walk-Ups

Don Hibbard

During the Second World War, Hawaii was confronted with a serious housing shortage, and with the end of the war the high demand for housing did not disappear, as returning servicemen started families of their own and many newcomers decided to make Hawaii their home, resulting in a dramatic increase in Honolulu's population. An indication of the extent of the housing shortage is revealed by the opening of Roy Kelley's 192-unit Ala Wai Terrace Apartments (1948; no longer extant), with its six four-story buildings on Hobron Lane in Waikiki. Not only were all the apartments immediately occupied, but the Kelleys had an enviable waiting list of 300 applicants. With such housing demand, many new residential subdivisions were developed and single family houses were supplanted by apartment buildings within the urban core, where zoning allowed. Prior to the war, apartments were primarily located in Waikiki, where they accommodated budget-conscious visitors as well as the more transient residential population. These walk-up apartments were frequently of masonry construction, although frame structures also were built, and most were two stories in height, with some going to a third story. (See the project introduction earlier in this book.) The Seaside Apartments (1939) designed by Dahl & Conrad at 413 Seaside Avenue, although now used for restaurant purposes, may be the best existing example of a pre-war Waikiki garden court apartment. Post-war walk-up apartments began to

Photo: Martin Despang

Diamond Head Leilani

Tropical modernism ensemble at the Ilima Apartments

appear in other parts of the city including Makiki, Moiliili-McCully, University, and Pawaa, all of which were zoned for apartments on the City and County Planning Commission's 1940 zoning map. By the end of the 1950s, apartments also began to appear in Pearl City, Aiea, Waipahu, Wahiawa, and Kailua. These buildings usually have a rectangular footprint, although occasionally employ an 'L' shape. They range in height from one to four stories, are more often than not constructed of concrete masonry units (CMU), and their dwelling units are single stacked, with access deriving from a walkway/lanai that runs the length of one side of the building on each story. Steps at one or both ends of the building access the walkway. Sometimes, in addition to the front walkway/lanai, each dwelling unit has a rear, private lanai. The buildings feature flat or low pitched gable or hip roofs with broad eaves, and any embellishment usually occurs in the end walls and/or lanai balustrades. End walls, which typically face the street, assume a number of different appearances. Veneers, such as black lava rock, brown basalt, and beige sandstone, are utilized on a number of buildings; others employ decorative screen blocks or shadow blocks to provide a visual accent, while the Hawaiian Holiday Apartment (1962) at 1420 Wilder Street features a concrete mural by Hon Chew Hee on its face. Lanai balustrades also utilize a variety of materials and assume different forms ranging from steel pipe with wood rails to sheet metal or wrought iron or extruded aluminum, but most commonly combine such masonry components as brick, CMU, and screen blocks. The vertical circulation is another

Pualei Circle neighborhood

Diamond Head Gardens

The Continental in front of Makua Alii (Project 106)

opportunity for embellishment, which often provides a vertical thrust to the otherwise horizontal composition. Jalousie windows prevail, while aluminum by-pass sliding doors to access rear lanai supplant hinged solid core doors as the decades advance. A few of the low-rise apartments of the period, such as the four-story apartments at 1335 Wilder (1966) designed by Walter Wong, the Makiki Apartments (1963) at 1122 Wilder designed by Howard Wong, the Oahuan Apartments (1956) at 1700 Makiki Street designed by Edwin Bauer, and the Kilsby Apartments at 1350 Kinau, are laid out to include a landscaped courtyard. Parking, if any, is usually in front or to one side, but by the 1960s was frequently placed at ground level underneath the elevated building. The placement of parking under the apartments partially resulted from a series of zoning code amendments passed by the City Council during

the period 1961–1963. With the adoption of the 1961 Comprehensive Zoning Code through CPC Resolution 937, parcels zoned Apartment District C with a minimum lot size of 7,500 square feet could be developed with low-rise apartments. The buildings were not allowed to exceed three stories or 36 feet in height, and their square footage could not exceed the square footage of the lot on which they were constructed. Developers had to provide one parking space for every unit in the building, as well as provide either ten-feet side lot setbacks for two story structures, or 15-feet side lot setbacks for three story complexes. In addition, a 20-feet front and rear yard setback was required. Dissatisfied by the fact that these regulations fostered having almost all the unbuilt area of a property devoted to parking, the City and County amended the CZC over the next two years to better regulate on-site parking. As a result

Kon Tiki (originally Ebbtide Waikiki)

Photo: DeSoto Brown, 1959

Makikian

of these changes, by 1963 parking was no longer allowed in the set back areas, which were reduced to ten feet on all sides, and a 1963 amendment required a planting area at least five feet wide be placed between the curb and any on-site parking, with vehicles entering or exiting the property from a driveway at the end of the planting strip. The set back and density requirements essentially limited apartment buildings constructed on a minimum size 7,500 square foot lot to about a dozen units and a two-story height. When the new no set-back parking regulations were added, apartment buildings using available space around the building for parking were typically restricted to only six units for standard size lots. To ameliorate this situation and provide an incentive to place parking under buildings, the City allowed the developer an additional story if parking was placed under the building. By 1966 these

Photo: DeSoto Brown

Victoria Apartments

low-rise apartments housed over a quarter of Honolulu's population. They remain a readily recognized and ubiquitous building form in the city and outlying areas. With their lanai/walkways instead of halls; single stacked, well ventilated units, and their broad overhanging eaves, these masonry structures are a practical response to Hawaii's climate and continue to provide economical housing for many individuals and small families.

Photo: DeSoto Brown

Bishop Manor

Princess Kaiulani Hotel

120 Kaiulani Ave
Honolulu, HI 968154
Gardner A. Dailey & Associates,
Roehrig, Onodera & Kinder,
Wimberly & Cook
1955 (1965, 1970)

A prime example of the hospitality and sensitivity that defined the heyday of statehood. Comprised of Hawaii's essential room – the outdoor lanai – the repetition of its simple and single element of gently undulating outlines of the balcony slabs creates an understated gesture alluding to the waves of the nearby oceans. It is the grand dame – sorry, the forever young princess – raw model of today's postmodern versions, which have recently become en vogue but as value-engineered versions with insufficient depth, they fail to keep the rooms behind cool enough from the sun. In this original in the composition of the three building parts, the inaugural 1950s part is blocking the macro mauka-to-makai airflow and faces the hot setting sun.

Photo: Martin Despang

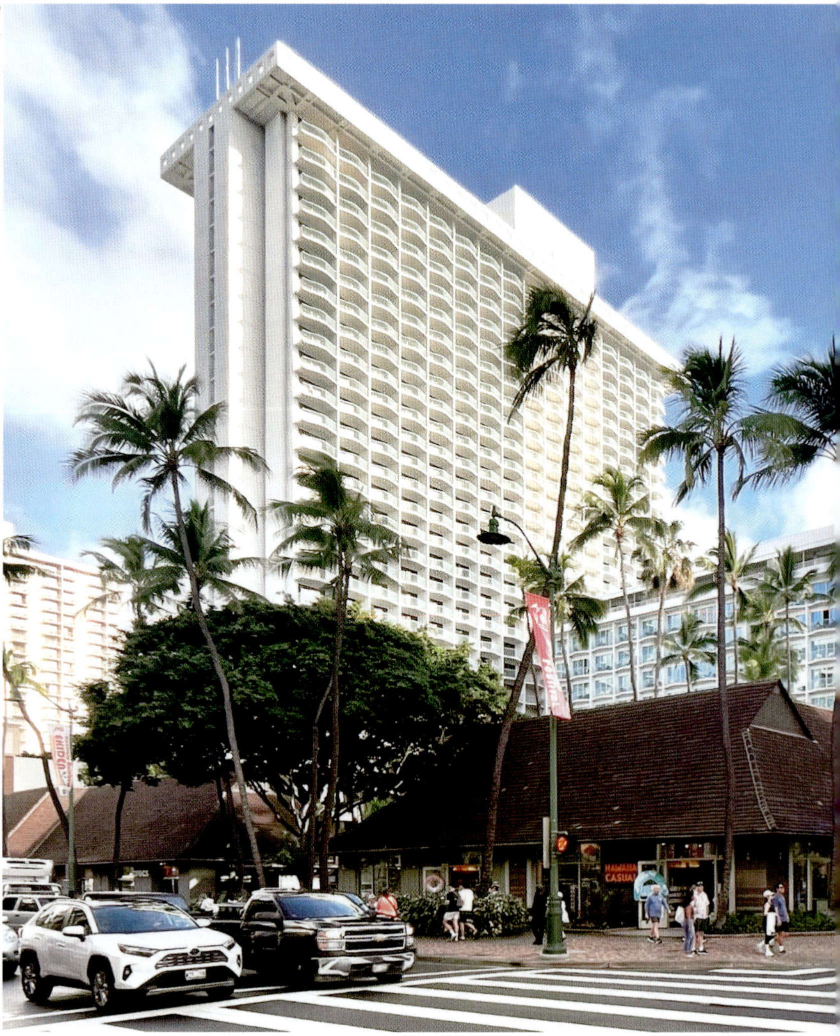

Later additions learned from this and are rotated 90 degrees to achieve perfection in both macro and micro bioclimatic performance. The 1960s parts along Ka'iulani Avenue, with the deepest lanais and partition walls, are a textbook example of how to stay cool. They make the recent 'Lilia' built two blocks mauka look bioclimatically stupid (see three episodes of TTH h(e)a's 'Living Wall Lilia Waikiki'), as the Marriott timeshare tower under construction across the street near Diamond Head repeats the bioclimatically least responsible west-facing 1950s part. The concluding 1970s tower, in addition to self shading, helps to sunset-shade the 1950s part. Generously set back from Kalakaua Avenue, an original 'jungly' wood sign is the only navigation advice through charming little shop pavilions to the oval pool area with its surrounding tiki interior that is unfortunately long gone. Speaking of which, the proposed demolition of the entire complex only to replace it with no additional rooms and far less awesome architecture is unbelievable in an era of growing concern for gray energy and 'circularity' given the monstrous mass of concrete. Recent large-scale rejuvenative redevelopments in Waikiki such as the 'Romer' or the 'Wayfinder' that treasure mid-century modern should send a clear message: this one is a clear keeper. *MD*

Photo: Olivier Koning

Board of Water Supply

630 S Beretania St
Honolulu, HI 96813
Wood, Weed & Kubota
1956

051 B

Featuring one of the earliest and more elaborate sunscreens in Honolulu, this building smoothly blends a multiethnic architectural vocabulary with a modern grammar. The sunscreen's Chinese fretwork effortlessly harmonizes with the Japanese portico and the Hawaiian motto 'Uwe ka lani ola ka Honua' ('The rain falls, the earth lives') – a celebration of Hawaii's multicultural society. The theme of water is introduced by the front fountain and continues in the green slate walls adjoining the entrance, while the interior features a large mural by Juliette May Fraser depicting the history of water use in Hawaii. A roof garden celebrates the islands' climate, as does a curving, elevated walkway, which runs between this administrative building and its neighbor and is dramatically supported by only a single pylon. The less noticed rear of the building utilizes more modest, but equally effective sunscreens, shielding the building from the morning light. *DH, TN*

Photo: Olivier Koning

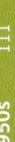

Waikiki Shell

2805 Monsarrat Ave
Honolulu, HI 96815
Law & Wilson
1956

052 C

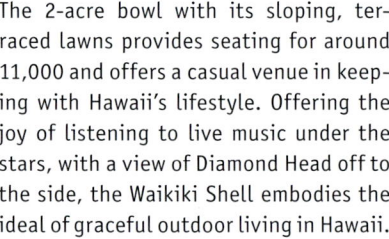

The 2-acre bowl with its sloping, terraced lawns provides seating for around 11,000 and offers a casual venue in keeping with Hawaii's lifestyle. Offering the joy of listening to live music under the stars, with a view of Diamond Head off to the side, the Waikiki Shell embodies the ideal of graceful outdoor living in Hawaii.

A distinctive telescoping, semi-circular-shaped roof shelters a 90-feet-wide stage and is fabricated from aluminum roofing sheets. Measuring 75 feet at its highest and supported from above by a steel-framed arch, the graceful structure seamlessly integrates with its lush tropical surroundings. In 2024, someone in the administration of the City, more concerned about a few drops of rain than the starlit ambiance of the Shell at night, covered the lower seating area with a tent-like structure, and so eroded another little bit of the charm of Hawaii. *DH, NG*

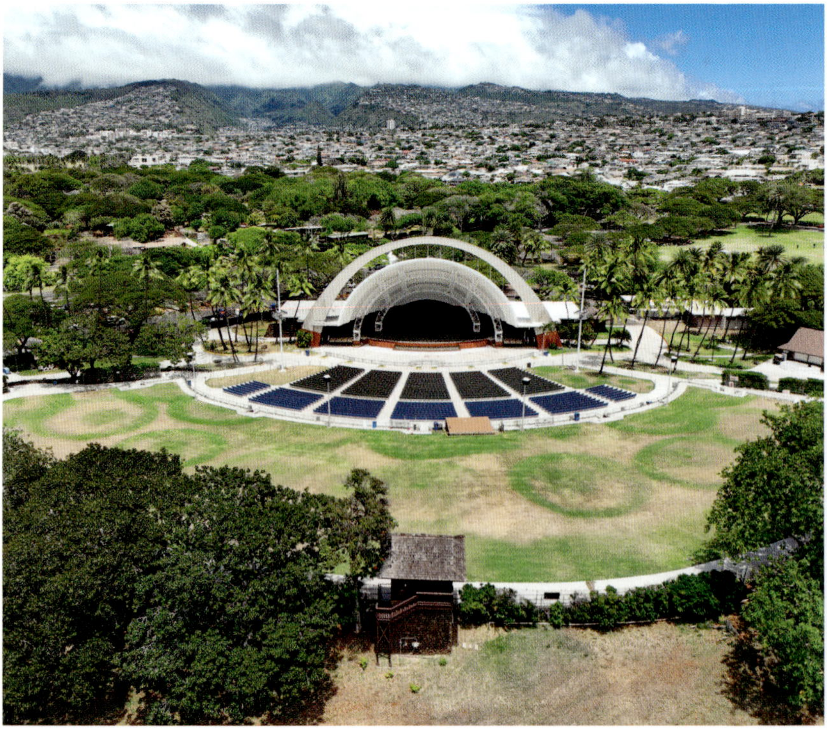

Marks Garage ↑↓   053 B

21 Chaplain Ln
Honolulu, HI 96813
Merrill, Simms & Roehrig
1957

Windward Shopping Center ↓   054 A

45–480 Kaneohe Bay Dr
Kaneohe, HI 96744
Wimberly & Cook
1958

The four-story Marks Garage stands as a splendid example of a mid-century, multi-deck parking lot in Honolulu and a rare reminder of the early efforts to address downtown Honolulu's automobile parking needs. In the year this 500-stall structure was completed, Oahu's automobile registrations stood at 159,227, a 329.8 per cent increase since the conclusion of the Second World War 12 years earlier. The reinforced concrete building exudes modernity with its cast stone fins screening the upper three stories of parking, while at ground level seven retail spaces feature walls clad in dark black, rough a'a lava, which contrast with the sleek, projecting, aluminum-framed display windows set on a diagonal to the sidewalk. The building transcends mere utilitarian functionality to visually vitalize the street over which it presides. *DH*

This composition is comprised of the Tiki Tops restaurant by the Spencecliff Corp., which is marked by two totems, linear shops with an undulating wavy sun and rain protection canopy, and its centerpiece, the Windward City Market mastered by structural engineer Richard Bradshaw as a super-thin shelled concrete roof. Creating a spanning column-free interior – with four filigree posts only added later – its four corner low points carry down the structural loads as the rainwater pragmatically and poetically flows into lava rock piles, constantly feeding the tropical vegetation that is overgrown thanks to it. A structure so minimal that it is only possible in the tropics, with no snow loads and minimal physical roof insulation required and a cool roof paint likely sufficient. The stuccoed postmodern pieces of cake that have been jammed

Photo: Martin Despang

054 A

into and around it in later years caused Wimberly's understandable disapproval according to Olivier Koning, so these need to be undone when the time comes for the next renovation. *MD*

Photo: DeSoto Brown

Hawaiian Memorial Park ↓

055 A

45-425 Kamehameha Hwy
Kaneohe, HI 96744
Administration Building
Wimberly & Cook, 1960
Mortuary
Ernest Hara, 1962

Growth on the windward side of the island of Oahu was hampered by the inadequacy of existing road facilities. Originally accessible only by the winding, narrow two-lane Pali Road, which could be completely shut down by heavy rain or a vehicle collision, improvements began in the 1950s with the concurrent construction of the Pali Highway and its four tunnels as well as the Likelike Highway and its two tunnels. Once these were completely open in the early 1960s, construction in Kaneohe and Kailua towns began to boom. Part of this growth was the opening of the Hawaiian Memorial Park cemetery in 1958. Starting with ample open acreage that could no longer be found anywhere in Honolulu, the cemetery grew even more in 1960. This was also the year its first structure, the Administration Building, opened. It established an architectural design motif, particularly in its folded concrete roof, that was mimicked by the 1961 Mausoleum with 600 outdoor crypts and the 1962 Mortuary with a chapel, kitchen, offices, and other amenities. Constructed of concrete, these buildings all presented a light, uplifting appearance. Thin tapering columns and walls of open breeze

blocks supported roofs in zigzag or repeated arch designs. They were very contemporary and modern for the time, which looked optimistically forward while turning away from the heavy classical architecture of the past. One advertised amenity that today would seem strange were the loudspeakers placed throughout the grounds that played appropriately reverent organ music recorded on eight-hour programs on audiotape, controlled from the Administration Building. The outdoor speakers were disguised by small clumps of shrubs planted around them. *DB*

Treehouse Apartments ↓

056 **C**

337 Lewers St
Honolulu, HI 96815
Bassetti, Morse, and Tatom
Structural: Alfred Yee
1959

From the year of statehood, here is a building like a tropical tree. While it is never possible to allow a structure to run seamlessly from inside to outside or vice versa in a temperate cold climate, this lovely structure clearly takes visible advantage of its permanently mild climate. The structure is tropical exotic at its very best. The primary structural columns have short branches on which the floor beams that carry the floors rest. Precast columns and prestressed beams integrated with composite cast-in-place slabs is Alfred Yee at his best. Recessed from the structure and clearly visible as independent is the building envelope of glass, concrete masonry units, and vertical guard bars. Le Corbusier's Domino House gone tropical. This is a best example of this very predominant mid-century typology of 'few story walk-ups' as the utmost efficient and effective mid-century way of housing the masses with decency and dignity. This gem is long gone unfortunately, but it is continuously kept alive in architectural education for the emerging generation. Architect Tatom later proved able to apply his sensitivity to the most extreme other end of the largest scale in the form of the Hawaiian Regents Hotel, which we also cover and this author looks at all the time while writing this from his lanai, never tiring of its timeless performative solid and void playfulness. Tatom applied lessons learned from this exquisite apprentice piece to later work beyond the Hawaiian Regents Hotel, like to Tamarind Square, which is also covered in this guide. *MD*

5

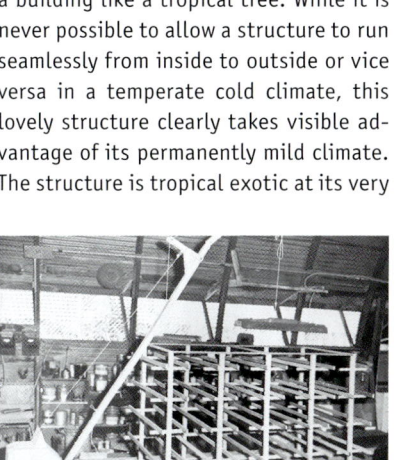

Photo: Docomomo

Photo: Docomomo

Ala Moana Building

1441 Kapiolani Blvd
Honolulu, HI 96814
John Graham
Structural: Alfred Yee
1959

057 B

No other building stands more for the inauguration of Hawaii's statehood. It was showcased in the opening credits of the original *Hawaii Five-O* (1968–1980) with its revolving La Ronde restaurant lit up in blue. The building tested that technology that was to be applied a year later to the World's Fair Space Needle in Seattle, but its architect Graham was not what would today be considered a boutique architect doing such buildings (with Heatherwick

and BIG's proposed Google London headquarters south façade seeming to have taken inspiration from this one) but was at that time America's most commercial designer of shopping malls. To survive the tropical sun, Graham protected its glass envelope with a covering screen of sun retractable aluminum louvers that were powder coated aluminum on one side and gold on the other. The rectilinear footprint following the trade wind direction of mauka to makai made its main east and west façades sufficiently self-shaded, with the louvers turned close but not closed to keep the sun out and daylight in. Consequently the building was a bioclimatic kinetic creature constantly changing its appearance by going with

and performatively against the daily sun paths. In the 1990s, the louvers were removed with the lame justification of maintenance used as the excuse to beef up air conditioning and distract from the theft of this feather in the building's cap; the current mere decorative lattice work was added instead. The flying saucer rooftop has also been out of commission for a long time and recently the building looks increasingly vacant, making one fear a destiny of demolition by neglect, as the self-styled Midtown Ala Moana development is suffocating it with an invasion of blue glass-box high-rises and its initial marketing website placed its logo over the building (as further discussed in the related 17 ThinkTech Hawaii h(e)a 'Midtown Flunk' episodes). This is all in total ignorance of its utmost iconic stature, most prominently illustrated in 1961's *Blue Hawaii* with the Maile character and her boyfriend, played by Elvis Presley, driving up nearby Mount Tantalus to have their romantic picnic strategically positioned in the vista of this first high-rise sticking out as a beacon of progressiveness. So, it is almost needless to say that critical reconstruction including returning the louvers and coating them with a hardly noticeable thin film photovoltaic coating would protect and preserve this cultural climatic icon by evolving its cutting-edge performance. *MD*

5

Hawaii Kaiser

Martin Despang

It would be easy to dismiss Mr. Kaiser as a colonial haole pouring his love over Honolulu after retiring from his continental US industrialist empire. And yes, that view could be supported by his fake Hawaiian Village lagoon and the similar one that, according to Curt Sanburn, was proposed but fortunately never built at Sandy Beach at the east end of his Hawaii Kai(ser) suburban sprawl. Despite his seemingly desperate attempts to sell his affection for Hawaii to his late wife by having all construction equipment painted in her favorite color (pink), taking a closer look at those two major developments in particular could and should give him more credibility. He started with his 1955 Kaiser Hawaiian Village. Breakers Hotel manager Ethel Nada recalled Kaiser

visiting and being inspired by Edwin Bauer's Polynesian Pop hostelry, so he applied it to his 'Village' next door and inspired others such as Spencecliff's Tahitian Lanai to join. The village's main masterpiece was certainly the 1957 Kaiser Dome, which no longer exists. While the aluminum tycoon's previously suggested aluminum automobiles with Jetson-like appeal and Hawaiian names remained fiction, this geodesic dome inspired by Buckminster Fuller materialized prefabricated from Kaiser's aluminum, with diamond-shaped panels bolted together at a cost of $4 per square foot. Kaiser did not witness the construction process because he missed his flight from California; that is how quick the dome was assembled. The dome was open at its base for the

Photo: DeSoto Brown, 1958

Kaiser Aluminum Dome, Kaiser Hawaiian Village

trade winds to cool it while the aluminum shells above protected it during the day-time heat. At night, once the surrounding car traffic slowed, Exotica music masters Martin Denny, Arthur Layman, and Dennis Baxter used its exquisite acoustics for their recordings. After Kaiser sold his 'Village' to Hilton in 1961, its inspiring spirit continued up until today and at present it is one of the most innovative habitable high-rises: the 1967 Lagoon Tower by Edwin Bauer. At that time, it together with 1350 Ala Moana Boulevard and the Ala Moana Building were pretty much the main actors in the city's skyline, therefore acting as a prominent backdrop in multiple episodes of the original 1970s *Hawaii Five-O* and 1980s *Magnum, P.I.* Like 1350 Ala Moana Boulevard, Lagoon Tower balances opacity and transparency carefully and cleverly to keep itself cool. Lagoon Tower had initially been conceptualized as condominiums and although functioning as a hotel today, it continues to be one of the finest examples of tropical exotic urbanism. Its lanai are pure poetry in the form of lily pad-like curvilinearity in plan as in section. Growing out between the buttressed pilaster slabs, they offer more secluded occupancy comfort toward the base and seamlessly butterfly freedom feelings toward the top of the building. Lagoon Tower has thankfully been kept pretty original, so nothing else is needed to further retain it. In addition to the Hawaiian Village hotel, Kaiser was also responsible for Hawaii Kai, where he was not just the developer but also

5

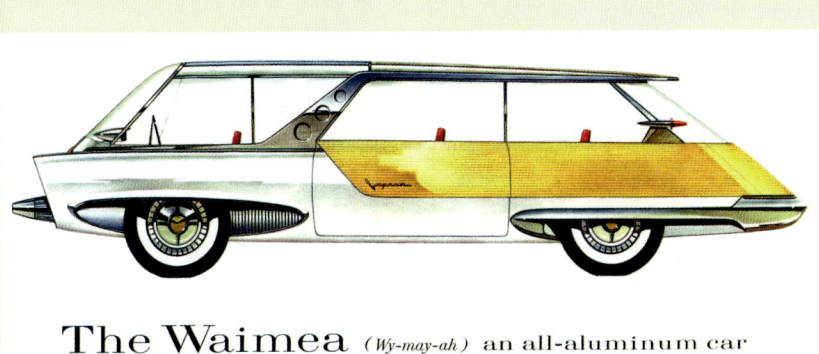

Photo: DeSoto Brown

The Waimea *(Wy-may-ah)* an all-aluminum car

The Waimea is a Kaiser Aluminum design that incorporates the design advantages of aluminum to achieve maximum utility. Front-located aluminum engine, tunnel-free aluminum floor, roof and body panels—all aluminum!

And you may be certain that you will be building cars like the Waimea, or components suggested in its design. Every year, more and more aluminum is being designed into American automobiles.

Ravenswood—source of highest quality aluminum

Ravenswood, West Virginia, is the location of what is perhaps the most quality-minded aluminum plant anywhere—the new Kaiser Aluminum reduction plant and rolling mill. Both by location and by layout, this plant is ideally situated to supply you the highest quality aluminum available today.

Ask us, if you like, this question:

"What Is The Difference In Aluminum From Ravenswood?" (and please turn to back page)

Kaiser Aluminum Co. Hawaii(an) fantasy concept car

Hawaiian Village Hotel, 1950s

Lagoon Tower's lily lanais

the builder. These first houses are quite a commendable effort to produce fairly affordable single-family housing that the Department of Hawaiian Homelands (DHHL) should be jealous of. They featured split level wide open spaces with exposed wood glulam beams spanning between party walls, as in the one by Rick Prahler. For Kaiser himself, admittedly being in another league, his own 1959 house in nearby Portlock is naturally larger in both lot and size but still modest in gesture in a Miesian sense, as depicted on the historic plaque at the gate. Right after his

Hawaii Kai house lots for sale, 1961

Koko Marina, 1973

HAWAII-KAI

...the most desirable address
in the Pacific!

Henry J. Kaiser's fabulous 6,000 acre resort
city currently under development out Koko Head
way unfolds a new and exciting facet every day!

Hawaii Kai ad, 1961

passing, the modernity of his house made
it a perfect set for the 'Samurai' episode of
the original *Hawaii Five-O*, which was the
very first to film but the sixth to air. Given
these noble proletarian-as-bourgeois case
studies, it would be unfair to blame Kaiser
for the increasing tastelessness of Hawaii
Kai's further developments. Had Kaiser continued to remain involved in the project architecturally, Hawaii Kai may have become
a single-story suburban Gold Coast.

Rick Prahler's Kaiser contractor home

Henry's estate

Henry's gate

Henry's porte-cochère

Henry's Miesian space

Henry's way to the helipad

Henry's rooftop

5

Photo: Olivier Koning

Pacific Club

058 B

1451 Queen Emma St
Honolulu, HI 96813
Ossipoff/Merrill/Roehrig,
Kinder & Onodera/Harry Seckel
1960

The Pacific Club answers the question of what is an appropriate regional architecture for Hawaii. Sited in urban Honolulu on a one-acre parcel and shaded by mature trees, the club's primary public space seems to be more a covered open space than a solid building, seamlessly intermingling with the outdoors via broad openings. Sited above an umbrageous parking lot, its capacious porte-cochère and wide entry stairs hospitably welcome guests to a flowing interior experience enhanced by judiciously placed artwork and vistas onto various courtyards and the landscaped grounds. Low ceilings, terrazzo floors, walls of coral, and also CMU mimetically perpetuating plastered lava rock, as well as refined koa accents provide the members of the oldest private club west of the Rockies with a most gracious and sedate social setting. *DH, MY*

Aliiaimoku Hale, the Territorial Highways Department Building

059 B

869 Punchbowl St
Honolulu, HI 96813
Law & Wilson
1959

Completed less than a month before Hawaii became the 50th state to join the union, Aliiaimoku Hale briefly housed the Territorial and then State Highway Department, before the nascent State government folded it into the newly formed State Department of Transportation. One of the more prominent early examples of sun screens in Hawaii and the first to use precast, prestressed concrete fins, the five-story building's 70-foot-tall, four-inch-thick fins were set in place by the use of a construction crane. In keeping with modern architecture's rejection of applied ornament, the building is only adorned

Photo: Bishop Museum, 1960

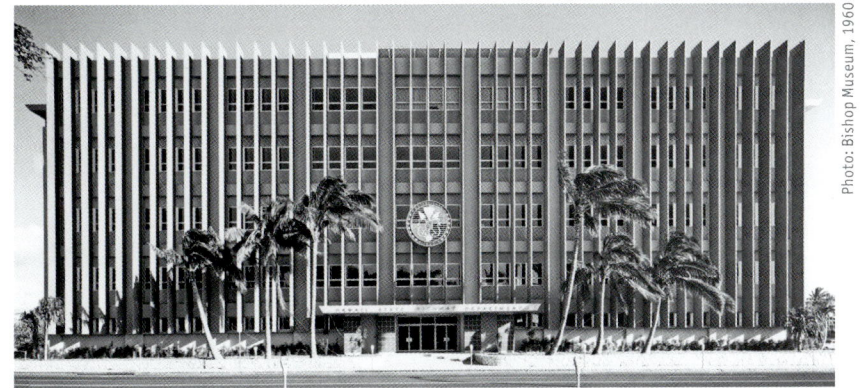

by custom designed breeze blocks on its end walls, and a 1,600 pound, 11-foot-in-diameter aluminum seal cast by the Oregon Brass Works in Portland, Oregon. The breeze blocks ventilate the fire escape stairwells, while Law & Wilson designed the aluminum seal for the department. *Hawaii Industry* magazine described the building to be as modern as the recently constructed Lunalilo Highway, Hawaii's first freeway, and indeed it was most up-to-date with four piers, clad in ceramic tiles, carrying the flat roofed, cantilevered portico, and an open lobby with terrazzo floors. The rear of the building is also worth checking out, where its slender, glass block windows are set in vertical rows, recessed on a diagonal to provide natural light to the offices with a minimum of glare. *DH*

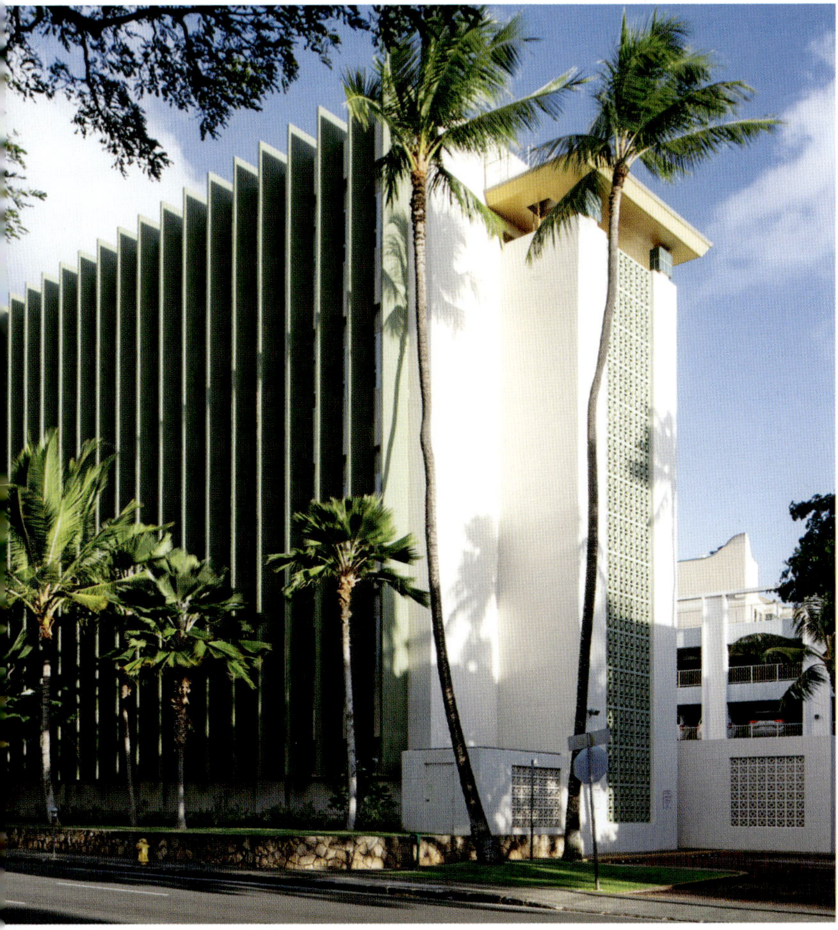

Photo: Olivier Koning

Tropical Modern 1960s

6

Cash Crops (Banks)

Martin Despang and Don Hibbard

This typology might be a most questionable choice considering your authors' chosen criteria of climate and culture appropriateness. But in optimistic and positive mid-century America, this typology of financial institutions in particular catered to what Modraveler.net calls 'consumer confidence' via ambitious architecture and made possible the tremendous housing and small business expansion that characterized the 1950s and 1960s in Hawaii. Banks such as Liberty Bank, Central Pacific Bank, City Bank, and Hawaii National Bank primarily catered to the Chinese and Japanese segments of the population and allowed their clients to more easily share in the growth opportunities of the period. Like with the typology of the beach pavilions discussed earlier in this book, this typology allowed numerous emerging architects – far more than the few mentioned here – to exercise their talents in ways that did indeed respond to the constraints imposed by banking programs and Hawaii's climate. A number of the new banks were incorporated into multistory buildings, with the banks serving as ground floor anchor tenants, as in Pete Wimberly's Waikiki branch of Bank of Hawaii, in his Varsity Building and Takashi Anbe's King Center, all of which are featured in the book. In many other instances, especially in suburban situations, the banks erected self-contained one-, two-, or low-story buildings to serve their customers closer to home. Examples abound and include the Ward Avenue branch of Liberty Bank (1963) designed by Merrill, Roehrig, Onodera & Kinder as well as Ossipoff's Kalihi branch of First National Bank (1961) at 2250 North King Street, with its Edgar Brownlee murals depicting the currency of Easter Island's lost civilization. The former shades its east facing façades with an overhanging second story supported by palm tree-inspired columns as well as decorative bris-soleil on the second floor, while solid walls keep the sun from penetrating its south and west sides. Similarly, the latter's only glass wall faces north, with solid walls on its other three sides. Here, the elevated second floor banking hall provides ground level, shaded parking. We illustrate many single-story examples with wide open, tall teller spaces recognizing the tropical setting in which hot air rises and preventing overheated heads. The

Waianae Bank roofitecture

Waianae Bank

Waianae Bank

First Hawaiian Bank branch in Waianae (1973) designed by Wimberly, Whisenand, Allison, Tong, and Goo is one of several to reinterpret indigenous shelters with their large roofs protecting the structure from the sun and rain. In an ancestral tradition, the structure is legibly orchestrated and celebrated. The structural materials of concrete columns and glulam wooden beams are kept raw and real and contrast with interior finishings of frameless glass; similarly, raw wood and blue floor tiles remind of Skidmore, Owings, and Merrill's Mauna Kea Beach Hotel as well as Killingsworth, Stricker, Lindgren, and Wilson's Mauna Lani Hotel where the blue tile floors have, most unfortunately, been ripped out in the recent renovation. First Hawaiian bank's branches in Kaneohe (1965), designed by Howard Cook, and Mapunapuna (1969), designed by Haydn Phillips, similarly employ graceful, sheltering flat roofs with broad overhangs. The latter is also noteworthy for having a solid wall of translucent Aurora marble that allows sunlight to filter through and naturally illuminate the banking hall. Banks increasingly moving to online banking poses a new threat to these splendid buildings and their high potential for repurposing, giving us one more reason to treasure these trophies.

6

Photo: Martin Despang

Photo: Martin Despang

King Center
1451 S King St
Honolulu, HI 96814
Anbe, Aruga, Ishizu
1960

060 B

upper stories have been primarily dedicated to doctor and dentist offices. The building's developer Herbert Hayashi also hired Anbe to design the neighboring Liona Apartments. *DH, RL*

A gold-anodized, expanded-metal screen sheaths the upper levels of the King Center and not only shades this five-story reinforced concrete building and its lanai corridors, but also serves as its primary character defining element. Manufactured by United States Gypsum, the 'Armorweave Sun Screen' was a popular shading device during the 1950s and 1960s in Hawaii, not only to protect buildings from the sun, but also to proclaim their modernity, instantly updating older structures. This building is one of only a few metal screened buildings to still remain in the city and is especially handsome with its tarnished copper scepter and script lettering proclaiming 'King Center' against the screen's gold backdrop. The aesthetic appeal of the well conceived composition is further enhanced by a number of other mid-century modern accents, ranging from the lobby's terrazzo floors and ceramic fountain (now without water), designed and executed by Isami Enomoto, to the dramatic, free-standing, butterfly roofed, concrete portico on the King Street elevation. While the ground floor of the building has been occupied by the Bank of Hawaii since the completion of the building, the

Photo: Olivier Koning

Waikiki Shore Condominiums 061 C

2161 Kalia Road
Honolulu, HI 96815
Kenneth Sato
1960

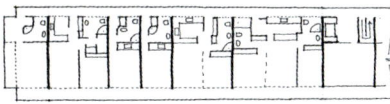

This is one of the most consequent single-loaded corridor examples. The open hallway circulation provocatively faces the Diamond Head neighbor's side of Roy Kelley's Outrigger Reef Hotel, which was built right after, with Kelley having lost a lawsuit to prevent this building after he had previously passed on purchasing its lot as he deemed it too small to build anything substantial on. Educated as an engineer, Sato succeeded in this ingeniously. The opposite Ewa side of the building, with its living room lanai's of studios to two-bedroom units, enjoys an unobstructed view of Fort DeRussy Park thanks to the army's ownership. This way, cross-ventilated units stay cool as the trade winds can pass through from mauka to makai and the circulation slabs shade at midday, reducing the heat of the setting sun to the very last daylight hours on the lanai side. Sato's expertise in thin shell concrete is demonstrated here particularly poetically in the zig-zag rooftop and entrance canopies as well as in the multi-story loggia towards the ocean. The building has been kept in its original condition and the recent, decent remodel of the lobby changed its former dark hermeticism to bright open airiness with Fleetwood sliding doors. This rejuvenated residential entrance includes a compelling collage of the heroic and humble history of the building. In *Blue Hawaii* (1961), Maile and her boyfriend, played by Elvis Presley, leave the adjacent Duke's Beach at Fort DeRussy with their surfboards with the steel skeleton of the building construction as the demonstrative backdrop of booming tourism. Increasingly, everywhere is glamorously gentrified, including recently next door's Outrigger Reef. But here things have stayed simple for strolling with the surf, souvenir and steak stores, all topped off with Susan and Co's Art Gallery. *MD*

6

Hawaii State Department of Health

1250 Punchbowl St
Honolulu, HI 96813
Merrill, Simms & Roehrig
1960

Despite its prominent location and utilization as the home of the State of Hawaii's Department of Health, this building's architect and build year were hard to find. This way, it proves to be truly in the tradition of the Hawaiian vs Western way of construction being a communal effort without the ego of individual authorship. Through orientation and fenestration, the building itself exemplary serves its mission 'to protect and improve the health and environment for all people in Hawaii'. In the macro, the linear mass of the building running mauka to makai is keeping this prevailing trade wind airflow. In its micro, the brise soleil screen of its south- and north-facing fenestration keeps the building shaded from the tropical sun. On both the southern and northern façade, the most elegant and thin vertical fins shade the rising and setting sun while the horizontal ones on the south façade take care of high midday solar radiation. The east and west ends of the building are most vulnerable to solar penetration so are consequently kept closed, dedicating themselves to

Photo: Olivier Koning

short term occupancy circulation. Here, the staggered massiveness of concrete is mitigatingly fluted and contrasted with stacked bond brick and filigree guardrail iron work as well as the corresponding total piece of artwork – the building name signage. The DOH has announced a $100 million renovation of what the news called 'a run-down building' and that the update is technically necessary. One wishes that they aesthetically retain the building's originality. We hope this attention helps raise their awareness of what a gem they have: a prime example of early statehood bioclimatic (non-indigenous) raw modeling. The state as the very best example, as it should be. *MD*

Photo: Martin Despang

6

Photo: DeSoto Brown

Photo: Olivier Koning

Chinese Consulate ↑↓

2746 Pali Hwy
Honolulu, HI 96817
Wong & Wong
1961

063 B

The former Chinese Consulate clearly conveys its function by utilizing modern building materials and techniques to convey traditional Chinese sensibilities. The roof with its inverted concrete barrel vaults is a stroke of genius, recalling traditional Chinese flared roofs, and is augmented by red columns, a moon gate, bronze lanterns, and a plastic laminate frieze with a lozenge pattern. The bright white pavilion-shaped building is further enhanced by sculpted gold-colored national plum blossoms, once again proving that applied ornament still retained a viable place in Hawaii's post-war, multicultural architectural milieu. Carp formerly graced the two rectangular fountains in the front. *DH*

The Town House Apartments →

1415 Victoria St
Honolulu, HI 96822
*Donald N. MacDonald &
John T. Jacobsen*
1961

064 B

This building is exemplarily for the many more of its kind that are the paradisal dream of all temperate climate architects, particularly those aiming for the highest energy efficiency of our time – the passive/active house standard where a structure protruding from inside out is necessary to be thermally disconnected, requiring extreme effort. Honolulu's most forgiving climate for human thermal comfort means that

Photo: Martin Despang

floor slabs can be continuous from the inside to the outside. Only when the buildings are hermeticized and therefore consequentially not covered in this book should they use ISO Schöck or similar as the product to structurally connect while thermally disconnecting balconies. In buildings like this subject to a trade wind breeze with sliding glass doors all around, there is principally no need for insulation. This building type, as per Curt Sanburn's introductory essay, is best described as stacked lanai with continuous vertical bar grade railings, providing its thermally and spatially porous boundary. The fenestration with mostly sliding glass walls is recessed in a variety of depths, creating a playful ephemerality. This particular building was nominated by Matt Noblett, who runs the German firm Behnisch Architekten's Boston branch, and photographer Olivier Koning, originally from France, likely because buildings like this are climatically not possible where they are from, so they speak of being truly from/for Hawaii. Imagine the traffic on the H-1 freeway out front changed to bicycle-only à la Copenhagen; it would be pure paradise. The vegetation on the lanais, allowed by the HOA, could fully take over and make the buildings fully blend in with Hawaii's nearby natural mauka. *MD*

6

Bishop Museum Kilolani Planetarium ↑

1525 Bernice St
Honolulu, HI 96817
Merrill, Simms & Roehrig
1961

065 B

Waikiki Grand Hotel →

134 Kapahulu Ave
Honolulu, HI 96815
Ernest Hara
1962

066 C

The Bernice Pauahi Bishop Museum, an outstanding institution of the Pacific and indeed the world, opened its first building to the public in 1891. Additional structures followed into the 1920s, but there was no new construction until the Kilolani Planetarium (now the Jhamandas Watumull Planetarium) was completed in 1961. With the US beginning its period of active space travel at this time, increased public awareness of this burgeoning field was seen as beneficial. The original building was comprised of a domed planetarium inside which 'stars' were projected for narrated programs, a smaller observatory dome containing a telescope, and a lobby to accommodate museum-goers awaiting the next program. Both domes were positioned atop circular bases built of local lava rocks and mortar in a nod to the Hawaiian environment. Two curved, flaring decorative outside columns supported a roof over an open concrete patio, and a large rounded outside planter bed also carried on the theme. Exterior additions in the 1970s began to obscure the planetarium, and a new ticket entry, gift shop and restaurant (the Jabulka Pavilion) from 1984 further hide the structure's original appearance today. *DB*

Thanks to the increasingly endangered species of altruist landlords, this building has been the home of this author until most recently since arriving in Hawaii a dozen years ago. It has truly proven to be a prime example for environmental and social inclusivity. With Kapahulu Avenue running exactly east-west, its accordingly south-facing street elevation is lanaied so sufficiently that it self-shades itself. The Ewa units face the cool north, embracing the pool. Its double-loaded corridor wing aligned with small studios is open to both ends on the mauka side, turning into the single-loaded mauka wing with larger units and morning sun. The original iconic building name sign on lava rock and a cantilevering canopy welcome visitors to the lobby with continued, unrestricted open access to all floors up to the communal sun deck. Urban nomads qualifying entertain on the lobby's Steinway piano donated by a previous tenant . As a condotel, the building has a wide mix of inhabitants and has only recently become vulnerable to the epidemic of gentrification. So, the future management should live up to legendary manager Don Pierce's practice of keeping all inhabitants safe and sheltered with a smile, including local residents like Vanda, who receives a small social security check. This will keep the Waikiki Grand uniquely inclusive. In the next renovation, one might want to be less surfacial and more substantial, bringing the building more fully back to its original self-sustained nature with the original convenience store at the Lemon Road side of the lobby. *MD*

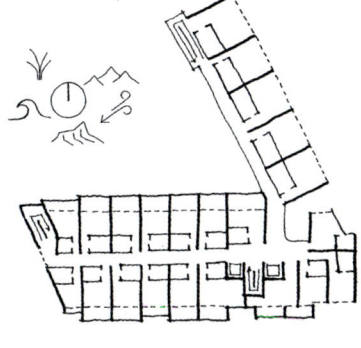

6

1961 Ad, Tropical Modern Hotel

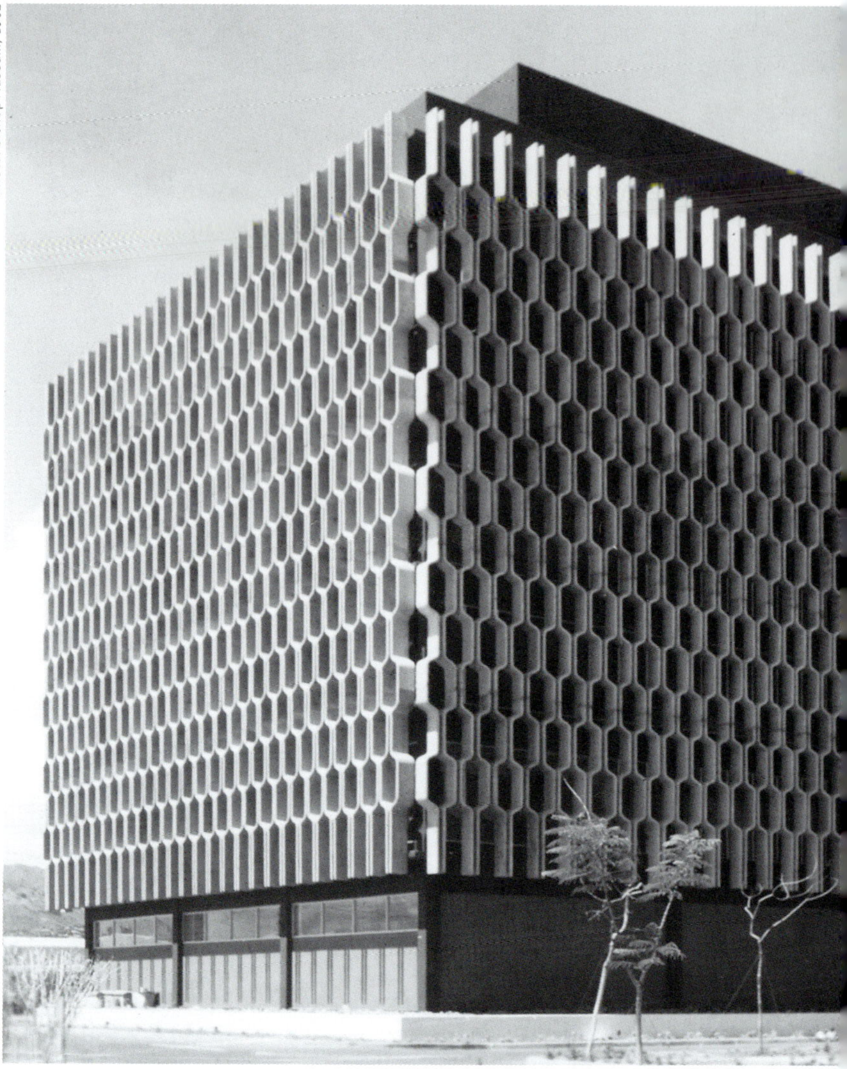

IBM Building

067 B

1240 Ala Moana Blvd
Honolulu, HI 96814
Vladimir Ossipoff
Structural: Alfred Yee
1962

The IBM Building was built in 1962 according to designs by Vladimir Ossipoff. Celebrated now as an iconic part of – and sales office for – the Hughes Corporation's extensive project in Kaka'ako, IBM is a distinctive feature of coastal Ala Moana Boulevard, a circumstance emphasized through an always-changing lighting program. Masterfully simple, the seven-story IBM Building was a distinct design solution for a specific place and purpose. The repetitious

shadows of the grillwork become as significant a part of the architecture as any part of the structure itself'. Scheduled for demolition in 2008, the building gained a significant following among Hawaii's preservation community, which staunchly opposed the property's loss. Luckily, the Hughes Corporation, which took over the larger project in 2010, was more sympathetic to the building than had been Ward Village's earlier developer, General Growth Properties. Architects Woods Bagot and Ferraro Choi combined forces to design the renovation of the building, adding a sculptural concrete penthouse to the roof and a second addition to the makai side of the ground floor. The latter features a courtyard flanked by an open lanai providing a space for receptions and other entertainment. The original grill design is employed as a motif in flooring and other decorative features of the renovated structure. The project was completed in 2014 at a cost of $24 million. *WC*

6

pattern of its precast-concrete grille was intended to express IBM's leadership role in the keypunch card-based computer industry of that time. The elaborate brise-soleil also shades the building's floor-to-ceiling windows from the sun. The short sides of the grille's hexagons were set at an angle to prevent birds from nesting on them and to allow for water runoff as a self-cleaning device. According to Ossipoff: 'The most important point of the building, however, is the character of the building itself. Not only does the systematic and repetitious pattern of the concrete grille [the brise-soleil] express the computer-world character of the IBM Corp', he told the *Honolulu Advertiser* in 1966, 'but it also gives the building a sense of belonging in the sun. The deep

University of Hawaii at Manoa

William Chapman

The University of Hawaii dates to 1907 and the founding of what was then the College of Agriculture and Mechanic Arts of the Territory of Hawaii. Established as one of many land-grant colleges in the US, the new college originally occupied a lot on Young Street in central Honolulu, near Thomas Square. Anticipating expansion, the college's board chair, Judge Henry E. Cooper (1857–1929), one-time minister of education for the Republic of Hawaii, pressed for the acquisition of a site in the then rural Manoa Valley, where it now lies. One of the first new faculty members was the Cornell graduate John Mason Young, who was appointed head of engineering. Young produced the first masterplan for the campus in 1909. This called for an expansive quadrangle aligned on an east-west axis extending from what is now Hawaii Hall to the east towards Manoa Stream – roughly the area presently comprising McCarthy Mall. Proposed buildings included a law school, a medical school, a veterinary science school, and an architecture school. He also included an observatory, located high above the campus on Wa'ahila Ridge, and a 'hydraulic laboratory' across Manoa Stream near what is now Burns Hall at the East West Center. The first building to be constructed was what became known as Hawaii Hall (now Hawaii Hall). Started in

1911, it was completed the following year in time for the class entering in 1912. Shortly afterward, attention shifted away from the proposed formal quadrangle to the buildings needed for the new school of engineering. Designed by Young's colleague Dr. Arthur R. Keller (1882–1961), the first of these was completed in 1915. In 1922, the then 'University of Hawaii' added the first new building to the original quadrangle scheme. Reversing the plan from that of 1909, Gartley Hall would occupy a site at the 'Ewa edge of the campus, perpendicular to recently named Hawaii Hall. George Hall, the university's first dedicated library building, followed in 1925. Designed by local architect Arthur Reynolds (1863–1925), who had also designed Hawaii Hall, this third neoclassical building complemented Gartley Hall, located opposite. In 1929, Dean Hall filled the area between Gartley and Hawaii Hall, providing space for the sciences: zoology, botany, entomology, geology, and anthropology. Crawford Hall, originally the 'Social Science Building' and the last of the quad's original five buildings, would wait until 1938. Several other university buildings and features were gradually added to the original Beaux-Arts campus. These included a gymnasium and a lecture hall/theatre

Bachman Hall before renovations

(now demolished). Miller Hall, built in 1939 and designed by John Mason Young in a combined Spanish Colonial Revival and neoclassical style, faced the theatre. A last major Beaux-Arts building was Gilmore Hall, built on the site of the present Art Building. Also designed by architect Ralph Fishbourne, Gilmore Hall served as the home of the agricultural extension service and College of Agriculture. Demolished in 1973, Gilmore Hall became something of a cause célèbre for the nascent preservation community. Other features of the older campus are the Founders' Gates, constructed in 1933, and the Andrews Outdoor Theatre, completed in 1935 – both also designed by Fishbourne. The 5,500-capacity Greek-style theatre (not an amphitheatre as many refer to it) was named after Dr. Arthur L. Andrews (1871–1945), first dean of the College of Arts and Sciences. The Charles Atherton House YMCA across University Avenue from the main campus should also be counted as part of the original Beaux-Arts campus. Dedicated in 1932 and designed by architect Guy Nelson Rothwell (1890–1971), the Atherton House provided the first housing for (male) university students. Many of the university's most distinctive buildings date from the postwar period, though they typically fill slots in the Beaux-Arts plan developed by John Mason Young. Bilger Hall was completed in 1951 to provide laboratory space and additional classrooms for the growing science interest at the university. The architect was English-born and New Zealand-raised local architect Mark Potter (1895–1966), known especially for his romantic, Arts and Crafts-style houses and cottages and for an earlier association with Harry Livingston Kerr (1863–1937), with whom he designed the neoclassical Mission Memorial Building of 1915. Strongly suggestive of modernism's Bauhaus roots, the three-story

6

Saunders seating

Saunders Hall before restoration

Saunders lanai learning

Sinclair Library before alteration

building displays a striking range of industrial awning windows that contrast strongly with the smooth stucco surfaces and projecting concrete canopy of the uppermost floor. Saunders Hall, built in 1974, is representative of the resurgent interest in diagonal planning in the 1970s, spawned by Chicago-based SOM architect Walter Netsch (1920–2008) – known at the time as 'Field Theory'. Designed by Ossipoff, Snyder, Roland, and Goetz and set at a 45-degree angle to the neoclassical University 'Quad', the new concrete building for social sciences made a bold statement on the then architecturally conservative campus of UH Manoa. Seven stories high (with a separate roof terrace) and distinguished by its deeply embossed concrete stucco surface, Saunders Hall is organized around a large open courtyard, with its open circulation corridors punctuated by corner projections hovering over the courtyard garden below. Sinclair Library was one of the first modernist buildings added to the growing campus in Manoa when it was completed in 1956. Originally called 'The New Library', Sinclair was the work of the young firm of Lemmon, Freeth & Haines (which evolved to become the prominent firm of Architects Hawaii Ltd.; more recently AHL). Sinclair Library would embrace the climate of the Hawaiian Islands, eschewing the new technology of air-conditioning and designing interior spaces in a way to permit future change. Distinctive features include the operable glass jalousies of the main reading rooms and the gently curving entry, composed of concrete, brick, and Waiānae sandstone. Helping to establish the firm's reputation, the library would eventually house some 500,000 volumes, making it the preeminent research collection in the Pacific. With the construction of a new library in 1965, extended in 1975 and expanded again beginning in 1991, Sinclair Library shifted to serve undergraduates and then media and art and architectural history. The university is now converting the building to a student learning center, without, unfortunately, its original climatically sympathetic features. Bachman Hall, built in 1948, was the product of the partnership of Associated Architects, with Vladimir Ossipoff (1907–1998) serving as principal designer. Bachman Hall is distinguished by its unusual arrangement of spatial volumes, employing a pierced screen, 'false' walls and windows, an open courtyard defined by square columns (and planted with contrastingly curving coconut palms), and a dramatic two-story entryway. The building has special significance for the architects' collaboration with French-born muralist Jean Charlot. The landscape partnership of Thompson and Thompson (Catharine Jones Thompson and Robert Oliver Thompson) designed the courtyard and

Endangered Kykendall Hall

lawn facing the building. The wood 'temporary' buildings, known as the 'Portables', dating to 1967, were a response to a significant jump in enrollment and expansion of program offerings in the 1960s. Designed by Duluth, Minnesota-born and University of Michigan-trained architect Richard N. Dennis, the Portables answered several needs and have changed functions over time. Shed-roofed with tongue-and-groove Douglas fir vertical siding, the Portables were a frank expression of tropical modernism. The Biomedical Science Building was designed by renowned architect Edward Durell Stone in the early 1960s. Original construction drawings date to October 1967 and UH Manoa took possession of the building in 1971. The building was originally a seven-story tower surrounded by a block-like hollow cube. Six courtyards filled the space between the outer perimeter and allowed for internal circulation and connection between the structures. The walls are scored throughout in designs reflective of Pacific Island pottery and textile designs. The tower has similar bands of decoration on each floor, surmounted by continuous ranges of high windows. In 2010, Group-70 (now G70) added the C-MORE (Center for Microbial Oceanography: Research and Education) Hale to the makai (ocean) end of the larger compound. Awarded LEED Platinum Certification, the new structure somewhat obscures the original structure. Keller Hall, once the home of the Department of Mathematics and the Department of Computer Science was completed in 1959 for a cost of $632,211. Designed by local architect Clifford F. Young (1918–2011), the contract was completed by Edwin Mamoru Tani (1924–2014), a 1949 UH engineering school graduate. The four-story building is distinguished by its paneled concrete cladding, its vertical aluminum fins, and its full-height stained-glass window by art professor Murray Turnbull (1919–2014) and his wife Phyllis. Sakamaki Hall, completed in 1977, is named for historian Shunzo Sakamaki, the first Asian-American faculty member to reach the rank of professor at UHM. The architect was Kaimuki High School graduate Robert Matsushita, who received his architectural training at the University of Oklahoma, studying under noted architect Bruce Goff.

6

Photo: Andrea Brizzi

Portables before planned demolition

East West Center

William Chapman

The East West Center (EWC), completed in 1963, was the masterwork of Chinese American architect I. M. Pei. Comprised of some five principal buildings and two pavilion-like structures, the center was part of the United States' effort to counterbalance Soviet influence in Third World countries, notably through the creation of the Patrice Lumumba University in Moscow. Funding came from the US government through the initiative of then-Senator Lyndon Johnson. Called the Center for Cultural and Technical Interchange Between East and West, the new teaching and research institute was signed into law by President Dwight Eisenhower, with additional funding coming annually from the US Department of State. The center took in its first students in 1960 before completion of the original five-building campus. The center always had a close relationship with the adjacent University of Hawaii at Manoa (UHM); in fact, two buildings, Moore Hall and Edmundson Hall, on the campus were paid for through funds earmarked for the EWC. Students at the EWC took classes at UHM and received their degrees from the older institution. Key buildings for the center were Jefferson Hall, Hale Manoa, the EWC Theatre (renamed Kennedy Theatre in 1963 a few days after the assassination of President Kennedy), Hale Kuahine, and Lincoln Hall. Burns Hall,

Photo: Andrea Brizzi

Lincoln Hall

Kennedy Theatre

named after Hawaii's Democratic governor, John A. Burns, came in 1977 at the makai end of the generous EWC site. John Hara, leading a team of other architects, was responsible for the compatible design. Jefferson Hall, which now houses the Hawaii Imin International Conference Center, was the last major building completed of the original EWC campus. Originally open to the outside, the main floor once featured a lounge for the East West Center's scholars, students, and distinguished visitors. (It was enclosed during renovations in 1985.) The Honolulu partnership of Young & Henderson, successor to McAuliffe, Young & Associates, assisted Pei in the realization of the multipurpose building, with local architect Clifford F. Young taking on much of the responsibility for the project. Jean Charlot, a noted Hawaii-based, French-born artist and a former student of Diego Rivera, the Indonesian artist Affandi, and New Zealand muralist David Barker, created the interior artwork. Japanese landscape architect Kenzō Ogata designed the Japanese Garden, located to the rear of the building. Named after the third president of the US, Jefferson Hall combines the austere symmetry of the New Formalism with hints of Chinese traditional architecture to convey the links between Asia and the West envisioned by the center's multiple champions and founders. Located toward the makai

(ocean-side) end of the 21-acre East West Center campus, Hale Manoa is a 13-story, elegant but still 'brutalist' structure designed by I. M. Pei. Clearly inspired by Le Corbusier's Unité d'habitation housing, Manoa originally housed 400 male students in the East West Center fellowship programs; females lived at the four-story Hale Kuahine further mauka. Completed in 1962, the impressive dormitory features double floors of rooms interspersed by four open floor areas (lanai) for cooking, eating, and socializing. With the reception and lounge areas on the ground floor, Hale Manoa provides a lively home for today's multinational (and now co-ed) residents – who still enjoy the cross ventilation offered by the lanai and the opportunities of meeting fellow students and visitors. Dependent on the trade winds for ventilation, the access stairs from the lanai areas can feel a bit restricting. Students prefer the ocean side for its views but often choose the mountain side for the cooler climate. The building has undergone few changes, other than the redecorating of the ground-floor lounge in 2004 and the provision of new kitchens in 2005. The dorm rooms cluster into separate living units of two double and five single rooms, all sharing a single bathroom area. Lincoln Hall, completed in 1962, was one of five original buildings designed by I. M. Pei. Intended as a residence for visiting

Photo: Andrea Brizzi

Garden side of Jefferson Hall (Structural: Alfred Yee)

scholars, professionals, and trainees on short programs, the building – named, of course, for President Abraham Lincoln – encompasses a four-story-high atrium space filled with plants. As with other EWC structures, the local firm of McAuliffe, Young & Associates played a significant role in Lincoln Hall's construction. The rooms are naturally ventilated by louvers set into the windowsills. The interlocking concrete blocks create an interesting square pattern on the infenestrated sections of the side walls, suggesting something of a debt to Frank Lloyd Wright's experiments with decorative masonry blocks. Designed by I. M. Pei with the local firm of McAuliffe, Young & Associates handling the on-site supervision, the 800-seat Kennedy Theatre (Hawaii has always used the British spelling) features prestressed concrete beams and girders, creating an expansive two-story covered lanai frequently used during events. The decorative treatment, including the slightly arched balcony support and Chinese-patterned beam ends,

Photo: Andrea Brizzi

University side of Jefferson Hall (Structural: Alfred Yee)

relate directly to Jefferson Hall across the street. Originally built to serve EWC conferences, the theatre quickly became a popular venue with the University of Hawaii Drama Department. A land-swap resulted in the university assuming ownership of the theatre, with the East West Center acquiring the land for Burns Hall, the administrative building for the center. The EWC complex also includes two intriguing small structures, one a Japanese teahouse situated in the Japanese Garden to the rear of Jefferson Hall, and the other a Thai open pavilion or 'sala' located in front of Hale Kuahine. The teahouse was the gift of Sen Sōshitsu, a 15th-generation grand tea master. The Thai sala was presented in 1967 on behalf of King Bhumibol Adulyadej (Rama IX). In March 2008, Princess Maha Chakri Sirindhorn, daughter of King Bhumibol Adulyadej, and Queen Sirikit dedicated a new sala designed by renowned Thai master Pinyo Suwankiri.

6

Hale Manoa

Hale Manoa

1711 East-West Rd
Honolulu, HI 96848
I. M. Pei & Associates
1962

Two of your authors fought over this building, so it is obviously one of our favorites. This paradise became the home of this author for his very first week on the island and if he had the chance, he would have never left. As part of the National Government's East West Center, the building is a dormitory that houses students of the center at the University of Hawaii at Manoa. Its 13 stories are split leveled with alternating 'private' and 'public' floors. The monk-like minimalism of the private dorm rooms contrasts with the generous public spaces for circulation, communication, and communal cooking with distant ocean views. Bathrooms are shared and in parts coed. Built in concrete, its three-dimensional fenestration grid keeps the Manoa Valley rain and sun principally out to the south and entirely to the north into the Mauka Valley – where this author was blessed to stay and enjoy the custom-made passive ventilation system that blocks the valley winds with fixed gazing, welcoming its cooling effect, which is adjustable from a slit below. The east and west facing façades most vulnerable to the heat of the rising and setting sun are consequently kept opaque. The ultimate tropical version of Le Corbusier's Unité d'Habitation. The public-private partnership dormitory under construction directly makai of it was unfortunately obviously blind and unable to see its obvious raw model masterfulness given its turned 90-degree orientation and resulting sunset-blasted fenestrations. So, this building will increasingly remain the perfect raw model for architectural education, its staff kindly giving tours, apologizing for the lack of renovation due to limited funding, which we reply with 'what a blessing', as this way the originality is preserved. In a city that sadly increasingly only the rich can afford, the operating management makes a big difference by making paradise come true for the emerging generation, altruistically charging only $30 per night for an inclusive experience

Photo: Martin Despang

Photo: Martin Despang

in a vintage I. M. Pei building. The national government in ownership is better not turning it into a high-end resort. If it becomes part of the DOGE sale of government buildings, the University of Hawaii surrounding it must, as a potential buyer, promise to do better than that close-to-completion new dorm next door – a building that has learned nothing from this neighbouring masterpiece, as far as orientation, fenestration, and inhabitation are concerned, charging double for isolationist prison-like cells. It is a contrast to these monk-like cells with splendid common areas high in the skies, with this concept of small, protected personal spaces around large, communal open spaces. Different from the new microwave highrises that have not earned their branding with Hawaiian names, Hale Manoa dearly deserves the name Hale, as it evolves those native practices. *MD*

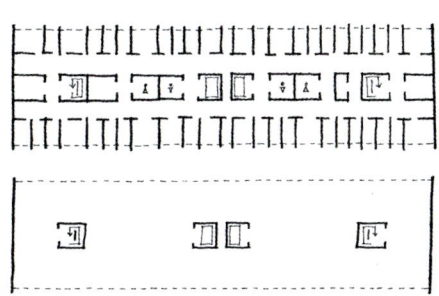
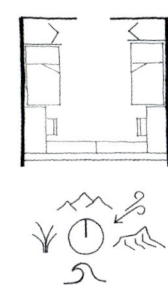

6

QR

Liona Apartments

952 Ahana St,
Honolulu, HI 96814
Anbe, Aruga, Ishizu
1962

069 B

This is one of the most environmentally and economically responsible island projects to date. A three-story walk-up with no elevator, no pool, and no air conditioning results in the lowest possible maintenance costs. The elongated building footprint follows a mauka-makai direction, making the main fenestrations southeast and northwest entirely jalousied with horizontal louvers. Above a sunken parking area, there are one-bedroom apartments with external hallway access, above which in turn are two stories of studios accessed through a double-loaded corridor. The south and north ends carry the open staircases that welcome the north-east trade winds through vents above the unit entrance doors and out the louvered fenestration. Dwayne 'The Rock' Johnson shares on YouTube that he grew up here until they were evicted for not being able to afford the rent. While he is kind and comforting of similar feelings among the youth

Photo: Rainer Kiessling

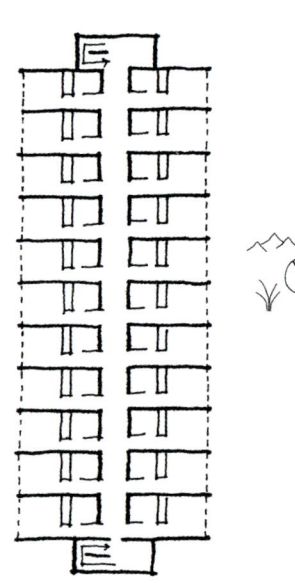

Photo: Martin Despang

of today, he remembers dreaming of living across the street in a 'gorgeous high-rise'. We need to talk to him further to see if retrospectively he did not want to, as the building across the street is the hermetic, exclusive fossil Hale Kaheka of 1982 by Norman Lacayo. Nor would one want to live in the two most recently erected surrounding buildings that are suffocating it: the monstrous 'The Park on Keeaumoku' high-rises, whose only benefit is that they somewhat shade the west face that is too sunny; they are built right up to the parking garage that emits pollutants and obstructs the view from the building. While Dwayne had the privilege of growing up in one of the most easy-breezy, inclusive post-fossil buildings in Honolulu, existential economic circumstances did not allow him to appreciate it at the time. The rent continues to be among the most affordable, enabling it to be home to the future 'The Rocks' he encourages on YouTube. *MD*

QR

Photo: DeSoto Brown, 1963

Waikiki Circle Hotel

2464 Kalākaua Ave
Honolulu, HI 96815
Park Associates
1963

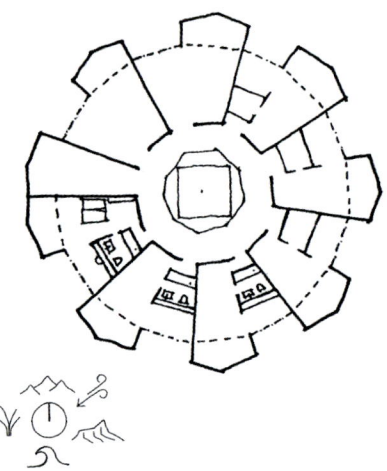

This is the first hotel owned and operated by a woman and an Asian: Emma Kwock Chun. Possibly consequently, it is not a hard-edged box, but rather a soft circle. From a central core the floors concentrically cantilever out, leaving a fully open outdoor lobby. Its lava rock-clad and fern-overgrown ground floor restaurant is elevated and fenestrated in such

Photo: DeSoto Brown, 1964

Photo: DeSoto Brown, 1965

a way that sitting at the tables, you see the beach and the Pacific Ocean rather than cars. All rooms have generously-sized lanais, their slabs super thin even including the conducts for the integrated lighting – something unimaginable in these days of clumsy pour-in-place concrete, as is currently happening a few blocks over at the Marriott timeshare tower construction. Initially growing by itself like a palm tree out of the sand of Waikiki Beach, its functional fenestration anatomy was equally natural: the guestrooms were equipped with curtained lanai sliding doors in one segment, as in actuality the circle is a polygon. The other segment with horizontal wooden jalousies allowed visitors to seamlessly self-adjust to any daylight and trade wind ventilation requirements. This mitigated the non-directional nature of a circular orientation with guest rooms facing all directions – those staying cool to the north, ones to the south through the lanais above, and those to the east and west otherwise baked by the sun rising and setting. In the next renovation, the circle looks forward to getting back its wooden jalousies and original Chun circle-infused cast-iron rod railings, replacing the recently installed, unintelligent glass parapets and the single wall AC units stuck into the stucco infill. This author cannot wait for it – writing these observations from another altruist rental, once again announced to be sold: Ernest Hara's The Seashore. The stacked lanais facing Waikiki Circle's mauka side, offering daily views of always open, easy-breezy housekeeping segments, are living proof of the stacked sky lanai lifestyle only possible in Honolulu. *MD*

USS Arizona Memorial of the Pacific ↓

071 A

1 Arizona Memorial Pl
Honolulu, HI 96818
Alfred E. Preis
Structural: Alfred Yee
1963

Its gleaming white countenance shimmering across the waters of Pearl Harbor, the USS Arizona Memorial of the Pacific reflects the heroic innocence of the 7 December 1941 sacrifice made by those who lie interred in the ship. Eloquently communicating its solemn message, this concrete memorial straddles the sunken hull of the USS Arizona. Resting on 150-foot-deep concrete piles, the precast and reinforced concrete memorial seems to float on Pearl Harbor's rippling waters without visible means of support. The gracefully simple catenary curve of its body reinforces an ethereal impression, while employing a variation of one of the architect's favored silhouettes, the butterfly roof. Through broad openings in the central portion of the memorial, visitors have bow-to-stern views of the sunken battleship sitting in its watery grave, still leaking oil. A trapezoidal opening in the memorial's

Photo: DeSoto Brown, ca. 1963

terrazzo deck even more directly links visitors to the rusting hulk a mere eight feet below them. Design details such as the triangular entryway, the absence of right angles, the unsupported corners of the trapezoid's stainless steel hand rails, and the interplay of the concave memorial wall and its convex base, as well as the solids between the openings recalling the silhouettes of Marine guards, are rarely consciously noted by visitors, yet add to the exquisite grace of their experience, subtly transporting them beyond the realm of the everyday into one conducive to serene contemplation. A seemingly straightforward, gracefully simple design, it successfully addresses and augments the emotions elicited by the physical presence of that 'day that will live in infamy'. Beyond the direct confrontation with history that it provides, the architecture of the memorial also operates at a symbolic level. The catenary curve of the roof, with its low point over the sunken ship, invokes the initial defeat followed by a triumphant rise, and the fragmented, jagged apertures illuminating the memorial wall express the violent destruction of the battle. The existence of the memorial owes something to Elvis Presley. Following the conclusion of the Second World War, the USS Arizona remained undecorated until 1950 when commander-in-chief in the Pacific Admiral Radford ordered a flag platform erected over the sunken hull. Six years later the platform was declared unsafe and removed. In response, the US Congress authorized the construction of an Arizona memorial and established a commission to raise private funds for its construction. A national campaign commenced on 7 December 1957, but after three years, was still far from its goal. On 26 March 1961, Elvis did a benefit performance at Pearl Harbor's Bloch Arena, raising over $64,000 for the memorial. More importantly, the concert sufficiently increased public awareness of the memorial to raise the necessary construction funds from the private sector, Congress, and the Hawaii state legislature. *DH*

Valley of the Temples Memorial Park

072 A

47-200 Kahekili Hwy
Kaneohe, HI 96744
Wimberly, Whisenand, Allison & Tong
1963

Sited on a gently rolling hill, readily visible from Kahekili Highway, the administration building for the Valley of the Temples Memorial Park imposingly rises from the surrounding green lawn to set a tone of reverence for the cemetery beyond it. A fusion of modern architectural principles and traditional Hawaiian forms, the building sits on a battered lava rock base, reminiscent of ancient heiau. At the front and rear of the building, centered, vertical gateways with an open, prestressed concrete framework and tapering side walls recall lele, the wood tower on a heiau used as an altar for offerings to the gods. The towers rise approximately 36 feet at the front and 19 feet at the rear. The recessed windows and cantilevered lanai with battered columns compatibly integrate the modern flat-roofed office function into the design. Originally, the building featured an interior courtyard that provided light and air to the offices; however, this has been enclosed to accommodate required functions. The building stands at the entry to the memorial park; at the back of the park, at the foot of the Koolau Mountains stands another temple, a reinforced concrete replica of the Byodo-in, a millennium-old villa and Buddhist temple in Japan. Designed by Robert Katsuyoshi and built in 1968, it serves as a columbarium. It also houses a nine-foot gold and lacquered wood statue of Buddha Amida, the largest wooden Buddha carved in the last nine centuries. *DH, DL*

Photo: DeSoto Brown

Photo: DeSoto Brown

Outrigger Canoe Club

073 C

2909 Kalākaua Ave
Honolulu, HI 96815
*Vladimir Ossipoff & Associates;
Wimberly, Whisenand, Allison & Tong*
1963

Asked by the canoe club to 'provide a quality of openness and an atmosphere of gracious Hawaiian informality', the architects of the Outrigger Canoe Club developed a tour de force of modern Hawaii regional design. Flat-roofed and single-storied, the coral and concrete walls unobtrusively dissolve into the surrounding landscape. Magnificently open, 'there is never a feeling of being "in a building". Walking through the club is an experience of ever changing spaces, interior and exterior, always related to sunlight and landscaping, always with a different view of the sea beyond,' so explained the Hawaii Chapter of the AIA in a 20 February 1966 article in the *Honolulu Star Bulletin*. The club's congenial, meandering sequence of integrated indoor-outdoor spaces exudes Hawaiian hospitality at its best as it moves from a plumeria-shaded, zigzag entry walk, through an open-air lobby to an outdoor restaurant and beachfront, hau-embowered terrace. Along the way, a Japanese dry stream garden as well as a clean-lined, low-ceilinged reception pavilion and landscaped courtyard are encountered. In 1908, the club sought to revitalize the sport of surfing on boards and outrigger canoes, by providing 'the small boy of limited means' access to the beach. Originally situated between the Royal Hawaiian and Moana hotels, it moved to its present location on the expiration of its lease in 1963, the victim of escalating land values. *DH*

Photo: WATG

6

Photo: Martin Despang

Varsity Building ↓ →

1110 University Ave
Honolulu, HI 96826
Wimberly, Whisenand,
Allison & Tong
1963

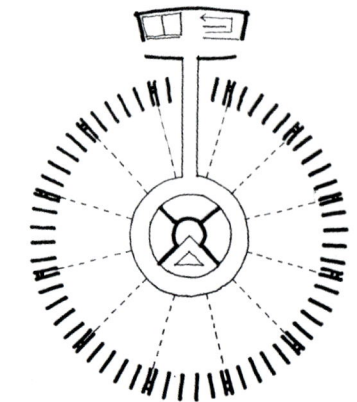

Developed on property owned by Consolidated Amusement, a theatre chain, the Varsity Building was named for the now-demolished Varsity Theatre next door, which had opened in 1939. In turn, its name had come from its proximity to the University of Hawaii, a few blocks away on the same street. The Varsity Building is cylindrical in shape, a trendy form in the 1960s and one of a group of

Photo: Olivier Koning

Photo: Martin Despang

Photo of Ronald Lindgren by Andrea Brezzi

similar structures in Honolulu from that time period, two others of which are also in this book. The main circular structure is attached at each floor to a separate rectangular elevator shaft that stands close by. At the building's opening in 1963, the entire ground floor was occupied by a branch of the First National Bank (today's First Hawaiian Bank), then actively expanding to serve numerous growing communities in the Hawaiian Islands. Although the bank has moved out, its original vault is still in place, as are the driveway and teller cubicles for drive-through banking services. Exterior plaster sun shades partly cover each window to cut glare and heat for the building's offices. This feature is noteworthy for being far-sighted, since electricity costs at the time were minimal and saving energy was not yet considered important. *DB*

Kahala Hilton ↓

5000 Kahala Ave
Honolulu, HI 96816
Killingsworth, Brady and Smith
Structural: Alfred Yee
1964

075 C

A near-gossamer grid of precast concrete, post-and-beam members soften the Kahala Hotel's façade and give it definition, ascending above the building's flat roofline, pergola-like against the sky. A low-rise lobby runs perpendicular to the beach, while 288 guest rooms rise ten stories behind it to form the head of the T-shaped building. The long pavilion-like lobby and adjoining lounge have 30-foot-high ceilings, and although not as open as many of the more recent resort hotels, windows and sliding doors do line the length of the teak-floored wing

6

Photo: Andrea Brezzi

and open on lanai to offer a free flowing, lambent atmosphere. The standard guest rooms and their baths, containing a minimum of 550 square feet, are among the largest in the islands and introduced his and her bathrooms to Hawaii's hotel vocabulary. The presidential suite has hosted all of the presidents between Lyndon Johnson and George W. Bush, as well as Queen Elizabeth, Emperor Hirohito, Prince Rainier and Princess Grace, Prince Charles and Princess Diana, and numerous other world leaders. The hotel lives up to the claim to be, 'a blend of architectural and tropical beauty', where guests can find 'classical elegance and relaxing comfort'. *DH*

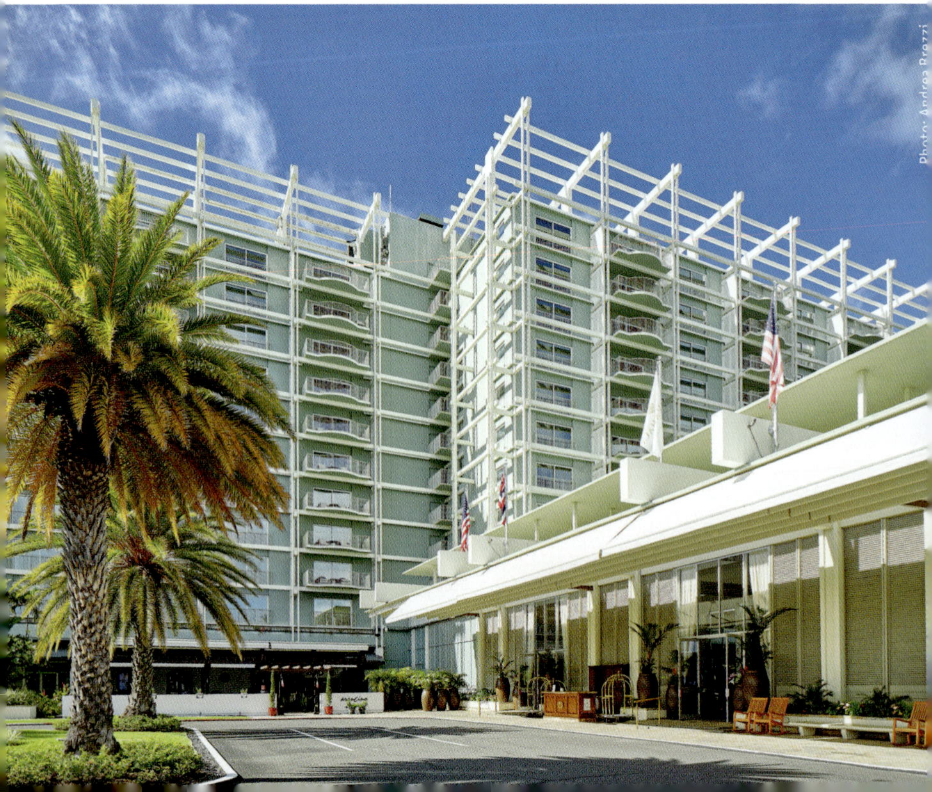

Photo: Docomomo

Ilikai Hotel

076 B

1777 Ala Moana Blvd
Honolulu, HI 96815
John Graham
Structural: Alfred Yee
1964

This concept of a three-legged star in plan is not unique to Hawaii yet fits into its tropical setting, with each wing in the shade/shadow of the other in the daily path of the sun. Linear lanais with vertical bar railings all around add to the tropical ambiance, with parapet panels periodically painted in Pacific Ocean turquoise opaque to add variety to occupancy options. The project by developer Chinn Ho was originally conceptualized as a high-end residential property with 1056 units. Struggling as such, it was soon reconceptualized as a hotel and now condotel. It played a prominent role in many episodes of the original *Hawaii Five-O* TV series and featured prominently

Photo: Olivier Koning

6

in the opening credits, with a helicopter flying towards it, catching Jack Lord (alias Steve McGarrett) at the top. And yes, his colleague detective Chin Ho Kelly was named after Chinn Ho. Jack Lord personally owned a unit in the building. For more nostalgia, Elvis Presley liked staying in the Ilikai and performing in its Y-shaped sibling, the Westgate Hotel in Las Vegas. The Ilikai's theatrical external elevator leads to what Graham topped his Ala Moana building with – what looks like a crashed flying saucer on the rooftop restaurant, adding to that 'ninth island' (as Hawaii folks call Las Vegas) flair. *MD*

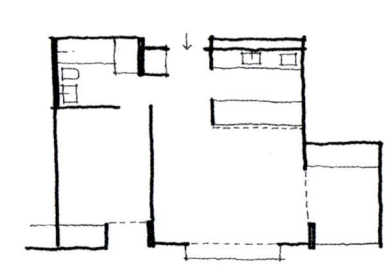

Queen Emma Gardens

077 B

1519 Nuuanu Ave
Honolulu, HI 96817
Minoru Yamasaki
Structural: Alfred Yee
1964

A splendid example of Minoru Yamasaki's work as applied to public housing, Queen Emma Gardens stands as one of the finest projects undertaken by the Honolulu Redevelopment Agency (HRA). Described by the periodical *Hawaii Business and Industry* as 'an outstanding example of urban renewal cum laude', it only came to be as a result of concerted public outcry against the quality of the initial design proposed by the agency. Yamasaki's adaptation of Le Corbusier's vision of high-rise housing freeing the surrounding ground space for landscaped park, this three-tower complex accommodates 587 residential units on an 8.3-acre city block. Emphasizing open green space, the complex centers on an expansive, tree-bordered lawn area with a meandering pathway above the parking structure, while the wooded Ewa side of the property is graced by two teahouses, connected by a meandering koi pond. The residential buildings themselves respond to their environment, having been sited parallel to the prevailing trade winds, they channel

6

Photo: Docomomo

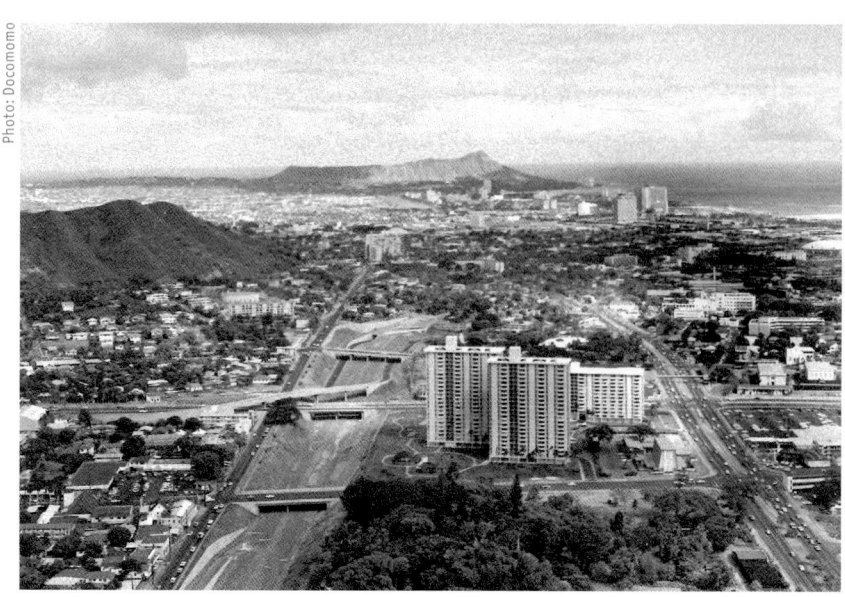

the balmy breezes through their double-loaded corridors. In addition, recessed lanai, graced by curving precast concrete sunshades and the delicate tracery of their aluminum alloy railings, not only provide interaction between the apartments and the outdoors, but also give the structures texture and relief. *DH*

Photo: Docomomo

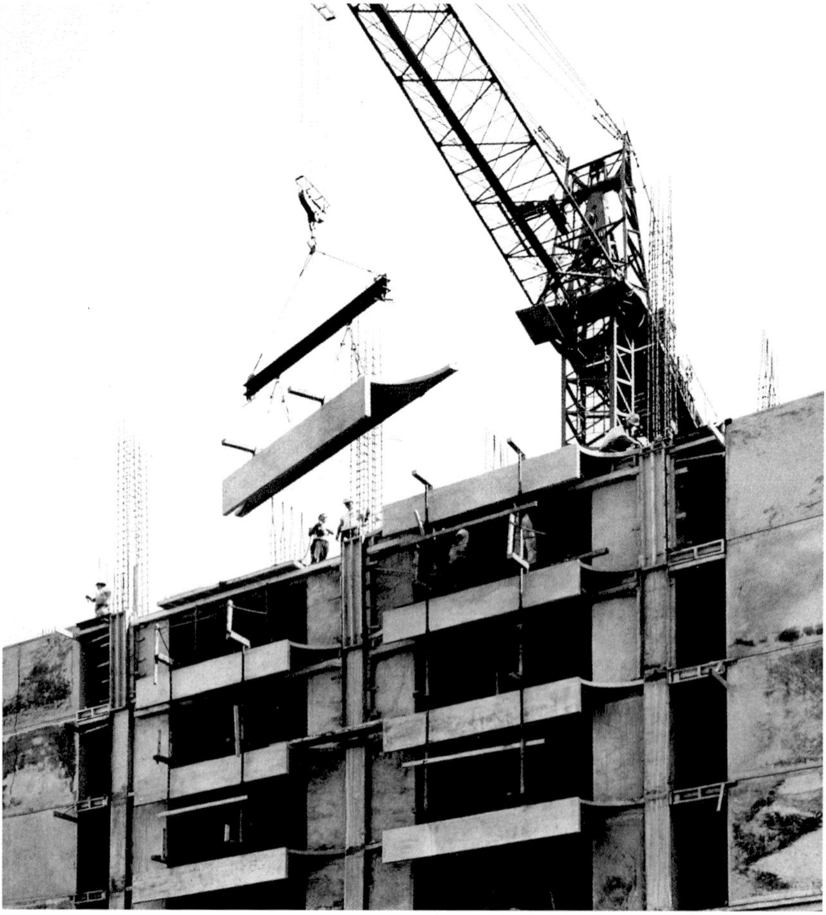

Blaisdell Concert Hall, Exhibition Hall

078 B

777 Ward Ave
Honolulu, HI 96814
Merrill, Simms & Roehrig
1964

Constructed on the historic Ward Estate, the Blaisdell Center was originally called the Honolulu International Center. Urban designed by John Carl Warnecke (see TTH h(e)a's 'Ward Wonder World'), the center is comprised of the arena, exhibition hall, and concert hall, the latter due to its introverted typology a monolith with an elegantly arched welcoming gesture with waffle slab ceiling illumination and custom glass pieces as screen walls. In a recent redevelopment attempt under Mayor Caldwell, the major intervention would have been the replacement of the exhibit hall with a new structure by Norwegian architects Snohetta, which did not come across as tropically exotic as their proposal for the Obama Presidential Library (ultimately built by Williams & Tsien in Chicago). The original hall was very tropical exotic and easy-breezy, with Nervi-like inverted umbrella columns structured in lushly landscaped water ponds. With the Calwell/Snohetta proposal shelved due to the cost explosion of the island's elevated rail project, all it might take is to make a virtue out of the dilemma by just undoing/dismantling the pretentious early 1990s hermitization decoration of this exhibit hall part to bring back the original composition of three pieces of architectural artwork. *MD*

Blaisdell Center Arena
777 Ward Ave
Honolulu, HI 96814
Adrian Wilson & Associates
1964

079 B

A jewel of entertainment and architecture, which, in this typology, is not affordable anymore as this building type is now primarily driven by value engineering and the unfortunate consequences of show-off superficiality. This piece demonstrates sublime substantiality from silhouette to sectional structural shape, with its prisma profile giving it a typologically-fitting boogie-woogie architectural good feeling. Even today, many music masters from all over the world gather here to perform in this spectacular venue. One of the most memorable acts to ever perform here was Elvis Presley in 1973 in the first concert ever to be broadcast around the world via satellite. Fans approach the venue in a procession through tropical flora and water

ponds, out of which the UFO-like arena seems to want to blast off and enhanced illumination starting at dusk makes it appear to float. Included in the funding shortage experienced by the threesome of the arena, concert hall, and exhibition hall, the recent renovation benefitted by receiving only a light touch-up. Here's hoping this write-up helps to maintain that attitude throughout further future renovations to continue with retrofitting versus revamping. *MD*

Photo: DeSoto Brown

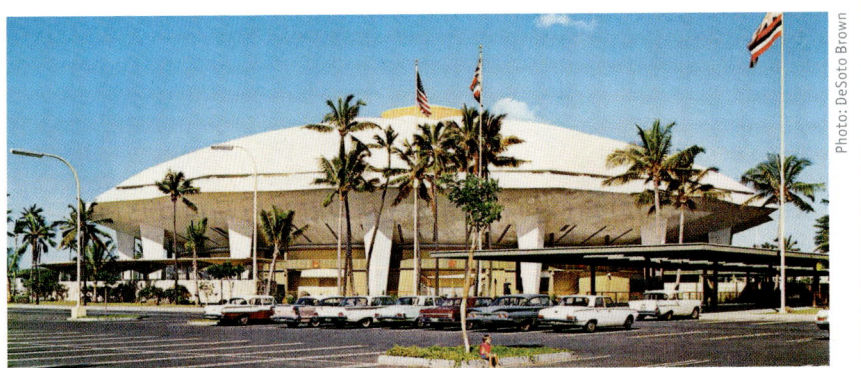

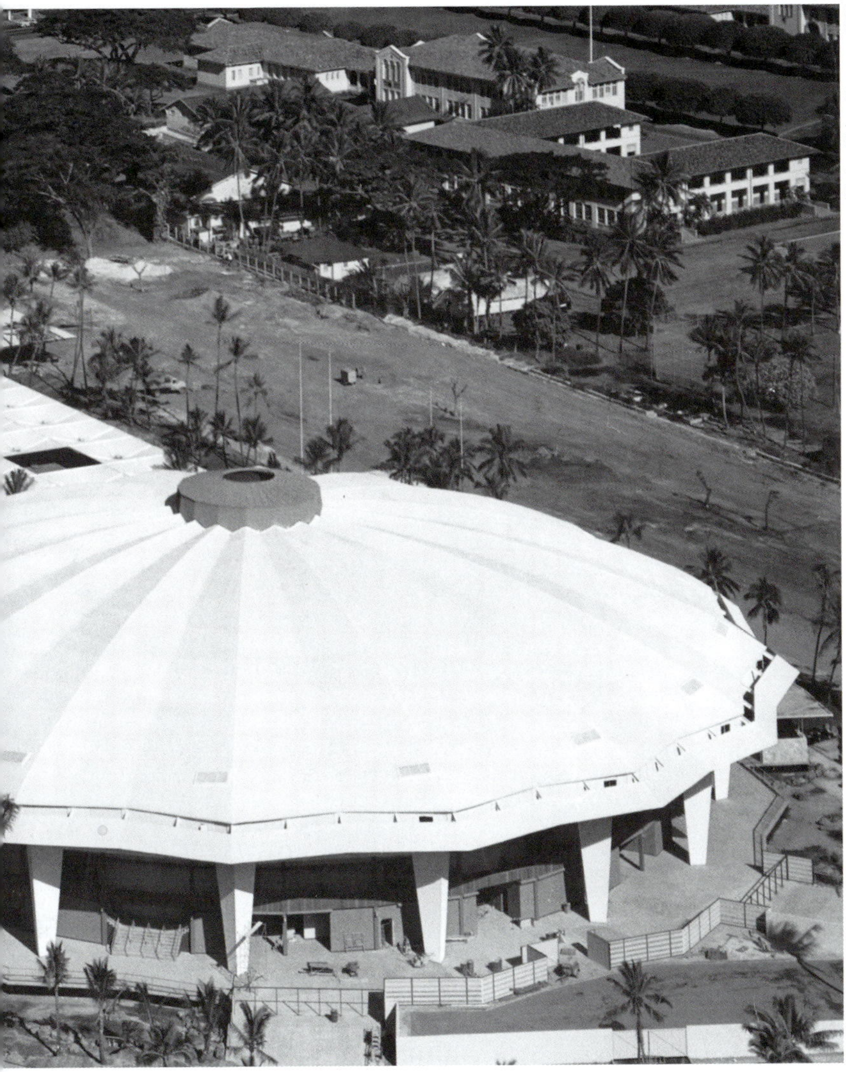

Photo: Bishop Museum, 1963

Honolulu city lights dress up the Blaisdell Center Arena

6

Photo: DeSoto Brown, 1964

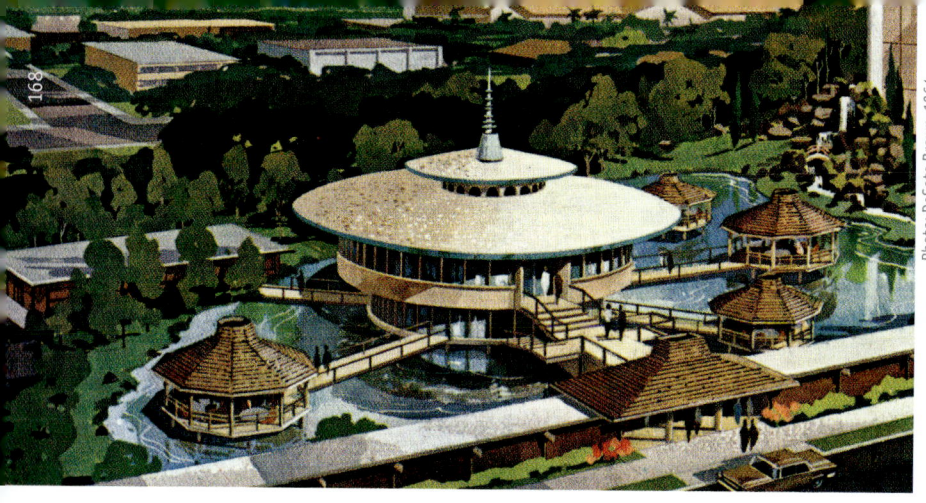

Pagoda Restaurant 080 B
1574 Kanunu St
Honolulu, HI 96814
Hideo Murakami
1964

Opened in 1964 in an actively growing part of Honolulu that had mostly been open, undeveloped land, the Pagoda Restaurant was on the same property as the 12-story Pagoda Hotel, which contained 203 units. A connected parking structure held 150 spaces, increasingly necessary in the congested city. The restaurant consisted of five round structures. The largest contained two floors of dining as well as two bars; four small private dining rooms outside

Photo: Olivier Koning

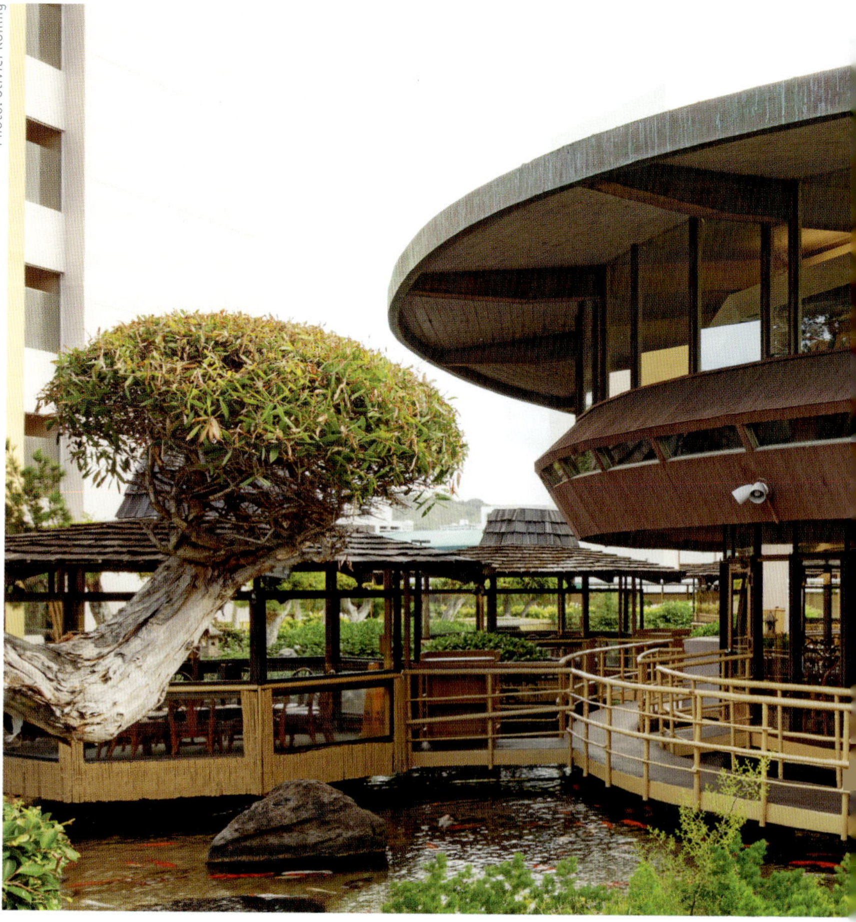

Photo: Martin Despang

were connected by walkways. The entire complex was surrounded by an artificial pond, which contained hundreds of colorful Japanese koi fish. These were fed on a regular schedule that patrons gathered to watch, as the fish thrashed and mounded up in a jammed frenzy. A small artificial hill, landscaped in the Japanese style, formed a visual focal point for diners. A waterfall ran down this hill into the fishpond. On the hill stood a decorative stone pagoda with 13 tiers, which provided the name for the entire business. For decades, the Pagoda 'Floating' Restaurant, as it was originally called – 'floating' because it didn't actually float on a body of water – was very popular with both residents and visitors alike. It was picturesque and unique, and served pleasant food. *DB*

6

Photo: Chunya Wu

Community Church of Honolulu

081 B

2345 Nuuanu Ave
Honolulu, HI 96817
Wong & Wong
1965

Punahou Circle Apartments →

082 C

1617 S Beretania St
Honolulu, HI 96826
Park Associates
1965

A masterpiece of innovation and expressiveness, the bold, upward-sweeping, battered lava-rock walls of this dramatic, dynamic, and cohesive composition seem to flow upward from the earth itself. Typical of post-Second World War ecclesiastical designs, its nave's side walls feature sliding glass doors to open the church to walled gardens. Prestressed concrete rafters make a broad, soaring ceiling possible and spring from shallow round arches rendered in a modern manner, which define the side aisles. A skylight illuminates the chancel, and stained glass windows by R. Douglas Gibbs Company of Glendale, California, enrich the rear wall and the clerestory with abstract depictions of Hawaiian flowers and creation scenes. The Community Church of Honolulu was established in 1934 as the Keeaumoku Church of Christ, an English-speaking offshoot of the Second Chinese Congregational Church. In 1938, the church assumed its present name, reflecting the congregation's decision to be 'open to all, regardless of race, class, or caste'. In that year they purchased the Chinese-style Chungshan Chinese Language School (1935; demolished) designed by Yuk Tong Char and made that Emma Street building their sanctuary until forced to move to the present location when the state purchased their property to build the new H-1 Freeway. *DH, CW*

Unlike the same architect's Waikiki Circle Hotel, this apartment is not of circular geometry but rather part of the neighboring circles of Punahou School, as its most popular student Barack Obama grew up in this building with his grandparents. In this way, he was shaped by an excellent example of superb sustainability. The single-loaded-corridor building's only short-term occupied open hallways are oriented towards the sunny southwest; the sun rising and setting east and west façades are treated as closed, with the building's main lanai life opening up to the cool northeast. The concrete lanai parapets are tall enough to provide privacy but are topped with a metal guardrail to meet code, while they are low enough to have one look over the surrounding landscape. These parapets stop before the unit partition walls and are infilled with vertical wooden slats serving as privacy screening for human or storage purposes. The living room's glass wall is one big fixed glass sheet allowing unobstructed mauka views, with its ventilation cleverly positioned at its bottom as wooden jalousies, with the concrete parapet aerodynamically serving as a diverter of the strength of the trade winds. The ground floor is kept communal and open, sheltered from the sun and rain by the floors above. The structural grid feels like a forest with tree trunk-like columns

cast masterly in a prismatic shape going along with the zig-zag entrance canopy in front. The necessity of some spalling repair work is visible. The owners will keep the building authentic, likely thanks to their awareness of their most prominent tenant, Barack. Similar to Dwayne (Johnson)'s childhood urban multidwelling a few blocks away (see project 069), the Punahou Circle Apartments maintains its tradition of humble upbringing, kindly keeping the rents moderate. *MD*

6

Photo: DeSoto Brown

C. S. Wo Building ↑↓

1500 Kapiolani Blvd
Honolulu HI 96814
Haver, Nunn and Jensen
Structural: Alfred Yee
1965

083 B

By the 1950s, C. S. Wo & Sons had become Hawaii's largest furniture store. In 1957 it opened an attractive, large showroom on Kapiolani Boulevard, an excellent example of mid-century modern design. Consisting of one large interior space with high ceilings and a mezzanine floor reached by two impressive curving staircases, the store offered the company's locally-manufactured furniture along with carpeting, lamps, and other items from the US and elsewhere. From the beginning, C. S. Wo planned to add several stories atop this initial structure. The additional stories, and other enlargements, opened in 1965. The bottom two floors were topped by three new floors, with the two topmost being rentable offices. A ramp on the left side of the structure led to the new second floor parking level. C. S. Wo added new types of merchandise to fill the enlarged space. The narrow office windows facing Kapiolani Boulevard were covered across their top third by concrete shades, taking into consideration that the afternoon sun would be directed into them every day. Such sun baffles are fitted to buildings in Hawaii too rarely, particularly with traditional central air conditioning being nearly universal and energy costs being a major consideration. Today the building sports another floor at the penthouse level, which is easily identified for its lack of sunshades. *DB*

Photo: Don Hibbard

Photo: Docomomo

Kaimuki Jade →

1139 9th Ave
Honolulu, HI 96816
Park Associates
1966

084 C

Herewith the architects return to the circular building floorplan of their previous Waikiki Circle Hotel by optimizing its geometric downfall: a small, trapped dark central corridor circulation. At the expense of a larger diameter, the building has a donut-like open core around which the open, single-loaded hallways circle so that the units get cross ventilation enhanced by the stacked effect of rising hot air extracted through the physical chimney function of the courtyard core. Following the universal archetypical typological tradition of courtyards

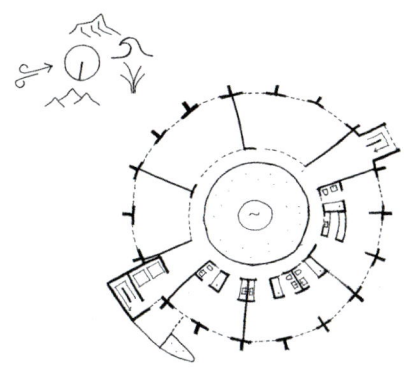

Photo: DeSoto Brown

throughout architectural history beginning with the Romans and Chinese, the Jade Apartments have a water feature in the form of a red brick pavement volcano in its center for physical and spiritual cooling. With the resulting naturally unspectacular peripheral exterior of the tube tower with its glass jalousie fenestration and vertical circulation outsourced to here, the building is a hidden gem that can be fully appreciated only from within. Recent unit renovations show that the glass jalousies have unfortunately been replaced with fixed glazing, which makes particularly the west- and east-facing units only bearable with fossil-fueled air conditioning, so owners are encouraged to retain/revert back to the original easy-breezy, cross-trade-wind-evaporative, water-fueled cooling way. *MD*

Photo: Olivier Koning

6

Photo: Olivier Koning

Jealousy of Jalousies

Don Hibbard

A jalousie window, also known as a louvre window in the United Kingdom, is a window that consists of parallel glass, acrylic, metal, or wooden louvers set in a frame. The louvers are locked together onto a track at either end, so they may be tilted open and shut in unison to control airflow through the window. They are usually controlled by a lever or crank mechanism. The name 'jalousie' derives from the French word jaloux, which means jealousy. Several hundreds of years old, the term was applied to blinds or shutters having adjustable horizontal slats for regulating the passage of air and light. When the window slats were closed they tipped downward. As a result, the person on the outside was unable to see the person inside. Conversely, whoever was on the interior had the benefit of being able to see the person outside. This presumably caused an unfair advantage and hence 'jealousy'. On the mainland, jalousie windows were most frequently used in mid-twentieth-century homes in Florida, southern California, and the Deep South. They were also widely used in mobile homes during the 1950s and 1960s before most mobile home manufacturers began switching to sliding and sash windows in the 1970s and 1980s. In Hawaii the jalousie window became the most popular window for use in tract houses and apartments from the 1950s through the late 1970s, facilitating an easy-breezy lifestyle by allowing the trade winds to flow through almost all of the window space. Van Ellis Huff (1894–1987), an engineer who graduated from the University of Florida, has been credited as the inventor of the modern jalousie window. Huff was inspired by a homemade wooden slat window he saw while on a trip to Bimini, a group of Caribbean islands 50 miles

Jalousie advertisement

Beautiful early jalousies, Liljestrand House

Craft crank, Liljestrand House

6

south of Florida that are included in the Bahamas. Once he returned to the millwork company he operated with his father-in-law, Huff designed an improved wood slat window with a pinion gear operator. In 1937 he applied for a patent for his 'Tropical Louver', which was awarded to him on 8 August 1939. He began manufacturing the custom windows for several Miami homeowners and architects,

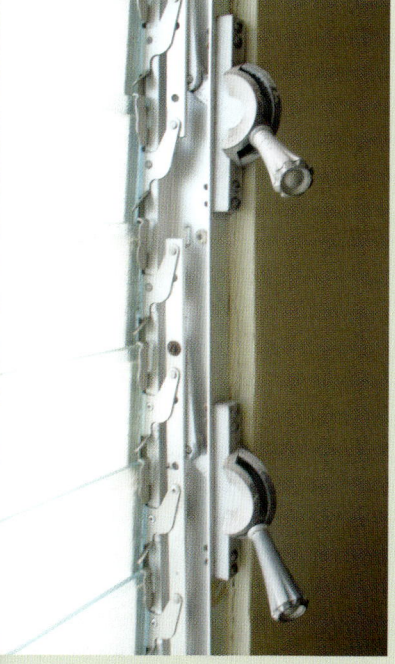

Kalanihuia handle

including Alfred Browning Parker, who began to specify the jalousies in their designs. Upon receiving a large contract in 1940 from the United States Navy for jalousies to be placed in barracks and officers' quarters at Guantanamo, Huff went into partnership with Charlie Miller under the name Pro-Tect-U Jalousie Company. Huff appears to have decided on the name jalousie as the term was then current in New Orleans for wood slat louvered shutters. The Second World War slowed the growth of Huff's jalousie manufacturing business, with the primary clientele being hospitals; however, during these years Huff designed a jalousie using glass rather than wood slats. With the conclusion of the Second World War, he traveled to California in 1946 and secured a contract with the Navy to provide jalousie windows for their new construction projects in Hawaii and at the naval bases in Guam, Johnson Island, and the Philippines. He completed this contract in 1950, visiting Hawaii and the other islands where his windows were installed. On a trip to Hawaii he met Ti How Ho, the owner of Surfrider Sportswear and the person who started the palaka shirt. Ho ordered jalousie windows for his house in Kaneohe, the earliest known private residential use of the windows in the islands. Ho also served as an officer of Pacific Jalousie Corporation, which was formed

1960's mass-market jalousies, Waikiki Grand Hotel

HHome (Jason Selley's round) with thermally modified invasive wood species jalousies

Hawaii, they became the preferred residential and apartment window by the late-1950s. Initially the windows were brought in from various manufacturers on the mainland with such companies as Pro-Tect-U, Win-Dor, and Lite-Ven-Trols offering them for sale. By 1953 City Mill, a local hardware store, was carrying the windows, and in 1955 Sears included them in their inventory. In 1957 Matsu Okumoto started Jalousie Hawaii, and within a year the company began manufacturing windows locally. They brought in extruded

in 1948 with former Florida architect James Fagothey as president. The company, which only remained in business until 1952, carried Huff's Pro-Tect-U jalousie windows. Paradise of the Pacific magazine in its coverage of the 49th State Fair in 1949 included a photograph of the company's exhibit and captioned it: 'a new development in ventilation'. During the 1950s a number of people began to infringe on Huff's patent, and a number of jalousie window manufacturing companies sprang into existence, many of them using aluminum or pot metal in their worm gear handles rather than the bronze rack and pinion handles used by Huff. With no energy or money to fight these infringements, 60-year-old Huff sold his business in 1954. After the appearance of jalousie windows in

Breezway wooden jalousies, HNL Airport

Photo: DeSoto Brown

Queen Kapiolani Hotel

aluminum from various mainland dealers and made the windows from this material. The company also brought in gear operators as these were not made locally; however, they did make their own lever operated handles. In addition to Jalousie Hawaii, a second company operated by Carl Fukumoto, Hawaii Metal Forming, started manufacturing jalousie windows in 1965. This company is no longer in business. During the 1980s Jalousie Hawaii stopped making jalousie windows as demand for the windows declined, the result of the popularization of home air conditioning and an increased concern for security.

These days, authors Martin Despang and Bundit Kanisthakhon encourage the emerging generation to reintroduce jalousies as the ultimate form of tropical exotic fenestration. The examples shown of glass and wood jalousies in their predominant horizontal and vertical way have been known since Elvis's bride Maile slammed them closed around their wedding in the Kauai's Koko Palms Resort in *Blue Hawaii*.

Photo: Graham Hart

Glass jalousies in a UH architectural project design

6

Kahala Beach Apartments

4999 Kahala Ave
Honolulu, HI 96816
Killingsworth, Brady & Smith
Structural: Alfred Yee
1967

085 C

Although in outskirty Kahala, for many like *Hawaii 5-0's* Jack Lord, who moved here from the Ilikai Hotel, this development is the epitome of a metropolitan tropical dwelling. Edward Killingsworth himself called it 'the four shoeboxes at the sea', and a pre-fab concrete construction photograph by its structural engineer Alfred Yee indeed made it originally look rather rational and less livable.

The finished foliage in the spacing courtyards turns the rationality into pure spirituality, its jungle-like feeling giving nearly full privacy, allowing one not to notice any tiger neighbors. According to Killingsworth's later partner, Ronald Lindgren, the architect's 'structural expressionism' of letting the beams project past their meeting with the column also softens the build mass. The entrance canopy as a firework of structural expressionism is flanked by reflecting pools like many of Killingsworth's projects back in his native Long Beach, California. The only disappointment in this masterpiece are the doomy double-loaded corridors only broken up by half-open side circulation.

Photo: Andrea Brezzi

Photo: Andrea Brezzi

6

Photo: Andrea Brezzi

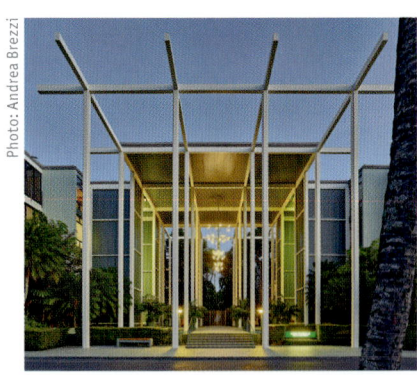

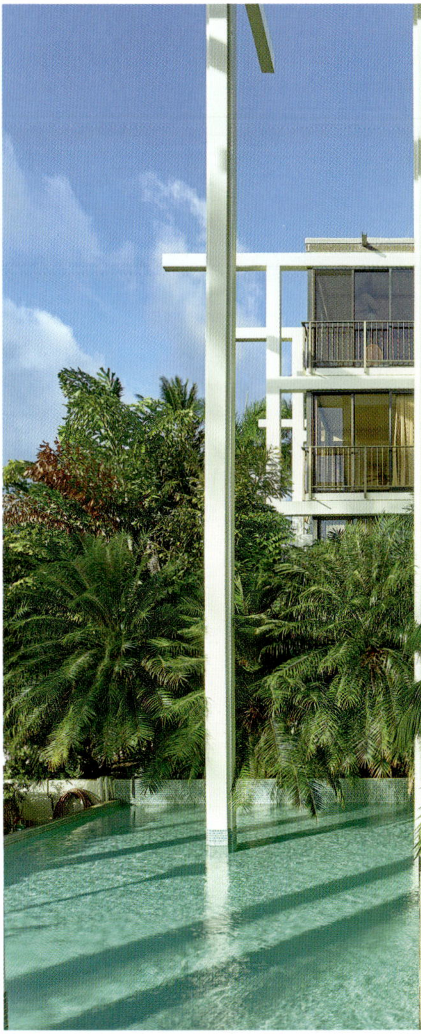

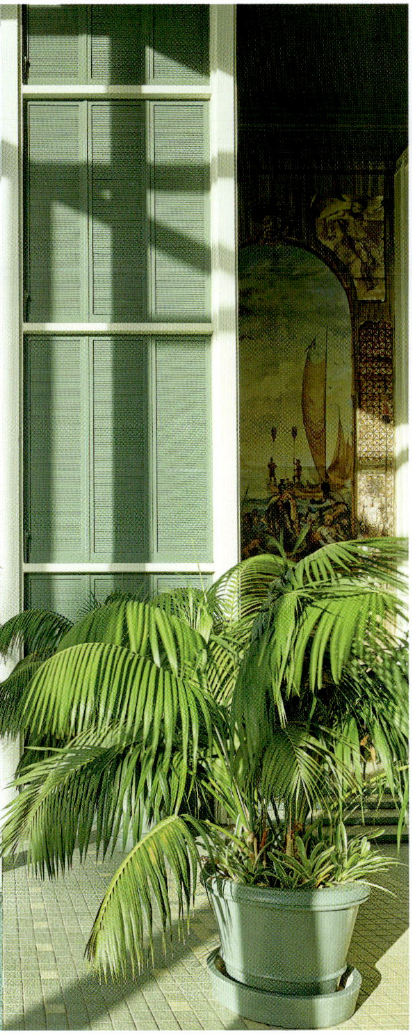

Photo: Andrea Brezzi

In discussions, Ron Lindgren suspected cost-value engineering as the cause and agreed that widening the corridors a little so as to have the hallway floors as slabs spaced away from the walls – by resting on rhythmical beams and atop a zenith lid from above – would have been the way forward in an ideal Killingsworth world. This, however, is a good minor problem to have given the bad: the Kamehameha Schools leasehold the building sits on expires in 2027 with the future uncertain. Our related 'demonstrations' of long ago with us as representatives of Killingsworth through Ron Lindgen/Stricker/Lindgren/Wilson, Docomomo, Bishop Museum as the University of Hawaii's School of Architecture need to be joined by many others in making it absolutely clear to Kamehameha Schools that tearing this gem down is an absolute no-go. In fact, the opposite is true: It so deserves to be restored to its original condition, undoing the enclosure of far too many of the lanais, thereby preserving this as the ultimate living case study of tropical dense urban dwelling. *MD*

Seaside Hotel

086 C

342 Seaside Ave
Honolulu HI 96815
Edward Killingsworth, Alfred Yee
1967

This speculative investment project is the only one Edward Killingsworth and Alfred Yee teamed up to do. Soon after they successfully sold it to United Airlines as lodgings for their flight attendants and pilots. Having been on a budget, their frugal strategy reinterprets the more closed indigenous hale strategy of minimized openings in order to keep the tropical sun out. The budget still afforded small lanais with vertical bar guardrails bolted to the edges, the only texturing of the otherwise monolithic mass. Killingsworth's signature post-and-beam expressionism, however, is applied to the crown and the base as the entrance

pavilion on a pedestal reminiscent of the Kahala Beach Apartments, but here enclosed glass jalousies. The most recent owner re-branded the hotel as the marginally different 'Shoreline Hotel', with an exalted color extravaganza to the lobby and the entrance and just recently repainted the lanai undersides blue, replacing the more pleasing variety of pastel colors. But color, of course, comes and goes, the building taking it in a relaxed manner thanks to its simple strong stature. To raise guest awareness and take pride in its architectural authorship, the lobby's coffee table design books may require the addition of the firm's only monograph, sponsored by Killingsworth's Ron Lindgren. Accordingly, in the next renovation, to comply with all of the other Killingsworth lobbies' easy breeziness, the AC in the entrance pavilion should be removed and the original glass jalousies reactivated to elicit a similar trade wind feel as the adjacent indoor-outdoor restaurant on the mauka end of the pedestal. Listen to Killingsworth's Ron Lindgren about it. *MD*

6

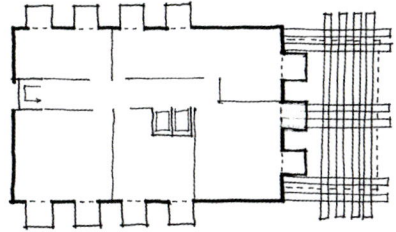

Photo: Martin Despang

Bank of Hawaii

2222 Kalākaua Ave
Honolulu, HI
Wimberly, Whisenand,
Allison & Tong
Structural: Alfred Yee
1967

087 C

The largest bank in the Hawaiian Islands, Bank of Hawaii completed a modest new one-story branch in the Waikiki district of Honolulu in 1950. Just 15 years later, the neighborhood had grown so fast due to the huge increase in tourism that the construction of a 15-story high-rise on the same site was considered necessary. The resulting $4.5 million structure contained a Bank of Hawaii office on the first two floors, along with a large Woolworth's variety store that included a substantial restaurant. Three floors of parking for 250 vehicles was a required amenity with traffic being a concern by

this time. Nine floors of offices comprised most of the building's interior space. The most unique and significant aspect of this tower is the exterior framework of precast concrete elements that were brought to the site and gradually assembled around the structure. Together they form a decorative and artistic façade. At the time there was public speculation as to what the pattern was supposed to represent, with most people guessing it was inspired by the crowns of pineapples, which were a major agricultural crop in Hawaii in the 1960s. However, a 1966 newspaper article described the design as 'early Hawaiian decorations'. Since the bank needed to continue to function during this period, it moved into the ground floor in late 1965, even as the building's upper floors were still under construction. A major focal point of the bank's lobby was an immense metal sculpture that rose 15 feet in height up to

Photo: DeSoto Brown, 1967

the mezzanine level of the interior. This artwork was readily visible to pedestrians passing on crowded Kalakaua Avenue outside. Titled *Legend*, it was created by commercial sculptor Edward Brownlee, responsible for numerous other commercial pieces in Honolulu during the midcentury period. As banks now continue to reduce the number of physical spaces they occupy, this once-grand Bank of Hawaii branch no longer exists today. *DB*

Manoalani →
1629 Wilder Ave
Honolulu, HI 96822
Johnson and Perkins
1967

088 C

Departing from traditional apartment typologies, within its 32 apartments the Manoalani includes ten four-bedroom units, each of which is two stories high. With only four apartments to a floor, each unit occupies a corner, allowing two exposures and good cross ventilation. To further enhance the airiness, on each floor wide, recessed lanai, some of which residents have now enclosed, define the

center bays of all four façades. Designed for family living, this 12-story, reinforced concrete condominium features a pool and provides two parking stalls per unit on its basement and first story levels. When initially built the building advertised its Diamond Head views. Architects Allen Johnson and Thomas Perkins not only designed the building, but were also its developers along with realtor Velva Bergevin. *DH*

6

Photo: DeSoto Brown

The Seashore

2450 Koa Ave
Honolulu, HI 96815
Ernest Hara
1967

089 C

This was author Martin's Beletage lanai location from which he contemplated his contributions to this book. Having appreciated the architect's previous work from a few blocks away at the Waikiki Grand Hotel (see previous report) and re-applying its successful strategy of orientation and fenestration here: the linear building block running double-loaded

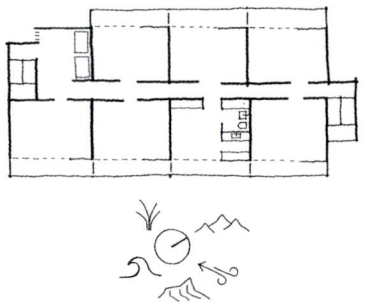

mauka-makai for ideal macro trade wind airflow leads to the units facing north and south, with each lanai slab shading the one below, particularly during the summer time of the year. The orientation makes it possible for balanced work on the lanai, remaining sun screened, dry and protected from rain blown by the trade winds, while still enjoying its cooling effects. The hallway is naturally ventilated through stacked turquoise breezeblocks – the main eyecatcher of an otherwise charmingly understated stacked lanai building. A simple concrete frame with concrete block infill as the solid bones guarantee the longevity of the building, which remains pretty much in its original condition. Architect Hara optimized his layout from the Waikiki Grand, where narrow deep units had the bathroom and studio living space behind one another; here they are next to each other with the kitchen back-to-back with the bathroom and opening up to the studio living room, resulting in the most generous lanai, which runs the full width of the

Photo: Martin Despang

unit. The closet parallel to the unit hall-way wall with fully glazed sliding doors doubles the urban panorama through its reflections, particularly of the scallop lanaied Waikiki Resort Hotel with its retained 1960s charm (also by architect Hara and constructed four years earlier in 1963). With the Seashore, Hara brings this Killingsworth Kahala Hilton Hotel floor-plan layout trick of a narrow versus deep floor plan within reach of the proletariat. Unlike the Waikiki Grand, which remained half hotel/half condominiums, the Seashore has fully converted to condos.

The large majority of units are individual short term rentals. Landlord Derrick (with Albert) and Denise's altruist attitude allowed this author to experience the stacked lanai way of living year-round, day and night, and to properly reflect on all the other buildings in order to share the observations with you in this book. The hang-looseness is prevalent around the urban enclave on its Ewa side, with a mix of eateries, a surf shop, plus the one in the building with its folks with the friendly shaka, making one feel extra welcome, like in a big family. *MD*

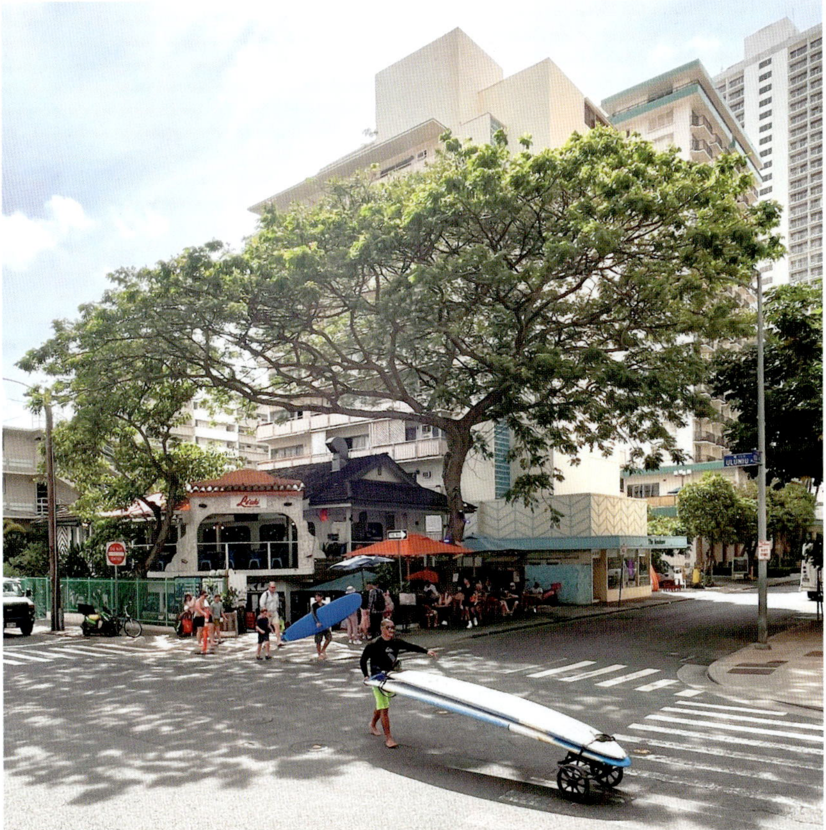

Thurston Memorial Chapel

1601 Punahou St,
Honolulu, HI 96822
(On Punahou School Campus)
Vladimir Ossipoff
1967

Started by Protestant missionaries in 1841, Punahou School (K-12) always held regular Christian religious services for students but, somewhat amazingly, did not have a dedicated chapel building until the opening of the Robert Shipman Thurston Jr. Chapel in the fall of 1966. Thurston's parents funded the construction in memory of their son, a member of the Punahou Class of 1941, who

Photo: Martin Despang

subsequently lost his life in the Second World War (1941–1945). The boxy structure extends out over the school's historic Lily Pond, which is fed by water from a spring named 'Ka Punahou' ('the new spring'), commemorated by an ancient Hawaiian legend. The strongly geometric interior, softly lit, is focused on the altar, which is situated below the congregation seated in the pews. To the right, the bottom edge of the exterior wall extends just above the surface of the pond, making the water literally a part of the chapel's interior. A paved open patio outside the chapel's entrances also houses offices and classrooms on its perimeter. This space can accommodate groups before or after a service; the facility is open to alumni and their families for weddings and memorials in addition to its regular use by students. *DB*

6

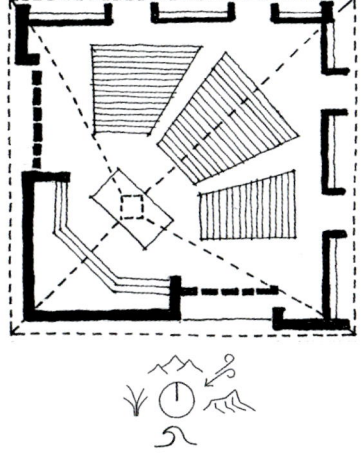

Photo: Martin Despang

Lagoon Tower

2003 Kalia Rd
Honolulu, HI 96815
Bauer, Mori & Lum
1967

091 B

During this author's morning mediations – beginning at the Halekulani and ending with the honu (green Hawaiian sea turtles) at Duke's Beach – this building always marked the turnaround point of the midsection of his jog around the Hilton Hawaiian Village's lagoon. His beach jogging recalls Tom Selleck's Thomas Magnum, just as the Mercedes Benz SL that often appears in this book as the P. I. mobile can be seen as a nod to Magnum's friend Orville 'Rick' Wright's SL. This particular model once belonged to Hawaii's longest-serving First Lady, Jean Ariyoshi, whose main contribution was the 'One Million Trees' planting initiative. Contributors Rainer Kiessling and Keli'i Keanu used the supplies as building materials for their mass timber housing project seen in the 'Reparadising' essay at the conclusion of this book. On the last weekend before taking his University of Hawaii School of Architecture students to the Technical University of Munich's SHIFT research for the upcoming falls, the author had to do without seeing his turtles because his university doc told him that while people used to cure their sinus infections in the ocean, it now seems to

be the case that they pick them up there. This makes him sad about his turtles having no choice but to live there. What does this have to do with architecture/the built environment? Actually, a lot, particularly given the criteria of climate and culture compliance with Hawaii's most paradisal natural environment that this book is based upon. As already hinted in the 'Kaiser's Hawaii' essay, this building is doing just that. While the most recent and concluding 'affordable housing' Howard Hughes high-rise is named after the cultural craft of 'weaving' inherent to Hawaii, it is reduced to façade ornamentation of an otherwise concrete and steel building with its single wall unit air-conditioning and this way hurting the honu further down the line. The Lagoon Tower name alludes to nothing but the artificial lagoon it is placed at, which is in fact very Hawaii(an). Its fenestration appears as interwoven from its concrete spandrels, buttressed pilasters, and lovely lily lanais just like nature. Not only beautiful formally, it is also environmentally performative by keeping the inhabitants in the interior of the building thermally comfortable. Imagine (look at the following project 1350 Ala Moana's historic photo from Ala Moana Beach Park) how the Kaka'ako skyline would have continued to develop this way. The architectural authors of the three buildings of that original skyline – 1350 Ala Moana

6

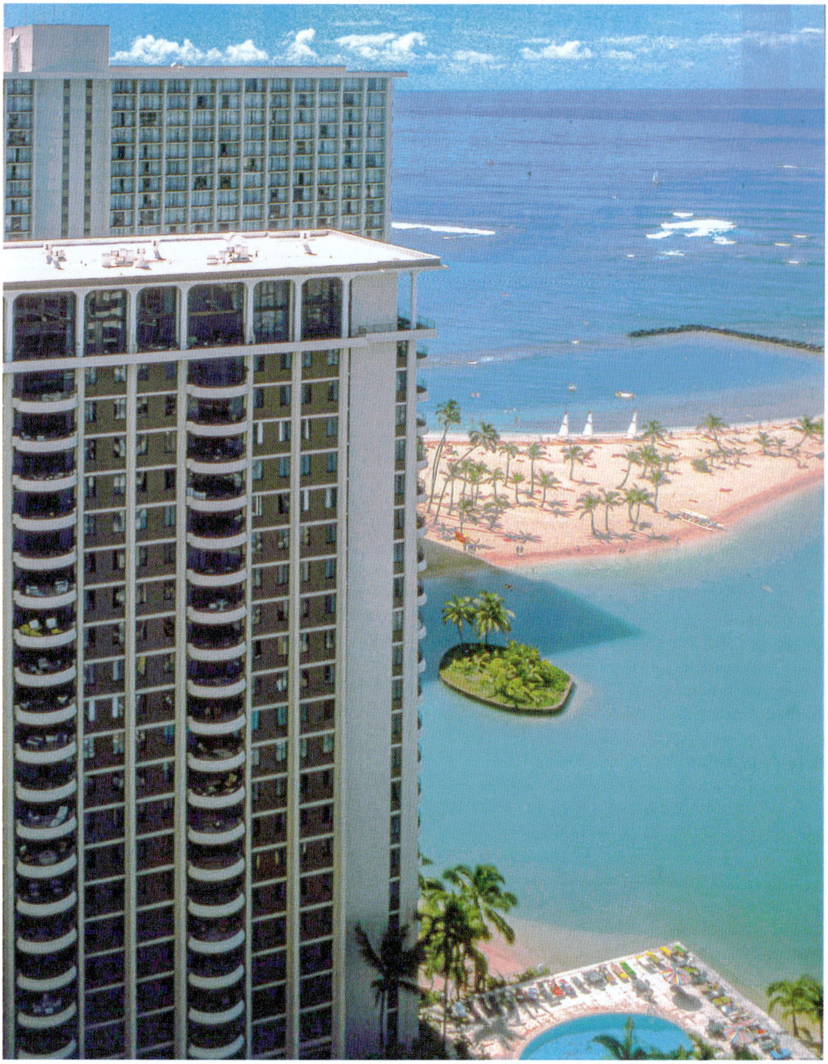

Photo: DeSoto Brown, 1975

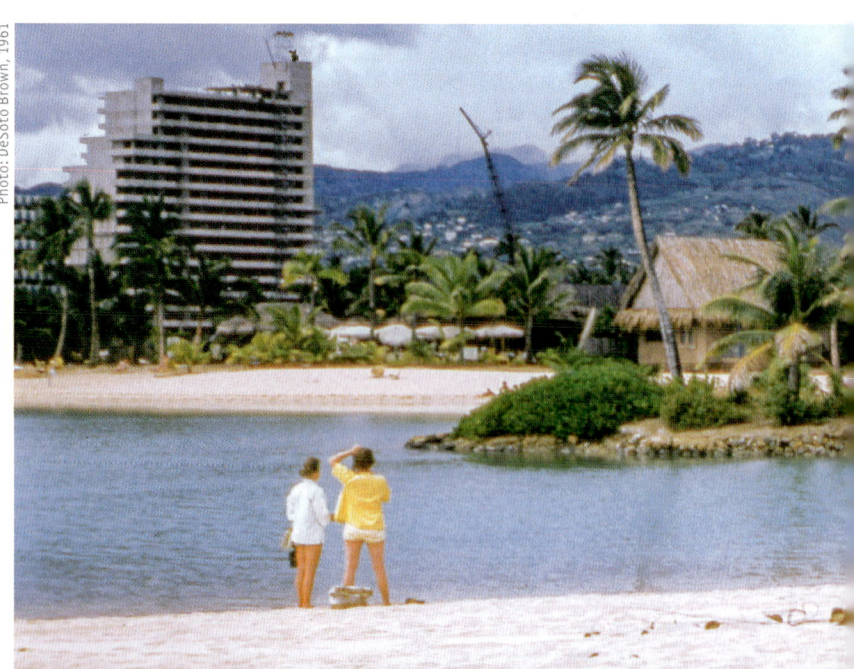

Photo: DeSoto Brown, 1961

Boulevard, Ala Moana Building, and Lagoon Tower –could not have been more different: an international starchitect, America's most commercial designer, and Lagoon Tower's architect being one of the most productive but humble and quiet architects in all of Hawaii. While all three buildings perfectly meet this book's criteria for performative bioclimatic excellence, the Ala Moana Building with its high-tech approach might not meet the SHIFT (Southern Hemisphere Information For Transformation) criteria of a return to low-tech. However, one could retrofit the original electric vertical sun blade louvers to manual in the same way one can downgrade power windows to cranks in cars. The two others, 1350 Ala Moana and Lagoon Tower, very much do meet SHIFT criteria. Constructing this building in exactly the same way, except instead out of its cement concrete a reimagined wood, would be a perfect manifestation of author DeSoto's point of the 'evolution of the island's tradition of innovation' (linked in the 'Reparadising' essay later in this book). The honu would appreciate it so very much. *MD*

6

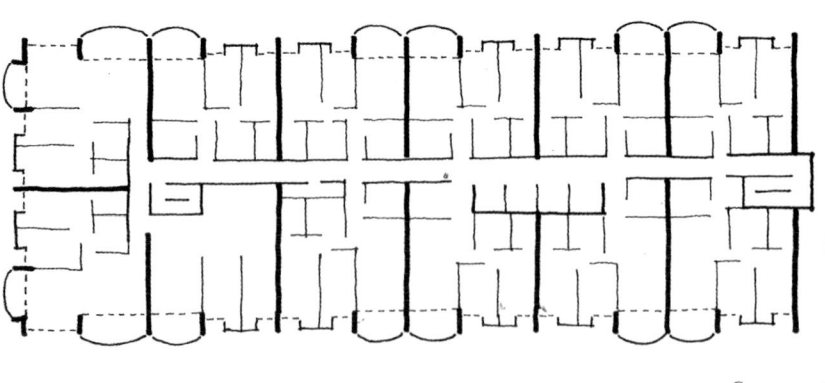

1350 Ala Moana

092 B

1350 Ala Moana Blvd
Honolulu, HI 96814
Minoru Yamasaki
Structural: Alfred Yee
1968

This is the most tropical exotic multidwelling building in all of Kakaako. Several original owners still reside here, as it was designed to welcome the trade winds while keeping the sun out. The ratio of opacity and transparency is carefully bioclimatically calibrated. Depending on the orientation, vertical and/or horizontal protrusions shade the recessed glass. What nearly all modern high-rises do wrong is over obsess about 'the view'. This structure does it right through minimizing microwaving glazing, providing views framed most innovatively by precast, craned-in closets that are literally and figuratively cool and an important façade element. Built five years after its predecessor, Queen Emma Gardens, this building perfects the lessons learned there, particularly regarding fenestration self-shading. As Alfred Yee shared with this author, while Queen Emma Gardens was initially more social housing with a variety of unit sizes down to studios without lanais or sliding doors, this project was more bourgeois from the beginning, with more spacious units, each with a lanai. Unlike the pretentious parking pedestals of contemporary highrises, this project provides the pleasantly downplayed proposition of lava rock-capped wood slats for screening the cars beneath a vast recreational landscape on top. Marked by the sign of the building simply stating the street address number, it does not need a sales-pitchy Hawaiian name like nearly all recently built highrises around it. The processional driveway leads to a classy lobby of timeless mid-century grandeur, with access to the elevators controlled by the front desk. Above, the double-loaded corridors provide access to units that are truly of the highest class and consequently cost, unlike those in new microwave glass high-rises. The building was a main architectural actor in the original 1970s *Hawaii Five-O* and the following 1980s *Magnum, P. I.* as the sole high-rise in Kakaako, self-confident enough to show itself in material authenticity with its concrete not painted or close to its ingredient gray. *MD*

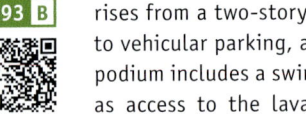

Pomaikai
1804 Ala Moana Blvd
Honolulu, HI 96815
Sam Chang
1969

093 B

rises from a two-story podium dedicated to vehicular parking, and the deck of the podium includes a swimming pool as well as access to the lava rock-embellished lobby of the tower. *DH*

At 19 stories, Pomaikai was among the tallest residential condominiums in Waikiki at the time of its construction. It was also one of the more open, with only two apartments per floor and lanai on three sides. Sliding doors allow each unit's living room and both of the two bedrooms to interact with the surrounding environment, plus the elevators on each floor open on an outdoor entry lanai. The residential tower

Harbor Square
225 Queen St
Honolulu, HI 96813
Killingsworth, Brady and Smith
Structural: Alfred Yee
1968

094 B

With the current post-Covid conversion of downtown office high-rises into residential buildings, these twin towers were a trendsetter more than half a century ago. Edward Killingsworth's later architectural partner Ronald Lindgren recalled the unit Ed owned here, which the office staff used when they were on the island for projects. Ron remembered the tower fronting Ala Moana Boulevard as the 'Executives' Tower', officially called 'Harbor Tower' and with curvy lanais, with the one behind it being the 'Secretaries Tower', officially named 'Town Tower' with rectilinear lanais reminiscent of the times depicted in *9 to 5* starring Dolly Parton, Jane Fonda, and Lily Tomlin. The rectilinear-in-plan Town Tower's unit layouts are like the Kahala Hotel rooms – longer than deep – while in the Harbor Tower room plans, the opposite is true. The tower's pioneering prefabricated structure by Alfred Yee was not quite up to the structural expressionist and environmental excellence of most other Killingsworth projects, which according to Ron Lindgren, was most likely due to the highly developer-driven

6

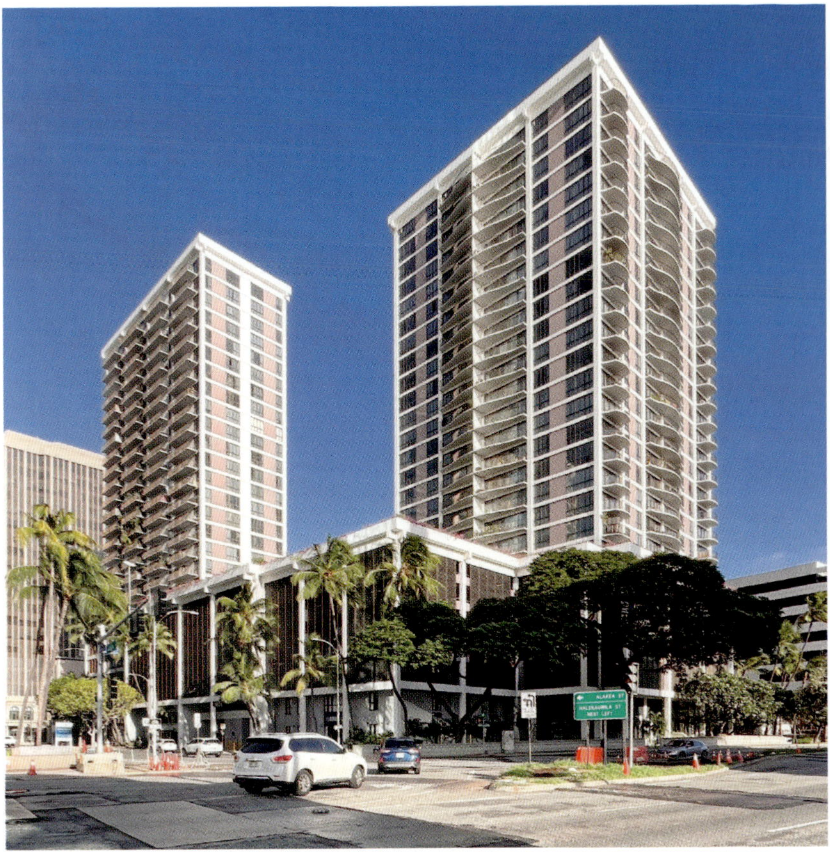

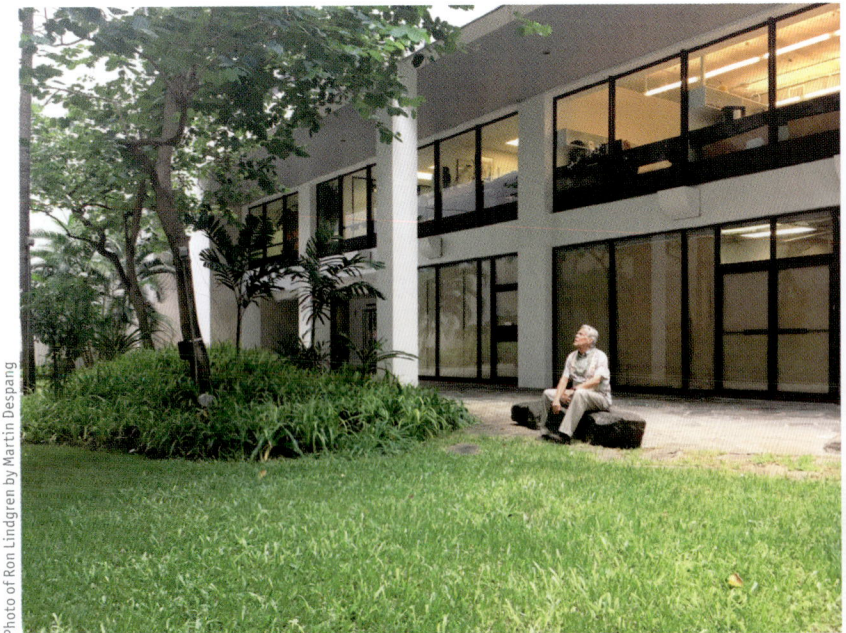

nature of the project. Ron recalls one of Hawaii's finest restaurants, once on the ground floor of the Harbor Tower, which gave downtown Honolulu that distinct mixed-use urban elegance that all new developments aim for yet struggle to achieve. Watch Ed Killingsworth's Ron Lindgren's inner scoop of it. *MD*

Photo of Ron Lindgren by Martin Despang

Outrigger Hotels

2335 Kalākaua Ave
Honolulu, HI 96815
2169 Kalia Road
Honolulu, HI 96815
Roy Kelley
1969

095 C

World-leading hospitality design architects Edward Killingsworth and Pete Wimberly both established their reputations here in Hawaii. With this project, we introduce a third protagonist who like Killingsworth and Yee with the Seaside Hotel (Project 086), was both architect and developer at the same time. For them, the Seaside Hotel remained a one-time attempt at this personal union between the architect and developer. Meanwhile Roy Kelley literally and figuratively built an internationally acclaimed hotel chain that was also rooted in the hospitality heyday of Honolulu. California-native Kelley moved to Hawaii during the Great Depression and worked for C. W. Dickey for a decade. In 1947 he undertook a design-build project and with his wife Estelle managed his very first hotel: the 50-room, five-story Islander Hotel on Seaside Avenue. This was followed in 1950 with his purchase of the Willard Hotel and conversion of the Edgewater Apartments into a hotel. He demolished the Willard and in its stead built a seven-story hotel named the Edgewater, which was the tallest building in Waikiki until 1955 when the Biltmore was completed. When the Waikiki Outrigger Canoe Club's lease was expiring and owner Queen Emma Estate's negotiations with competitors

Photo: Olivier Koning

failed, Kelley secured the deal and built the Outrigger Waikiki Hotel in 1967 as the first of many more hotels in Waikiki, the Hawaiian Islands, and the world to carry the brand name Outrigger. Kelley's success was to add middle-class hospitality to the originally predominantly high class of the Moana and Royal Hawaiian. Using smaller budgets, his hotels are simple, highly efficient double-loaded corridor 'long houses'. Different to today when balconies are value-engineered away, Kelley afforded balconies as small lanais, which were were effective in providing the hotel's main performatively patterned ornamentation, with their signature style curvilinear and angled plans that favored ocean views, but sometimes compromised their self-shading capability. Another motif that the pragmatic Kelley used poetically was convexity, as with the ocean end of the Outrigger Reef Hotel. Or the concavity like the front end of the Outrigger Waikiki on Kalakaua Avenue as an intricate sequence of concave compartmentalizations of its cast concrete being visually activated by the daily traveling of the sun. Also, the axially symmetric open egress end of the hotel corridor featuring breezeblock sills lit by the amber-colored

security lighting. The sculptural opacity created was juxtaposed by the maximally dematerialized glazed openness of the podium that served as the setting of Elvis's *Blue Hawaii* travel agency where his girlfriend Maile works, looking across the street at the International Market Place. The iconic nature of that glass ground floor fenestration was picked up again in the opening credits of the original Hawaii Five-O TV series with a speeding police car's blue patrol light reflecting on it, illustrating Curt Sanburn and DeSoto Brown's statehood childhood perception of Kalakaua Avenue as the coolest street on Earth. Entertainment having been an integral part of Kelley's concepts, the legendary Dukes restaurant at its makai end is a prime example of beach engagement and waterfront activation. New York's Blue Note Hawaii jazz club moved in around the time that this author moved into that neighborhood and has since been another invigorating tenant. The Ewa side alley for beach access is garnished with a Banyan ice cream shop and an aligning row of surfboard lockers in front of the backdrop of these lavish lanai and it seems that its all it takes to keep the building sufficiently in style, and with that protected from the frequent face lifts notorious to the hospitality industry. That might be why the Kalakaua

shopfront fenestration has experienced only relatively irrelevant and reversible postmodernization over the years. Unlike the Outrigger Reef with its long-gone exotic escapism, which Susanne remembers as the 'underwater' dive bar on the parking garage level, which social media reminisces about watching its 'bikini babes swim while one was knocking back a Mai Tai'. Instead, since then and on the other entrance end, the porte-cochère hale hut extravaganza feels like the 1990s-/2000s-era Disneyfication of Beach Walk. The most recent all-encompassing overhaul into the 'treasure island' theme meant well but has gentrified Kelley's grittiness, most extremely noticeable with the Shorebird beachfront restaurant and its $20 buffets with self-grilling fish station and the centrally-powered belt-driven ceiling fans charm replaced with the far too much 'monkeypod'. The formerly neighboring and more upscale but equally outdoorsy restaurant now turned into a hermetically-sealed wedding chapel is as ignorant as the neglect of the obvious seawater level rise at this location, with sewage infrastructure washed out making it increasingly impossible to live the former postcard frontyard beach life. It is rumored to have been heatedly bargained between Kelley and Dillingham back then. *MD*

6

AO freescaping between Outrigger Reef and the Halekulani

Royal Hawaiian Tower

2259 Kalākaua Ave
Honolulu, HI 96815
*Wimberly, Whisen and,
Allison, Tong and Goo*
1969

096 C

When the Royal Hawaiian Hotel opened in Waikiki in 1927, the distinctive pink structure was surrounded by open lawns, mature trees, and quantities of well-kept shrubs. With the passing of decades, however, the increasing urban growth around these expansive gardens led to the construction of encroaching buildings and less open space. In 1968, Sheraton Hotels announced a planned redevelopment of the Royal's property. On one side of the historic hotel the immense 31-story Sheraton Waikiki would be built, while on the other, a smaller 17-floor tower (the Royal Wing) would be constructed. It was also stated that the original 1920s Royal Hawaiian would eventually be demolished for another 30-story edifice. The first two of these were actually built but fortunately, the third never was. The Royal Wing (now the Mailani Tower) was constructed on the site of what had been the old-time Uluniu Women's Swimming Club. This land also provided space for a swimming pool to be added to the Royal, something never considered in the 1920s with the entire Pacific Ocean to swim in, just steps away. Connecting this new addition to the existing Royal Hawaiian was achieved by an open colonnade running next to the Coconut Grove lawn. Its support columns are, naturally, painted pink. In addition, the tower itself is decorated by repeated horizontal bands along its seaward façade which carry the signature color as well, so that observers will know it is a part of the beloved 'Pink Palace'. The Mailani Tower was constructed so that all its rooms face the ocean. As was originally intended, its more modern layout and room sizes brought the Royal Hawaiian up to date, should any potential guest not be happy with the idea of staying in accommodations dating from the distant 1920s. *DB*

Photo: Olivier Koning

Makaha Valley Towers

097 A

84-770 Kili Dr
Waianae, HI 96792
Arthur B. Hansen
1969

After developer Chinn Ho's urban Ilikai condotel proved to be a success, he repeated the idea here with an approximately 500-unit building in the most rural area at the outmost western end of Oahu in Makaha. The project was built right after Chinn Ho's adjacent resort endeavor, which is entirely gone today except for a few archeological traces. Left over is this line of skinny, single-loaded-corridor units up against the foothills of the Waianae mountain range. The cast-in-place concrete structure is segmented by the spacing of vertical circulation staircases that celebrate the open air. The horizontal open-air hallway circulation accesses stacked lanais of sizes from single-room studios to multiple-room units with floor-to-ceiling sliding glass curtain wall infills. The corner unit's fenestration retracts to permanently-open lanais, while the centered units get side ventilation through the multiple glass sliding doors in combination with glass jalousies on the hallway side. While building tall in a rural area is conventionally perceived to be inappropriate, upon further observation it presents the optimal conservation of our most precious land in Hawaii. Examples like this where the towers are not eyesores in a flat landscape on top of the topography, but rather at its base making them a more successful integral part of the landscape. *MD*

6

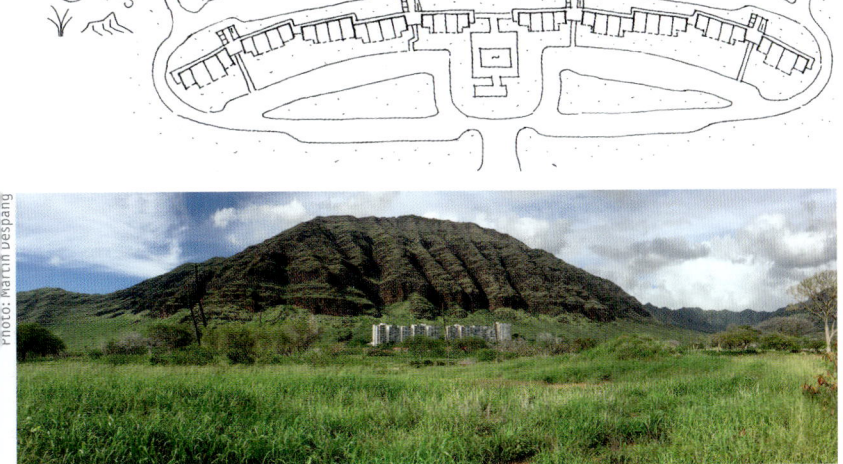

Photo: Martin Despang

6

Hawaii State Capitol

415 S Beretania St
Honolulu, HI 96813
*John Carl Warnecke and
Belt, Lemmon & Lo*
1969

098 B

Open on all four sides, the transparency of the Hawaii State Capitol not only celebrates Hawaii's exceptional climate, but also our open, democratic society. Governor John Burns in his opening address to the Fourth Legislature noted 'the open sea, the open sky, the open doorway, open arms, and open hearts' – these are the symbols of our Hawaiian heritage. In this great State Capitol there are no doors at the grand entrances that open toward the mountains and toward the sea. There is no roof or dome to separate its vast inner court from the heavens and from the same eternal stars that guided the first voyagers to the primeval beauty of these shores. It is by means of the striking architecture of this new structure that Hawaii cries out to the nations of the Pacific and of the world, this message: 'We are a free people ... we are an open society ... we welcome all visitors to our island home.' Reflecting Hawaii's unique status as a part of the United States, but not part of America, the Hawaii State Capitol blends the traditions of both the nation and the state in a modern manner. It interprets, in an island way, the architectural precedents

of most state capitols, with their classical columns, central rotundas, and legislative assembly halls to either side. The 60-foot-high coconut palm columns, the encircling water recalling the vast Pacific, the volcanic-shaped and lava rock-clad legislative chambers, and the open, sky-blue-tiled rotunda ceiling embody the tropical essence of Hawaii. However, more than a glorification of the physical place, the building proclaims the spirit of Hawaii. Not only is the building's central rotunda open to the sky, but also features four floors of equally open galleries and hallways, providing free access to legislative offices and rooms, and allowing all to see the comings and goings of the legislators. *DH*

'Hands off' event, April 2025

6

Surfrider Tower

099 C

Tower Wing 2365 Kalākaua Ave
Honolulu HI 96815
*Wimberly, Whisenand, Allison,
Tong & Goo with Roehrig, Onodera & Kinder*
1969

Thanks to its guest room lanai, the former Surfrider Hotel provides Waikiki with possibly its most dynamic and visually-enticing high-rise façade. Running perpendicular to the beach, both sides of this 21-story high-rise's narrow shaft feature continuous bands of individual lanai, with their open, outdoor release visually broken and splendidly enhanced by vertical, precast concrete grills. The lanai seems to zigzag down the façade with each room and each story alternating between curvilinear and right-angled lanai set on a diagonal. Resonant with the interplay of open and screened, light and shadow, the intricately coordinated and delightful composition terminates with pointed ends, and is capped by a bold, overhanging cornice. Originally a separate hotel developed by Kenji Osano, this 436-room building is now incorporated into the Sheraton Moana Surfrider as the Tower Wing. *DH*

Photo: Olivier Koning

Queen Kapiolani Hotel

150 Kapahulu Ave
Honolulu, HI 96815
Ernest Hara
1969

Dignified yet casual, the 315-room Queen Kapiolani Hotel's neoclassical Hawaiian façade presents an engaging tropical composition. Its formal, façade length, three-story-high colonnade is softened by a backdrop of precast-stone panels in a stylized foliage pattern, as well as a recessed entry embellished by lava rock and plantings. The hotel's 18-story, T-shaped tower sits on a three-story-high podium that reduces the building's sense of mass and pulls the tower back from the street. Cantilevered lanai offer not only a variegated surface, but also ample outdoor opportunities for the guests. The vehicular drop-off at the rear of the hotel opens onto a front desk, an unusual and efficient feature. Mayor Frank Fasi, whose commentary on Waikiki high-rises was not always favorable, lauded this hotel as 'an asset both to our visitor industry and to the community'. *DH*

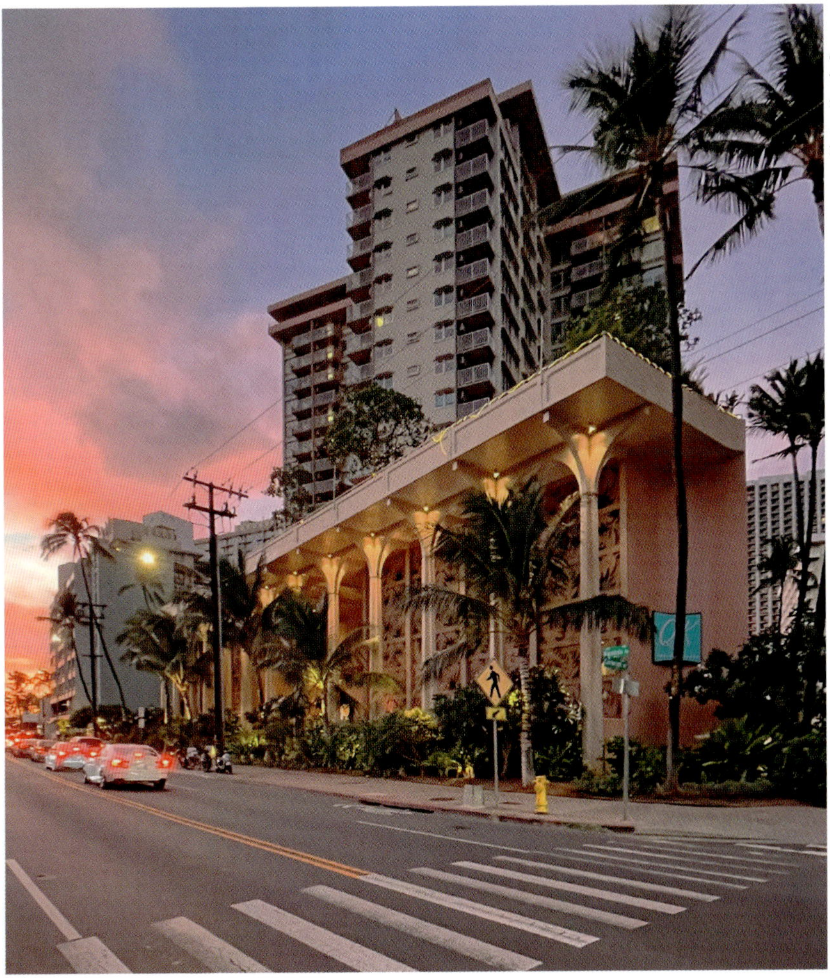

6

Tropical Modern 1970s–1980s

7

Photo: Martin Despang

Benjamin Parker Elementary School

45–259 Waikalua Rd
Kaneohe, HI 96744
Hideo Murakami
1969

Rising from the ashes of the 1926 school, the victim of arson in the early morning hours of 1 August 1966, the Benjamin Parker Elementary School reflects the product of public pressure applied to the State Department of Education (DOE) by the school's PTA, the Kaneohe Community Council, staff at the school, the Kaneohe Outdoor Circle, and Oahu Planning Conference. The community not only urged the department to transcend its ordinary, rather utilitarian machines for learning guidelines and policies, but prepared a 25-page master plan report, calling for a complex designed to be 'the architectural focal point of the community, the beauty spot of the neighborhood, and a quality environmental experience for the students'. They envisioned buildings that through the use of colors, materials, landscaping, and architectural details would instill a sense of 'beauty and something exciting and lasting' in the students' consciousness. The community secured sympathetic ears in the administration of the DOE and also the State Legislature, and architect Hideo Murakami, who formerly studied with Frank Lloyd Wright at Taliesen, provided the community with a superbly designed elementary school. Its pronounced and battered lava rock columns and walls command attention, contrasting with the smooth, cream-colored second story with its canted, cantilevered corner lanai, brise-soleil fins, and flat roof's wide, projecting fascia. A Juliette May Fraser tile mural that depicts a post-contact Hawaiian scene adorns the front wall of the school. All the classrooms and dining room are cross-ventilated with wall-length bands of wood louvers, and covered walkway-lanai access the single-stacked rooms. In keeping with the community report, the kindergarten classrooms were placed in their own building, and each room was fronted by a capacious, recessed lanai, where the pupils could play during inclement weather, as rain is a common condition on the windward side of all of Hawaii's main islands. Restrooms and a drinking fountain are also conveniently incorporated into each lanai's design. *DH*

Nanakuli Intermediate and High School

102 A

89–980 Nanakuli Ave
Waianae, HI 96792
Hideo Murakami
1970–1976

The four flat-roofed, donut-shaped buildings on the Nanakuli Intermediate and High School campus reflect the enthusiasm and energy associated with the first years of the school. Responding to the Baby Boomer generation's coming of high school age, the new school and its readily recognizable, modern stylish, circular buildings were built incrementally over a period of six years, with each new building intended to accommodate the addition of another grade level to the school. Each building essentially housed one high school grade level, with most academic subjects for that grade taught in the building, resulting in a 'school within a school' atmosphere. Originally the master plan for the campus called for a dozen round buildings to house the elementary, intermediate, and high schools; however, this plan was abandoned after the implementation of the sixth increment and the completion of Building C. Architecturally, the single-story buildings present a sweeping horizontal profile, rising from and merging with their surrounding environment while the encircling ridges of the Waianae mountain range dramatically serve as a backdrop. The courtyards in the middle of the buildings each have their own distinct character and landscaping and offer a sense of belonging and identity. The courtyards also are used as student assembly areas and facilitated cross-ventilation in the years before air conditioning was introduced to public school buildings. In the courtyard of Building A, the Administration and Library Building, the copper/bronze *Tree of Knowledge* sculpture was conceived and fabricated by Satoru Abe in 1971 while he was at Waianae High School, where he had been retained as the first person in Hawaii to participate in the federally-funded Artist-in-the Schools program. *DH*

7

Photo: Kikuyo Hibbard

Ka Hale Moi

666-670 Prospect St
Honolulu, HI 96813
George McLaughlin
1970

103 B

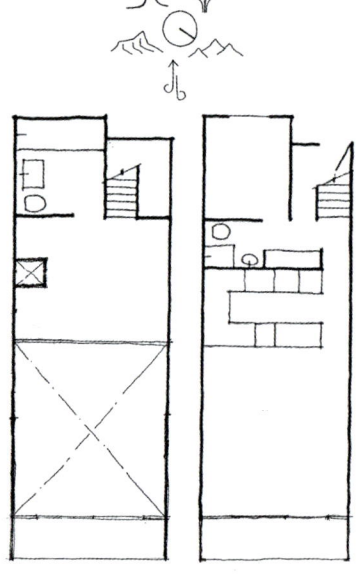

Confronting the Western way of living sandwiched between stacked floors spaced eight feet apart, this building dwells on the vernacular hale/A-frame knowledge of tall ceilings for maximum human thermal comfort based on the physical effect of warm air rising and then being blown out by the trade winds. The structure's open circulation hallways and elevators face the shaded Punchbowl Crater and each unit is accessed on every other floor. The interiors of the units open up into two-story lofts

7

dramatically overlooking Honolulu's civic center. The unit to take the fullest advantage of this way of flushing the spaces with cool trade winds is the one renovated by Tadpole Studio, who freed most walls and floors from their unnecessary coverings, exposing their concrete thermal mass to be cooled by the trade winds, which is so efficient sometimes that the adjustable jalousie fenestration has to be closed. Sunsets are most spectacular from the large makai opening, with its solar overheating mitigated by roll-down sun screens. This is science and the arts in tropical exotic harmony. *DH*

Photo: Mike William

Ala Moana Hotel
410 Atkinson Dr
Honolulu, HI 96814
John Graham
Structural: Alfred Yee
1970

104 B

at a sharp angle and projecting out of the dividing pilaster slab walls. The double-loaded corridor layout follows the mauka-makai macro airflow, resulting in optimal micro-orientation fenestration with units facing the sunless north or shaded

Your author stayed at the Ala Moana Hotel on my very first ever nights in Hawaii, waiting for a job interview and coming from cold spring nights in Arizona. Once back in the hotel for the night he realized the air conditioning thermostat was set at an usual thermal comfort temperature that it had felt outside all the time, day and night. It made him turn it off and open the lanai sliding door, causing him to fall asleep in paradise and think that this is the place he wants to be for good. Although the structure was the first high-rise in Hawaii that exceeded 350 feet and has nearly 1,000 units in its tower, it does not feel massive like most new glass high-rises because of its slick slab-like massing and its texturing by lanais cut back by the lanais on the south; only a minority of units at the ends with their makai and mauka view come with the price of a hot sunrise and sunset. While it is commendable that the tower has been kept in its original condition, it is recommended that its glass parapets should be undone for the original easy-breezy bar ones at the next touch-up. *MD*

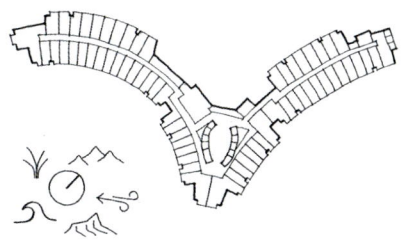

Sheraton Waikiki

2255 Kalākaua Ave
Honolulu, HI 96815
Wimberly, Whisenand, Allison, Tong & Goo
1971

105 C

Nothing was more symbolic of Hawaii's explosive tourism growth in the twentieth century than the Sheraton Waikiki in 1971. Only 16 years earlier in 1955, Waikiki had seemed to be booming with the opening of four 10-story buildings. But now, after scores of other highrises had been built, at 31 stories and with 1,904 rooms, the Sheraton was – somewhat amazingly – the largest resort hotel in the entire world. It contained over 5 miles of corridors and hallways. Sheraton already operated the Moana Surfrider, the Princess Kaiulani, and the next-door Royal Hawaiian Hotel in Waikiki, along with the Sheraton Kauai and the Sheraton Maui. In spite of its great size, the Sheraton Waikiki was designed not as a monolithic rectangular block but instead as a swooping structure with two rounded curves. The official term used in the office of its architectural firm was that it was a 'butterfly'. Whether from land or from the ocean offshore of Waikiki Beach, this somewhat unorthodox configuration gives every viewer a different perspective with every glance. A feature that many guests enjoyed was the exterior glass-walled elevator that provided views of the bustling Waikiki district and the green Koolau Mountains in the distance. A plush rooftop restaurant, the Hanohano Room, provided sweeping panoramas from the tallest structure in Waikiki. Oddly for such an enormous building, the Sheraton's lobby is small and rather confined. The lobby's garish, multi-patterned interior decor was criticized at the time of its opening, but the effect was justified by the claim that it was necessary since Waikiki was competing with Miami Beach as a destination. *DB*

Photo: Olivier Koning

7

216

Makua Alii

1541 Kalākaua Ave
Honolulu, HI 96826
Frank Slavsky
1969

After an invitation from a student's grandma to visit this her place, the entire class thought that this is a place that knows how to grow and stay old, thanks to it being forever young. Given the mostly depressing recent senior living developments, this is provocatively encouraging, showing how to do a social, solar senior dwelling well. Shaped like a boomerang bend in plan, the single-loaded corridor on the makai side acts as a linear street with parklets for plants, sitting, and street-watching from this front yard. Behind is the open-plan living space, with interior walls that do not touch the ceiling to allow hot air to rise and be cross ventilated. The mauka side has that clever 'wind

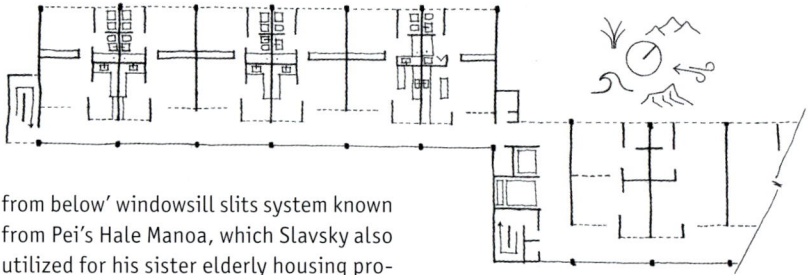

from below' windowsill slits system known from Pei's Hale Manoa, which Slavsky also utilized for his sister elderly housing project Keola Hoonanea. The building's crown inclusively functions as a communal laundry with trade winds providing drying. The base is a lush landscape for daily exercise and extended socializing, while at the Keola Hoonanea, residents also grow their own food on the grounds. Paradise already on Earth for the proud proletariat. *MD*

Photo: Martin Despang

Marco Polo Condominiums ↗

2333 Kapiolani Blvd,
Honolulu, HI 96826
Architects Hawaii
Structural: Alfred Yee
1971

The Marco Polo building at 2333 Kapiolani Boulevard represented both a significant addition to Honolulu's cityscape and an innovative approach to condominium development and sales promotion. Covering a landscaped site of nearly five acres, the 36-story, S-shaped tower contains 568 separate apartment units, a manager's residence, and four commercial units. The uppermost 'penthouse' units are two-story duplexes featuring three bedrooms; other units are two-bedroom, one-bedroom, and studios. Unlike more recent

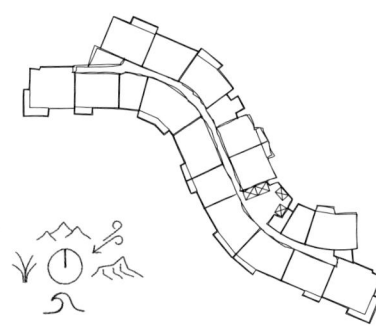

developments elsewhere in Honolulu, most of the units at the Marco Polo have lanai(s), facing either the ocean or the mountains. An original plan called for a single-loaded exterior corridor, but to maximize the number of units the developers opted for a more traditional enclosed central corridor serviced by four elevators and a separate lift for freight. In addition to the main block, the complex includes a large parking structure topped by basketball, tennis, and pickleball courts and a driving range for residents. There is also a circular pool on the makai side as well as a garden pavilion that echoes the very 'structuralist'-inspired porte-cochère (itself a visual skeuomorph of post and beam construction). The impressive property was developed by the firm of Reed & Martin on the site of a former Chinese club. The architects were Lemmon, Freeth, Haines & Jones in cooperation with John Carl Warnecke & Associates – the team that designed the new Hawaii State Capitol Building. One of the architects, Charles 'Ty' Sutton, called the building a 'double-hula design'. Promoted as 'Hawaii's first planned unit development', the property imitated resorts of the period, emphasizing 'lifestyle' and 'convenience'. The original complex included a restaurant and cocktail lounge, a barber and beauty salon, a coffee shop, and a delicatessen. Entering the market at a time of economic downturn, the developers offered 95 per cent financing and reached out to the city to help cover some units as 'affordable housing' – a decision that led to an interesting mix of tenants in Marco Polo's early years. The double-loaded corridor and lack of a fire suppression system – not required by Hawaii law for another four years – led to a tragic fire in 2017, in which four people died and over a third of the units were damaged. The complex has since experienced a massive series of renovations and improvements to make it safer in the future. *WC*

1010 Wilder

1010 Wilder Ave
Honolulu, HI 96822
Architects Hawaii
1974

108 B

Advertised as a 'prestige residential condominium' with only 41 units, the 18-story 1010 Wilder sits on a George Walters' landscaped 1-acre terrace on the slopes of the Punchbowl. The middle floors' setback and the top floor's dramatically cantilevered lanai break the lines of the building and provide it with a distinctive profile. Recessed lanai on all floors extend across the façade, affording views of the city as well as offering indoor-outdoor synergies. Lanai-corridors run across the rear of the building, allowing the single-stacked units to enjoy cross ventilation. High-speed elevators run up both ends of the building, and for the first nine floors, each one serves only two apartments, while from the tenth to 18th floors, where there are only two apartments per floor, the elevators open directly into the spacious units. *DH*

Contessa Apartments

2825 S King St
Honolulu, HI 96826
Anbe, Aruga, Ishizu
1971

A thicker, taller skinny tower, this structure comes across as a single standing tree with its soft-edged lanais wrapped all around its perimeter, which is filled in between rising pilaster strips like leaves to branches. The lanais have differing depths differentiated by the purpose of the rooms: from those serving bedrooms and bathrooms with shallow balconettes sufficient for a small chair or window cleaning to the spacious ones acting as extensions to outdoor living rooms. One is always surprised by how omnipresent the appearance of this building is from various viewpoints in the city, as in these shared impressions from Iolani School, where the young Curt Sanburn went and was intrigued to see it growing when it was under construction, or from the University of Hawaii at Manoa, but also check it out from the Royal Hawaiian Center's Seaside Avenue axis. The structure also physically fulfils its aesthetic organic promise with four larger units on each square floor, which are able to get natural trade wind cross ventilation. Getting close to the building, one realizes how the building is very close to heavy interstate traffic, impacting its easy-breezy health. So, it would benefit from the island going back to foot traffic only – the dominant mode of transportation not that long ago – in combination with a post-fossil multimodal mass transportation system. *MD*

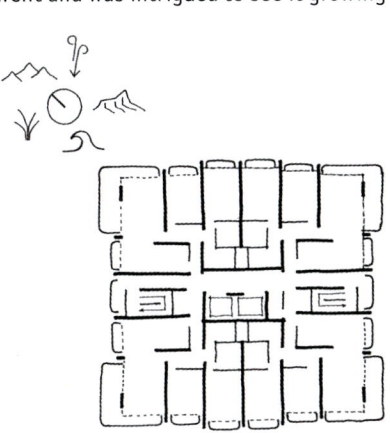

Photo: Olivier Koning

7

Photo: Olivier Koning

Hawaiian Regent Hotel

2552 Kalākaua Ave
Honolulu, HI 96815
John Tatom and
Richard Chamberlain
1971 (1979)

110 **C**

Covering five acres and offering 1,310 rooms, the Waikiki Beach Marriott is the third-largest hotel on Oahu, surpassed only by the Hilton Hawaiian Village's 2,860 rooms and the Sheraton Waikiki's 1,636 rooms. Its two towers rise 25 and 33 floors from a three-story base that epitomizes the open, flowing spatial freedom of the tropics. A porte-cochère flows directly into a spacious lobby and its adjoining, equally open bars, lounges, and cafes. Each activity area commands its own space, but at the same time is completely enmeshed with the surrounding environment, both built and natural. A lushly landscaped courtyard at the makai end of the hotel adds to the blue-sky openness, as does the splendidly landscaped third-floor terrace with its swimming pool and outdoor dining. Spacious, cantilevered lanai open the guest rooms to the outdoors and provide texture and animation to the building. *DH*

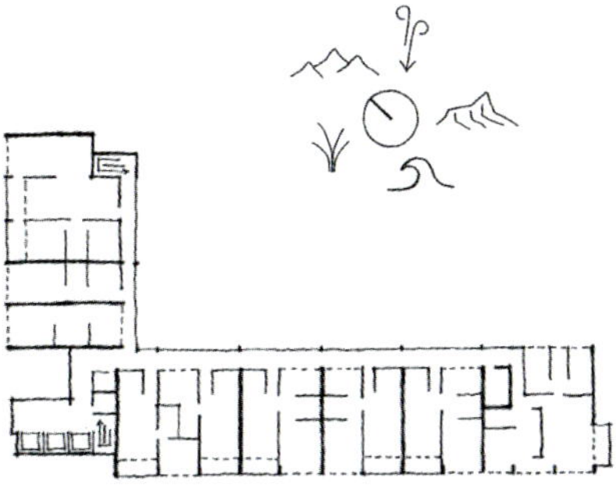

Banyan Tree Plaza

111 C

1212 Punahou St
Honolulu, HI 96826
DMJM with Cesar Pelli
1974

Project architect Cesar Pelli blessed Honolulu with two nearly identical,
L-shaped high-rise complexes: Ala Wai
Plaza from 1970 and later this one. Both
even share their orientation with their

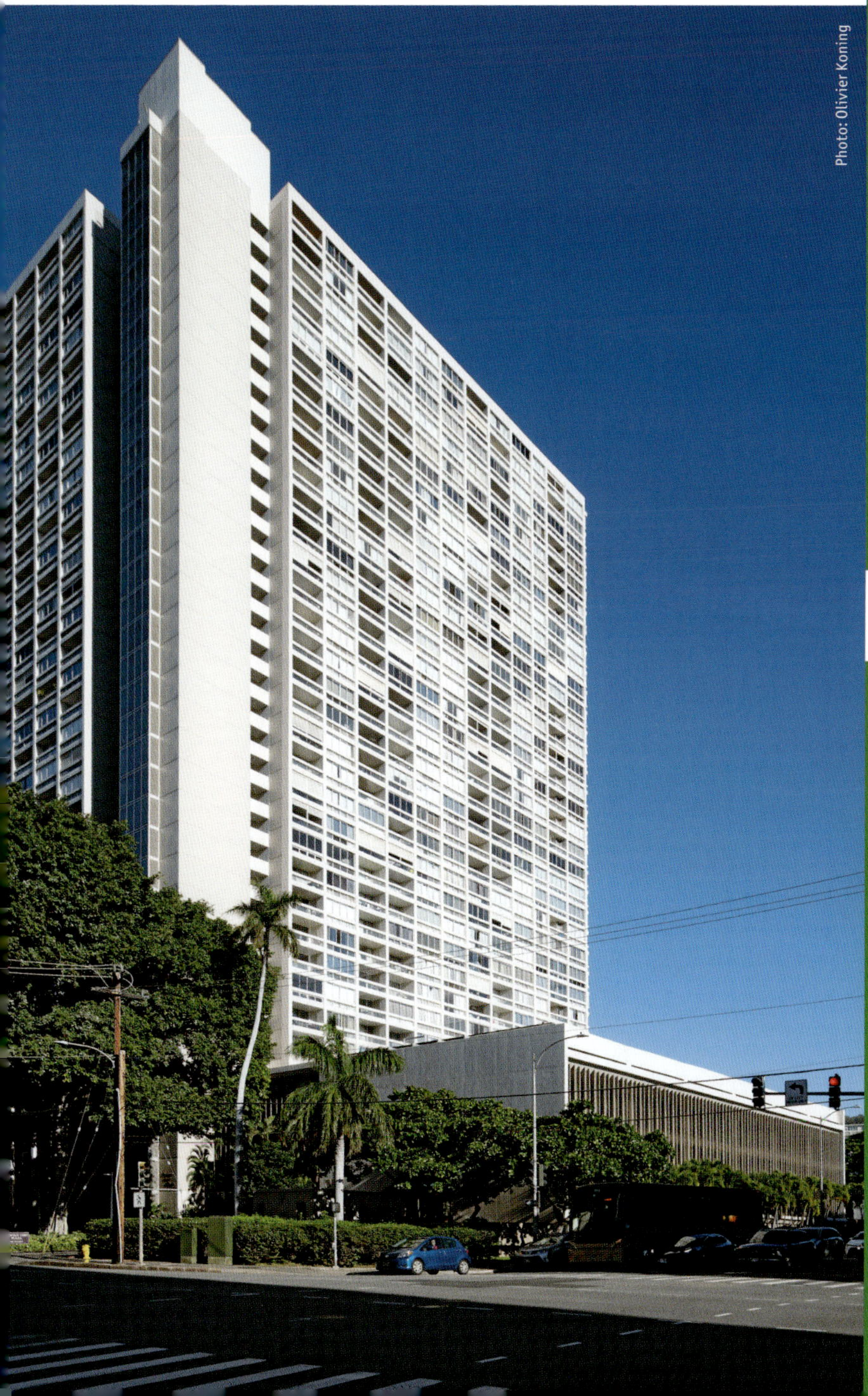

7

111 C

single-loaded open corridor circulations to the northwest and northeast, and the units toward southwest and southeast use their lanai slabs to shade the high noon sun and their vertical partition walls to shade the rising and setting sun. Both offer attractive maisonettes, with the Ala Wai one coming with the cost of more solar overheating. The 1973 AIA Awards jury chaired by Alfred Preis wrote of the Ala Wai one: 'An elegant high-rise, which forms a part of the unique urban complex of the Ala Wai Grouping. Slender and crisp. A direct statement of high-rise living. The planning is unique as to the views to each apartment. Lacks a feeling of regionalism. Does not provide for outdoor activities and landscaping. Office-like and lacking residential scale.' It feels like an equally timeless assessment for both. Although, with the Banyan Tree Plaza project, the lush landscaping is impossible to miss in the unforgettable drive around the ancient Banyan Tree from which the project derives its name. Recently Honolulu's Department of Permitting and Planning chief Timothy Hiu ruled that external egress staircases may no longer be enclosed, but rather open to the air again, as when the islands were pursuing statehood. So, these iconic glazed staircase towers in themselves should be unmuumuued and become great cardio workout spaces for their residents. *MD*

Hotel La Croix

112 C

2070 Kalākaua Ave
Honolulu, HI 96815
Jo Paul Rognstad
1973

Rognstad has been an architectural chameleon during his career, with this project being part of his ziggurat phase. He later/last became Mr. Value Engineer with his rubber-stamped, square-plan hermetic high-rises, among them his own very distinct residence at Century Center Tower (1978). However, in these four buildings he afforded the opposite: a rather complicated creation, at its widest at the base and tapering back to thinnest at the top. This was his final ziggurat – his others being the Bamboo Hotel on Kuhio Avenue (1965) and the Diamond Head Beach Hotel & Residences (1969) on the Gold Coast. Here, the guest room lanais face southeast and northwest with both ends of the building protected from the hot setting sun without openings except one lanai. The building is consciously celebrating its structural expressiveness with all loads cascading down to big beams, recalling San Francisco's Rockefeller Center. Like many buildings from that time, the hotel has experienced the aging of its concrete, and the current spalling repair has removed its iconic notched lanai partition wall guardrail beams and replaced

them with glass in line with the current epidemic and in this case it is even tinted. Hopefully the owner becomes aware of what a gem they have with the building and will bring back the guardrail concrete beams in the next remodel, this time evolved with basalt reinforcement within and basalt dowels for the infill. *MD*

7

Photo: Martin Despang

Diamond Head Vista
2600 Pualani Way
Honolulu, HI 96815
Warner Boone
1975

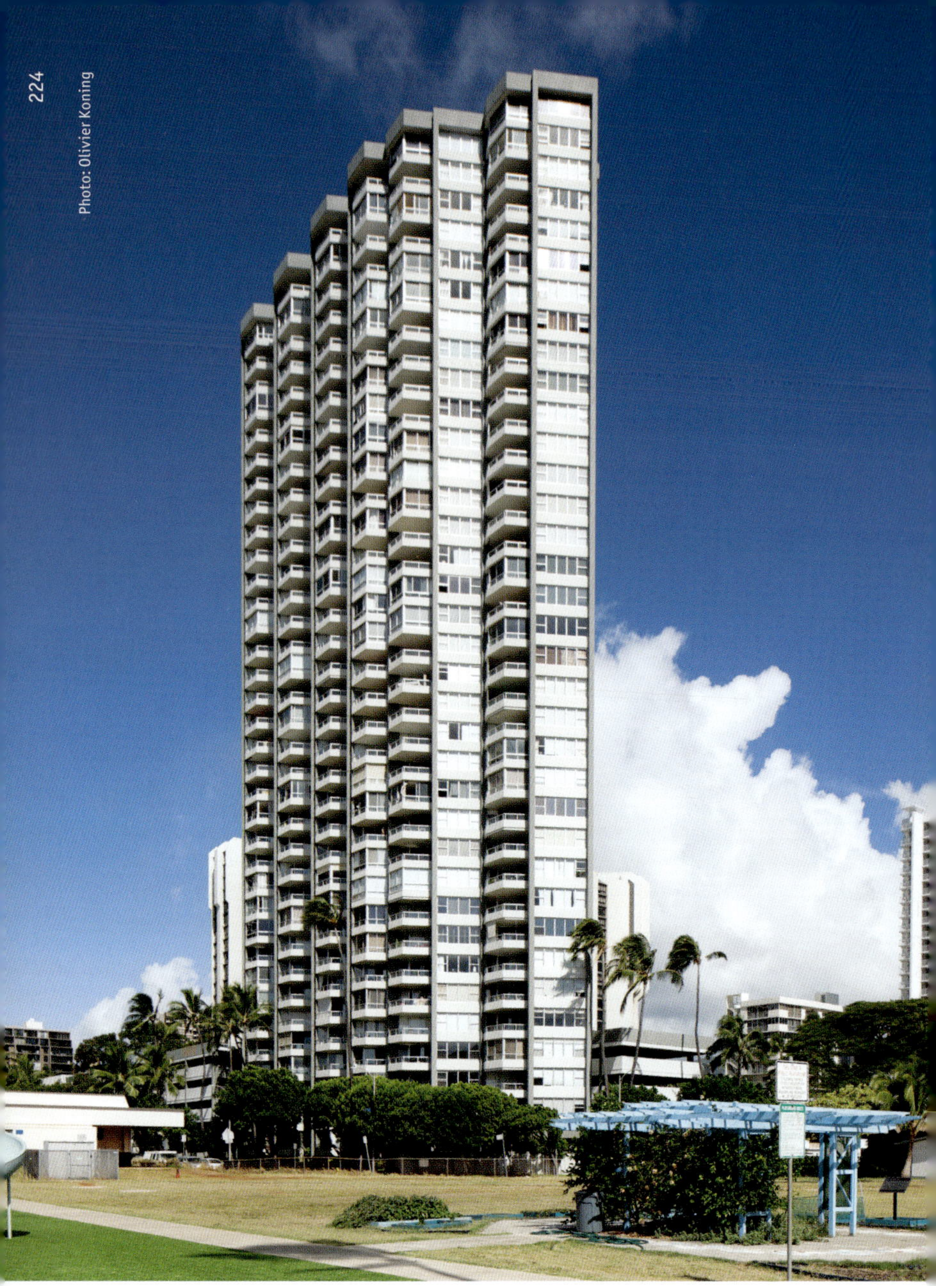

113 C

The Diamond Head Vista Apartment's staggered façade offers a visual respite from Waikiki's multitude of high-rise boxes and allows most of the 173 single-stacked units the view of Diamond Head, proclaimed in the building's name. The angular, cantilevered lanai rhythmical-ly establishes a geometric interplay of

enclosure and openness, tempering the vertical thrust of the 37-story condominium. Oriented with its rear towards the trade winds and serviced by a lanai/corridor, the single-stacked apartments offer ideal cross ventilation possibilities. The enclosure of a few lanai by individual owners adds a spontaneity to the façade, which so far has not detracted from its strong regularity and the interplay of solid and void. The building is one of several post-statehood condominium projects to zigzag their lanai across the façade. Others include the Consulate (1965) and Barclay Apartments (1969), both by Lemmon, Freeth, Haines & Jones, and the Royal Vista (1969) by John Rummell and Warner Boone. *DH*

the midst of Waikiki, is the focal point of a flowing ground level arcade. Four towering entries access the block-long arcade, which seems more a continuation of the sidewalk than the first story of a hotel with two 39-story, octagonal towers and 1,230 rooms. Unique coral-block walls lend a local accent to the lush street-facing entrances with their suspended bronze sculptures by American sculptor Edward Brownlee. Developed by Chris Hemmeter, the Hyatt's $75 million mortgage, secured to pay off the construction loans, was at the time the largest mortgage ever issued in Hawaii and the second largest for a hotel in the United States, requiring interest payments of close to $1,000 an hour. *DH*

Hyatt Regency Waikiki Beach Resort and Spa

114 **C**

2424 Kalākaua Ave
Honolulu, HI 96815
Herb Lawton in association with Wimberly, Whisenand, Allison, Tong & Goo
1976

The grand atrium, the architectural signature for the Hyatt chain and the hottest spectacle on the 1960s, 1970s, and 1980s hotel scene, only rises seven stories at the Hyatt Regency Waikiki, but it is completely open to the sky. Invigorated by a three-story waterfall and smaller cascades, this palm-filled tropical oasis in

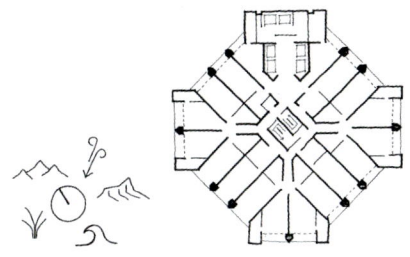

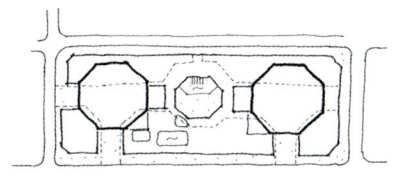

7

Photo: DeSoto Brown, 1976

Island Colony Hotel
445 Seaside Ave
Honolulu, HI 96815
Jo Paul Rognstad
1979

115 C

This is the prime example of Rognstad's stacked lanai assortments, as Curt Sanburn calls them in his interview with Rognstad for a 2015 *Civil Beat* article. The tallest building in Waikiki and locked into its rectilinear planning grid is a clumsy rectangle in plan. But with its southwest and northeast ends mostly closed, it opens up with its lanais toward the southeast and northwest. These are sufficiently deep and augmented with the vertical unit partition walls keeping the rising and setting sun out like few other buildings in Waikiki. Like too many, this building has been compromised by the addition of glass parapets. To remedy this, these elements should be undone and replaced with the original vertical bar ones, potentially as basalt rods. Following its own positive, progressive example of critical remodeling here: the recladding of the original blue-tile pagoda roof top hat with photovoltaic panels in an intelligent, integrative way. *MD*

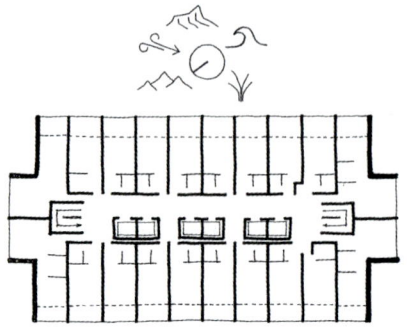

Waikiki Townhouse

2421 Tusitala St
Honolulu, HI 96815
Jo Paul Rognstad
1980

This is a pioneering example of this typology of skinny towers that have become fashionable all over the world in recent years, such as Vinoly's 432 Park Avenue or SHoP's 111 West 57th Street in New York City. While those in New York do not make sense climatically, those in our tropical environment have potential because of their airiness thanks to their

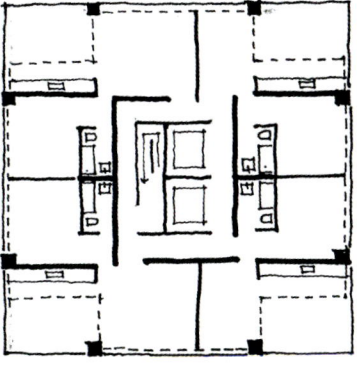

shallow floor plan depth. This Rognstad design seems to be a crossover of his Jimmy Carter era spirited 'stacked lanais' and 'skinny towers' and precedes his Ronald Reagan-sickened muumuu skinny towers, such as his residence at Century Square (1981) or his super-skinny Waikiki Marina Tower (1984). The Townhouse expressively exposes its lanai at its four

7

116 C

corners in a structurally stressed way. The original floor plan takes advantage of the adjacent kitchen's sliding door opening to the lanai, becoming an outdoorsy cooking/living space. The remaining bays on the east, south, and west directions with their glazing flush to the concrete frame get too much sun, made worse by too many owners counterproductively enclosing their lanai with glass. Bring all lanai back to their original unenclosed form and add external roll-down shading in front of these fixed glazed bays to enhance the human thermal sleekness of this slick skinny building, which Curt Sanburn says is Rognstad at his best. *MD*

Franklin Towers ↓ →

117 A

990 Ala Nanala St # 1A
Honolulu, HI 96818
Peter Hsi
1982

Aliamanu Crater once held the Hawaiian Islands' largest natural body of water, called Salt Lake for its brackish, salty water. But starting in 1964, a private developer started the process to fill in this lake to replace it with a golf course, something which would never be allowed today. Although the project was very slow in occurring, the end result was a golf course surrounded by a mix of private homes and condominiums of varying heights.

One of these is Franklin Towers, which uses a unique floor plan. This essentially is that two separate towers are connected side by side in what appears to be a single building. But each of the two towers is served by a different elevator, and each floor it stops on has only two apartments. This means there are no corridors in the building, only a small elevator lobby for each pair of units. Seen from outside, there are four vertical units of apartments, and each of these is offset from the one next to it, creating a staggered effect. The building therefore does not present a completely flat façade, nor does it consist of the usual rectangular block like hundreds of other towers in Honolulu. Apartments are fairly large, each containing two bedrooms and two full baths. At 40 stories, Franklin Towers is taller than most of the other condos in the Salt Lake neighborhood and thus provides fine views from its upper floors. Being on the boundary of the golf course also means that no other structures will ever block the view towards the mountains. *DB*

Tropical Brutalism

8

Financial Plaza of the Pacific 118 B

130 Merchant St
Honolulu, HI 96813
Leo S. Wou & Associates
1968

Designed as the initial step and centerpiece of an effort to spatially open and revitalize downtown Honolulu, the block on which the Financial Plaza stands boasts 43 per cent open space. To accomplish such a feat while accommodating the headquarter needs of five independent companies (the Bank of Hawaii, Castle and Cooke, Territorial Savings & Loan Association, Wilcox Development Corporation, and the American Savings and Loan Association) required seven years of negotiations to structure what was the largest commercial condominium agreement in the world for its time. Featuring three buildings, ranging from six to 21 stories in height, the brutalist-style buildings with their sandblasted, brown aggregate walls exude a sculptural quality with their cantilevered upper stories and bold supporting elements. The Financial Plaza was the only block of Victor Gruen's four-block downtown Honolulu revitalization plan to be fully realized. However, its open presence influenced its neighbors, First Hawaiian Bank and Bishop Square, to place substantial portions of their property into open space as well. In addition to pioneering a more spacious, pedestrian-friendly downtown, the Financial Plaza was also one of the first projects in the commercial district to introduce outdoor sculpture with the 1970 installation of

Photo: Martin Despang

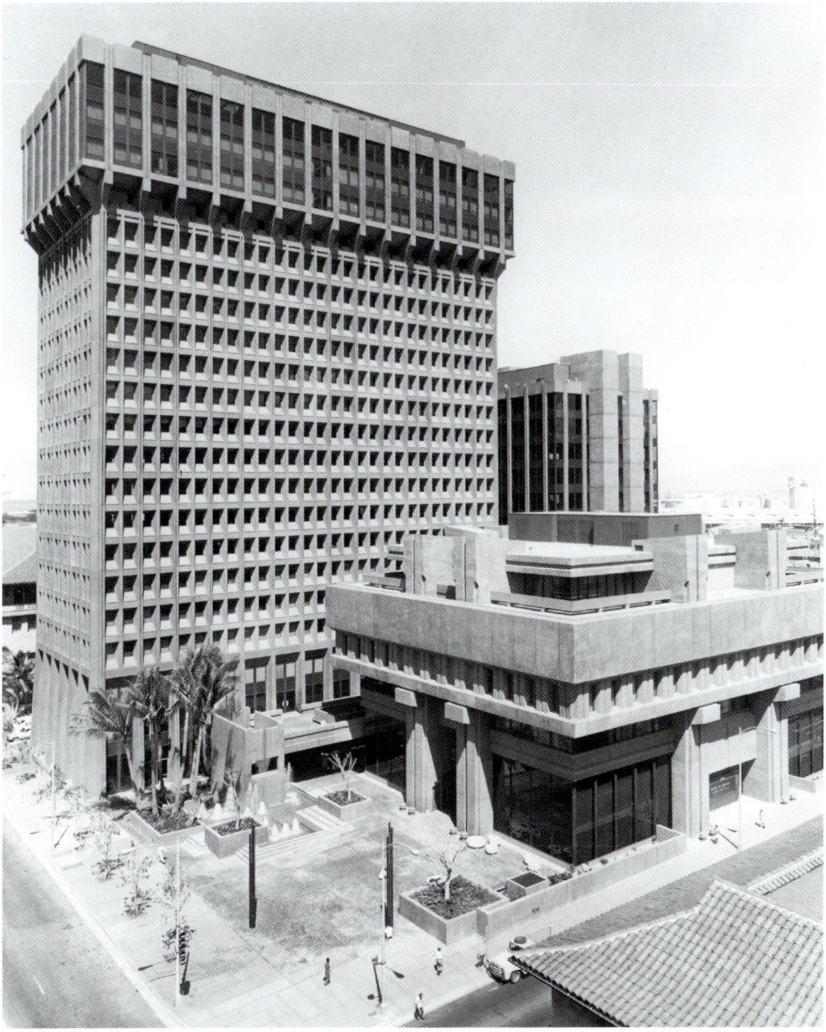

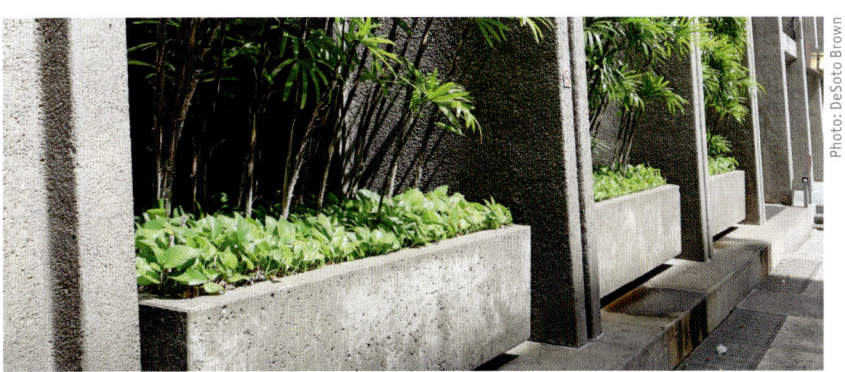

Photo: Bishop Museum, 1968

Photo: DeSoto Brown

Bernard Rosenthal's striking, 11-foot *Disc of the Sun* presiding over the Bishop Street corner's 'fountain court' with its modulated planting and Arnaldo Pomodoro's three cylindrical compositions on the Fort Street side, plus Laurence Halprin's Fountain. The plaza's unique layout and flair have resulted in a vibrant hub for both commerce and community engagement. It reflects a deep understanding of urban dynamics as well as a commitment to developing a multifunctional urban environment catering to both aesthetic and practical needs. *DH, LZ*

HONOLULU INTERNATIONAL AIRPORT

Honolulu Airport

300 Rodgers Blvd
Honolulu, HI 96819
Theodore Vierra (1962)
Vladimir Ossipoff (1970–1978)

119 A

The start of passenger jet airplane service in 1959 immediately made the existing Honolulu International Airport, constructed during the Second World War in the early 1940s, obsolete. A much enlarged facility was built nearby to utilize the existing runway system, and it opened in October 1962. This complex was designed with an impressive exterior appearance, with an 11-story office tower topped by the air traffic controllers' facility as a central focal point, flanked on either side by a low passenger check-in lobby. However, the tremendous growth of air traffic and technological advances in aircraft soon overwhelmed this airport, leading to significant additional construction in the 1970s. This began with a multistory parking garage that forever obscured the original view of the main terminal. In keeping with the architectural trends of the 1970s, much

of these renovations and reconstructions were done in the prevailing brutalist style. Exposed concrete, often with chipped vertical ribs, was contrasted with smooth terrazzo floors and touches of polished wood benches and railings. Earth tones of orange and brown appeared in the new departure lounges in carpeting and light fixtures, along with ceramic tiles. New wings housing arrival and departure gates utilizing covered jetways were constructed to accommodate the huge Boeing 747 aircraft that began service in 1970. The main terminal was also revamped to fit the already-established pattern of departing passengers being served on the upper level while baggage claim areas were on the ground floor. Despite the great changes this project brought, some positive elements were retained. These included the well-kept public gardens just below the main tower and the extensive use of open space both indoors and out, exposing airport patrons to the unsurpassed gentleness of Hawaii's climate that is such a memorable part of any tourist's first impression on arrival. *DB*

Photo: DeSoto Brown

Hawaii Hochi Building

`120` B

917 Kokea St
Honolulu, HI 96817
Kenzo Tange
1972

As the Kingdom of Hawaii's sugar plantations boomed starting in the 1870s, the need for more workers became acute as the local population was not large enough to provide them. This shortage led to immigrants being recruited from other countries, signing labor contracts before they left their homelands. The Japanese became the largest group of such workers, eventually comprising 40 per cent of Hawaii's population by the 1920s. As they finished their sugar contracts and ventured into the business world, many became owners of small stores, restaurants, construction companies, and many other lines of work. These entrepreneurs evolved into a growing middle class. Those who had come from Japan naturally continued to speak their native language, and many of their offspring learned it at home, which was reinforced by attendance at Japanese language schools in the afternoons. This population was served by radio programs, movie theatres, bookstores, and locally-published Japanese newspapers. One of these was the Hawaii Hochi, which began publication on 7 December 1912. Beginning in 1925, an English section was added. During the Second World War (1941–1945), prejudice against the 'enemy's language' forced a name change to the Hawaii Herald, but the original title was restored in 1952. Naturally, the population that could read Japanese could only shrink over time, and this impacted the Hochi. Regardless, in 1972 an entirely new headquarters building was constructed in the Kapalama industrial area at a cost of $1.2 million. Typical for this period, the structure is brutalist, composed of plain concrete. It faces onto the Kapalama Canal and from the street seems to be rather small. In fact, unseen behind this deceptive façade is a large building that originally held printing presses. The company stayed in business by printing numerous other small newspapers for different audiences and clients; 15 of them when the new building was completed. The inevitable end came on 7 December 2023 when the last issue of the Hawaii Hochi was published, 111 years to the day from its initial issue. The surrounding neighborhood is slated for significant redevelopment by the landowner, and it can be hoped that the Hochi's vacant plant can be saved for reuse. *DB*

Pacific Davies Center →

`121` B

841 Bishop St
Honolulu, HI 96813
Francis Donaldson and Au,
Cutting & Smith
1972

Bundit Kanisthakhon, having gotten to know Steve Au the closest, confirmed that Steve could associate himself with being categorized as a hippie. This structure, with its vast podium covering one entire block, is making Corporate America's most beloved child, the urban office tower, as hippie as possible. The concrete façade serves as a self-shading structural exoskeleton in conjunction with its core providing column-free office spaces. One can see the building as the emancipatory embodiment of Jane Fonda, Dolly Parton, and Lily Tomlin's in the movie 9 to 5. The building has been taken by the trend of converting commercial to residential in US downtowns. The architects in charge must be thanked for keeping as much originality as possible, like sculptor Van

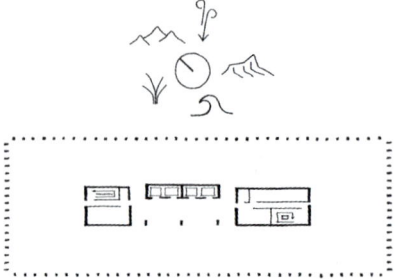

Photo: Martin Despang

Sant's cast-in-place alto-relievo murals celebrating the original owner's plantation business. The most recent foreseeable oversaturation with downtown dwelling provides the unique opportunity to proceed differently than to continuously chop up the wide-open spaces into speculative exclusive territorializations of capital concentrations, but rather to honor the building's unique wide, open spaciousness with alternative cooperative models, ideally tested on one floor offering neo-indiginous ways of living. Hippie Steve would love it. *MD*

8

Photo: Martin Despang

Frank Fasi Municipal Building 122 B

650 S King St,
Honolulu, HI 96813
NBBJ, Seattle/Honolulu
Structural: Alfred Yee
1973

The Municipal Building in Honolulu, Hawaii, is a striking 16-story tower renowned for its innovative design and engineering. A hallmark of modern architecture, it exemplifies how thoughtful collaboration between architects (NBBJ) and structural engineer (Alfred Yee) can create flexible, column-free spaces that blend functionality with aesthetic appeal. The building's design allows for expansive, uninterrupted floor areas, contributing to both its visual elegance and practicality. Column-free Design: One of the most remarkable features of the Municipal Building is its column-free layout, which offers 136,000 square feet (12,700 square meters) of open space. This was made possible through the use of prestressed joists and post-tensioned girders, structural innovations that allow for large, open floor plates. This design not only facilitates the building's versatility in use but also creates an uninterrupted visual connection between the mountains and the ocean. Design

Approaches: The Municipal Building integrates several cutting-edge design features that enhance both its efficiency and sustainability. 1. Precast Construction: Structural engineer Alfred Yee played a pivotal role in incorporating precast elements into the building's construction. This innovation accelerated the construction timeline and increased efficiency, contributing to the project's overall success. 2. Team Collaboration: The building's success is also attributed to the close collaboration between architects, engineers, and mechanical specialists. This teamwork ensured the seamless integration of systems such as plumbing and HVAC, saving both time and money during construction. 3. Beam Design: The use of both rectangular beams and I-beams provides structural stability for the floors, while circular openings in the beams accommodate essential building

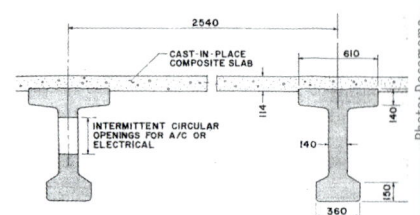

PRESTRESSED FLANGED JOISTS
FOR CLEAR SPAN OF 26ᵐ

Photo: Olivier Koning

8

utilities, such as HVAC and electrical systems, seamlessly integrating functionality with design. 4. Concrete Savings: By employing advanced engineering techniques, the building reduced its concrete usage by 47 per cent, lowering construction costs and minimizing its environmental impact. 5. Moment Frame: A simple yet effective moment frame design was incorporated to ensure the building's resilience against lateral forces like wind. This design provides stability without compromising the building's clean, modern aesthetic. Key Structural Elements: 1. Prestressed Joists: These long beams span between 64–77 feet

28

22

45

(19.6 and 23.6 meters), supporting heavy loads while maintaining open spaces on each floor. 2. Post-tensioned Girders: Spanning up to 121 feet (37 meters), these large, high-strength beams create expansive floor plates without the need for internal columns. 3. Foundation and Support: The building's foundation consists of a low concrete slab and four strong corner columns. The ground floor encloses only essential core elements such as elevators, plumbing, and ducts. This minimalist approach enhances the building's visual stability while allowing it to rise gradually, giving it a sense of lightness and openness. The Municipal Building in Honolulu stands as a testament to the power of collaboration between architecture and engineering. Its use of prestressed joists, post-tensioned girders, and composite slabs has created an open, column-free environment that remains adaptable to changing needs. Originally designed with open, public spaces intended for interaction, many of these areas were later converted into private offices to take advantage of the building's stunning views. Today, the Municipal Building is recognized as an important architectural and engineering landmark, demonstrating how innovative design solutions can create a functional, visually compelling, and sustainable structure. Its legacy endures as a symbol of the enduring synergy between architectural creativity and structural ingenuity. The Municipal Building was originally designed with open, public spaces that encouraged interaction and collaboration, allowing occupants to take advantage of the stunning views along the circulation along the ribbon windows with potential cross ventilation. As we hear confirmed from those

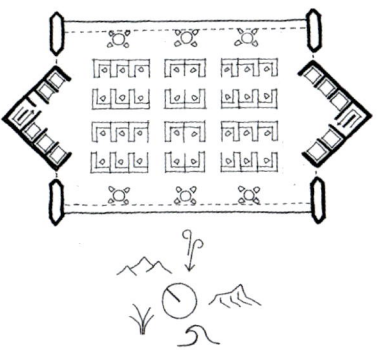

who worked on the project, the original design fully utilized the column-free spanning structure as that open office landscape sparkled with low cubicles. Unfortunately, this never materialized and was at the last moment changed to the opposite, reversing the layout to conventional office layouts with dark, double-loaded corridors, leaving only the individual rooms with framed views to enjoy the surrounding landscape. Looking forward, there is growing interest in future renovation cycles that could restore the building's original open layout and free-flow design. The sketched plan retrofitting the space to return to its original vision would enhance opportunities for collaboration, engagement, and flexibility – while also fostering a greater connection between interior spaces and the breathtaking views that the building was designed to embrace. This vision extends beyond the workplace itself, as creating more open, connected spaces would also strengthen the building's role as a civic and community hub for Honolulu. *BK*

8

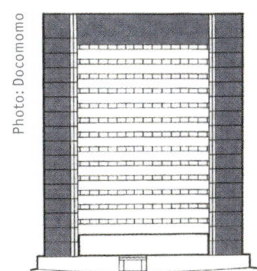

Moment frame diagram

Alfred Alphonse Yee

Bundit Kanisthakhon

The Evolution of Architecture in Honolulu: A Critical Reflection on Change and Innovation

The architectural landscape of Honolulu has undergone significant changes over the years, with one of its most influential figures being Alfred Yee, a structural engineer whose innovative approaches helped shape the city's skyline. His work marked an era when architecture was driven by creativity and bold experimentation. However, since then, the trajectory of architectural practices in Honolulu has shifted. This shift reflects broader systemic changes within the industry, which, in many cases, have limited the potential for such innovative design today.

Frank Fasi Municipal Building, 1973

The Decline of Collaborative Design and the Fragmentation of Vision

Historically, the collaboration between architects and structural engineers was seamless, as exemplified in Alfred Yee's work. Yee's ability to marry aesthetic appeal with structural integrity helped redefine Honolulu's architectural identity. This close collaboration resulted in solutions that were both functional and visually compelling. However, today's architectural landscape is defined by a more sequential workflow between architects and engineers, rather than the collaborative, side-by-side approach that once characterized their relationship. The rise of specialization and compartmentalized roles has often diminished the holistic design vision necessary for a cohesive project. This division has led to a narrowing of creative potential, as collaboration is increasingly sidelined in favor of more segmented, task-specific approaches.

Risk Aversion and the Stifling of Innovation

In recent decades, a culture of risk aversion has increasingly defined the architectural profession. As concerns over insurance, liability, and legal implications have grown, architectural firms are more focused on mitigating potential risks than fostering innovative design. This shift has led to a more conservative approach, emphasizing safety and code compliance at the cost of the bold, innovative designs that once defined Honolulu's architectural landscape. Where Alfred Yee embraced experimentation in structural engineering, today's designers often find themselves navigating a restrictive landscape, with novel ideas becoming buried under bureaucratic regulations.

Regulatory and Environmental Constraints

Another significant factor in the evolution of Honolulu's architecture is the growing complexity of building codes and environmental regulations. While these codes are crucial for ensuring safety, they have, in many cases, limited design freedom. Architects often find themselves forced to compromise on their creative vision in order to comply with these regulations. For example, energy efficiency codes, while essential for sustainability, have made it

8

Photo: Docomomo

Vessel

Construction of the long-span airplane hangar

Highly durable and low-maintenance

Interior of Guam airplane hangar

increasingly difficult to incorporate traditional design elements such as open, naturally ventilated spaces – once a hallmark of Honolulu's architectural style. In the face of such constraints, architects and engineers must balance modern demands with the unique environmental context of Hawaii. Traditional Hawaiian architecture, which emphasized open-air designs and natural materials, was inherently suited to the island's climate. However, contemporary efforts to modernize these traditions are often impeded by complex regulations, resulting in designs that fail to fully harness the potential of the region's climate and resources.

A Shift in Professional Practice: The Loss of Individual Leadership

The transition away from the era of 'one-man engineering leadership', exemplified by Alfred Yee, marks another key change in the profession. Yee's ability to oversee and shape projects with a unified, visionary approach is increasingly rare today. Architects and engineers now often work within large, corporate firms, where individual vision is frequently sacrificed in favor of corporate interests and efficiency. This shift has led to the compartmentalization of design, reducing the bold, innovative spirit that once characterized Honolulu's architectural landscape. Additionally, the current emphasis in architectural and engineering education on obtaining professional accreditation, rather than fostering independent creative thinking, has further stifled innovation. The focus on standardized knowledge over critical problem-solving has encouraged conformity, diminishing the kind of visionary experimentation that defined Yee's work.

Revisiting the Legacy of Alfred Yee

Alfred Yee (1925–2017) remains a pivotal figure in the history of Honolulu's architecture. His pioneering work in structural engineering, especially his use of precast concrete, allowed for the construction of taller, more efficient buildings. Projects such as the Queen Emma Garden, the Ala Moana Hotel, and the Municipal Building showcase his ability to adapt engineering principles to Hawaii's unique environmental challenges. One of Yee's most notable contributions was his development of precast concrete connections, including the innovative splice sleeve that allowed for more efficient construction methods. His work not only improved the structural integrity of buildings but also facilitated faster and more cost-effective construction. Yee was also known for his ability to integrate multiple disciplines early in the design process. His collaboration with architects, engineers, and mechanical specialists ensured that systems such as plumbing and HVAC were seamlessly integrated, saving both time and cost during construction. The Municipal Building is a prime example of this integrated approach. Yee's

work extended beyond Hawaii. One of his notable projects was a long-span airplane hangar in Guam, which continues to stand as a testament to his enduring design principles. According to local precast concrete plant managers, the structure has proven to be highly durable and low-maintenance, and plans are underway to replicate this design in Honolulu. Additionally, Yee patented various floating barges to transport materials from Hawaii to the mainland. His innovative honeycomb prestressed concrete vessels as depicted in the images below offer potential solutions for addressing global challenges such as rising sea levels, which threaten cities worldwide. In conclusion, Alfred Yee's legacy remains central to the evolution of Honolulu's architecture. While today's architectural landscape may be constrained by regulatory, professional, and cultural shifts, Yee's innovative spirit continues to inspire and challenge future generations of architects and engineers.

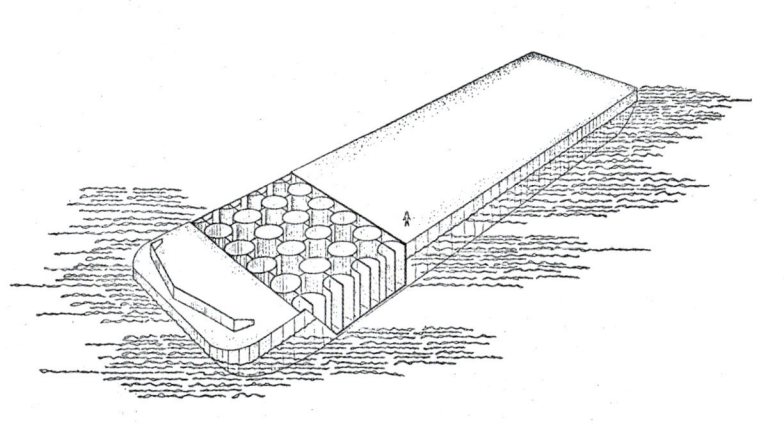

Honeycomb prestressed concrete vessels

Solution for rising sea levels

Honeycomb design applied in the field

Hale Koa Hotel

2055 Kālia Rd
Honolulu, HI 96815
Belt, Lemmon & Lo
1975

After the United States' annexation of the Hawaiian Islands was completed in 1900, both the US Navy and Army began the aggressive construction of some major facilities. One of the Army forts built along the south shore of Oahu during the early twentieth century was Fort DeRussy in Waikiki. Comprised of 72 acres of land purchased from, or condemned from, private owners, the former fishponds of this wetland were filled beginning in 1906. Five years later, two powerfully reinforced concrete batteries were completed to house huge artillery guns to theoretically be used for the defense of Honolulu against enemy ships offshore, should a war occur. These destructive weapons were so powerful that had they ever actually been fired, the concussion from each blast would have shattered windows and caused structural damage throughout Waikiki. Ironically, by the time war actually did come to Hawaii on 7 December 1941, technology had changed so rapidly that the Ft. DeRussy guns had become obsolete. It was airplanes that were used by Japan in its surprise attack, and it was airplanes that would be the primary weapons throughout the Second World War. This left Ft. DeRussy as primarily a recreational facility for the constant military population on the island during and after the war, and in 1950 it was officially designated as such. From then on it hosted military personnel and their families in its beach facilities in addition to beds for visitors on vacation. This latter function again soared during the Vietnam War in the 1960s and 1970s, when men on leave from Asia could meet up with their wives for a romantic break from their often grueling duties. In October 1975 the first tower of the Hale Koa Hotel opened with 416 rooms over 15 floors. The hodgepodge of aging wooden structures along the beach was gradually cleared away, with their functions now consolidated into the hotel. The military running such a facility in a very popular tourist area was the source of national controversy more than once during the 1970s. A second structure, the Maile Tower, opened in 1995 to go along with the existing building, now called the Ilima Tower. The two structures face each other across a plaza, and on the ocean side, an immense banyan tree is incorporated into portions of this shared space. In many ways the Hale Koa fulfills all the same needs and demands of most of Waikiki's clientele, with banquet rooms, a pool and other amenities, and even entertainment and a regular luau. It does so at a lower cost for its guests, who are undoubtedly grateful for that. While the continued existence of Ft. DeRussy can be rightfully questioned

Photo: Martin Despang

American World Airways was another major tenant, occupying the entire 11th floor and part of the 10th. The airline insisted on the right to install large outdoor signs on the building as part of its lease agreement, the permit for which was submitted just before the new Honolulu Comprehensive Building Code went into effect. The latter subsequently prohibited signs of this size, which in this case consists of illuminated letters 3 feet in height for the words 'Pan Am' (50 feet in length) and 'Pan American' at 95 feet. After Pan American Airways ceased operations in 1991, this Honolulu office building unintentionally became a kind of memorial to what had been a major international corporation. The Pan Am building is an example of brutalist architecture, but with the notable difference of not using the common gray concrete usually seen in such structures. Instead it could be called 'blond brutalism' for being a light sandy color like most of the beaches of the Hawaiian Islands. Close inspection will show the various darker stone elements of the concrete aggregate. The overall light color makes the structure less somber and fortress-like as many dark concrete brutalist buildings are criticized for being. The open base of the building along its Kaheka Street frontage, lifted two stories from the sidewalk, contributes to its sense of lightness. A perforated horizontal edge extending from the rooftop succeeds in furthering this effect. *DB*

in such a densely urbanized location, it must be said that the beach along its shoreline is open to the public as it legally must be, and the grassy open spaces, mature trees, and well-kept grounds are an asset that ironically would no longer exist had not the Army retained the property. Commercial development pressures would otherwise have led to a total build-up of this land decades ago. *DB*

Pan Am Building → 124 B
1600 Kapiolani Blvd
Honolulu, HI 96814
Hogan & Chapman
1969

In 1963, a large tract of 29 acres of land in central Honolulu, subdivided into 72 lots for commercial development, became available for sale as the Kapiolani Business District. One of these parcels would be the site of what was initially known as the American Savings building. The 17-story structure, opened in March 1969 on busy Kapiolani Boulevard, housed the American Savings & Loan company on its ground floor, which led to its original name. But at the same time, Pan

Photo: Martin Despang

8

Honolulu Municipal Parking

346 Alapai St
Honolulu, HI 96813
Anbe, Aruga, Ishizu
1979

125 B

The opening of the new Hawaii State Capitol building in downtown Honolulu in 1969 was a great achievement, but this was just the start of an even larger project. This was to gradually construct a new Civic Center to not only provide the Capitol with an appropriate and attractive setting, but also to consolidate government offices into a central location. The Civic Center redevelopment gradually took shape in the 1970s. Blocks of existing structures were demolished after privately-owned properties were condemned by the government, existing streets were straightened or removed, and new government structures were built in open park-like settings. In many cases, these latter buildings followed the prevailing brutalist architectural style that was common internationally at that time.

The government employees who would be working in this area were often going to use private cars for travel, which would require a substantial amount of parking. Rather than put up the usual unappealing multi-story concrete structure, an innovative and successful solution was used – the parking would be placed mostly underground, and disguised by lawns and trees. Two levels were constructed: one

Photo: Martin Despang

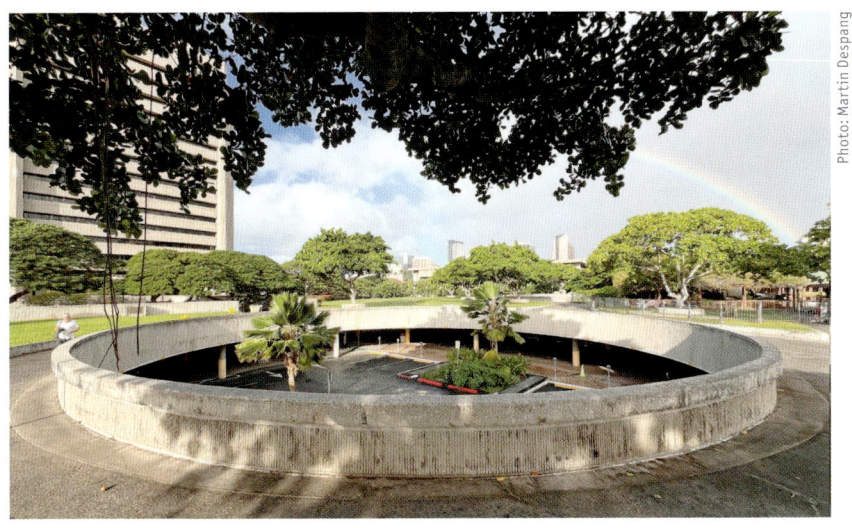

below ground and the other at street level. The entire concrete structure was then covered by earth, sloping upwards on all four sides, and here, lawns were cultivated. Monkeypod trees, already selected as the main type for the landscaping in this area, were planted along the perimeters. The result was a major success, with very little evidence of the storage of vehicles discernible to passers-by; the impression is that of a public park. The concrete structures that are visible – entrance and exit ramps, stairways, and other openings – are all recognizably brutalist, with vertical chipped ribs in the unpainted gray cement. But unlike the many brutalist buildings that critics love to hate, the contrast of the elements of raw concrete with the grass and trees surrounding it is actually pleasing. *DB*

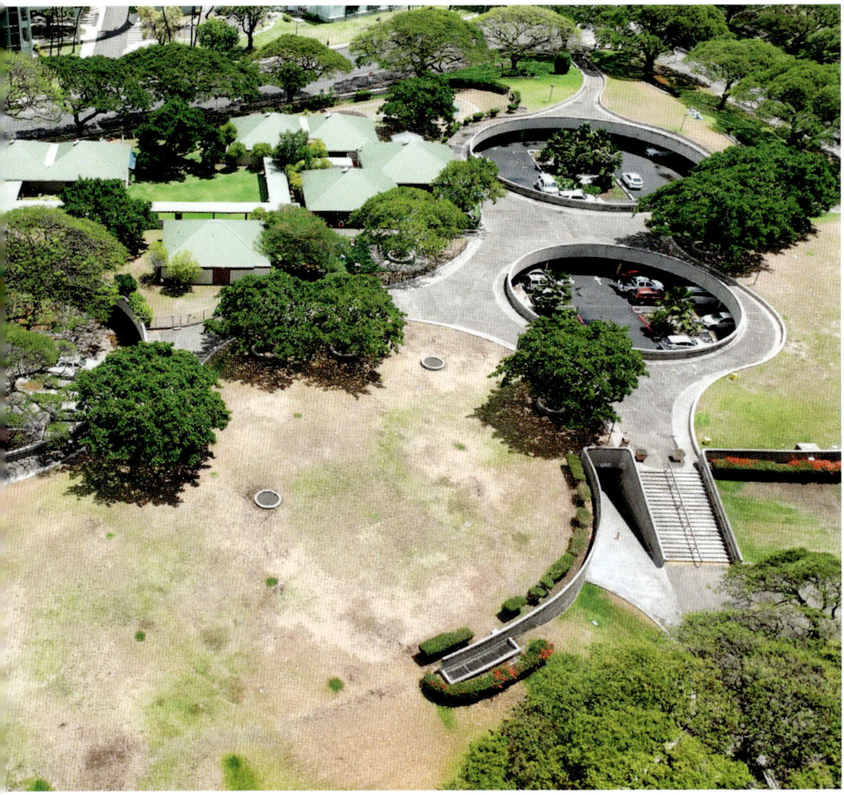

Photo: Kikuyo Hibbard

Kawaiahao Plaza

567 S King St
Honolulu, HI 96813
James K. Tsugawa
1979

126 B

Being located at the edge of the City and County of Honolulu's Hawaii Capital Special Design District required this downtown office/commercial complex to be developed in a low density manner with ample open space. In an effort to preserve and enhance the serene environment established by the neighboring Mission Houses historic site and other nearby historic properties, the architect and developers, James K. Trask and Francis E. Denis, devised a plan in which more than half of their sprawling 114,000-square-foot lot was devoted to open space. The complex's two low-rise buildings are judiciously placed in their garden setting, with the L-shaped, four-story building not only set back from King Street but also at a diagonal, which resulted in an inviting frontal sequence presenting an angular dynamic to the street. The building's boldly alternating bands of tinted glass and dark, precast concrete provide a sleek horizontality, which further reduces the building's presence, while a 40-foot-wide mall between the front building and its six-story office/parking structure forms an intimate space that wends through the complex, reinforcing the cohesiveness of the whole. The integration of garden pathways that connect the plaza with the Mission Houses is a highlight of the landscape design, which also features a permanent outdoor stage. The office/parking structure furthers the design agenda with its compelling parallel lines smoothly gliding along South Street. With the completion of the project, Bernice Pauahi Bishop Estate purchased the underlying land as well as the majority equity in the buildings and relocated its administrative offices here. *DH, LZ*

615 Piikoi
615 Piikoi St
Honolulu, HI 96814
Ernest Hara
1979

127 B

This fine vulcrete tropical brutalist building's inherent gestural bioclimatic pattern is its protruding fenestration frame grid, which principally has its horizontal parts shade to the south and its vertical parts to the east and the west, like its contemporaries at 1972 Davies Pacific Center, 1975 Finance Factors Building, 1978 Pioneers Plaza Building also do. It is charming that John and Mayumi Hara have moved their office into this their father's/grandfather's creation, which continues to be the most 'Back to the Future' among all the new blue, glass-box high-rises in the Midtown Ala Moana development. *MD*

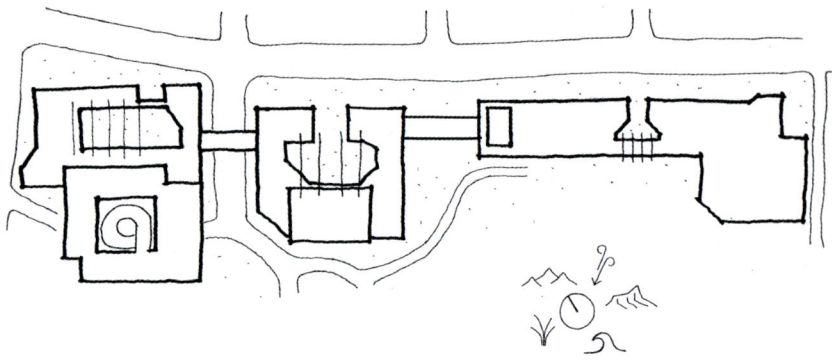

Royal Hawaiian Center

2201 Kalākaua Ave
Honolulu, HI 96815
Wong & Wong
1980

128 C

We are here zeitgeistly talking seriously substantial sublime Jimmy Carter era. The seemingly impossible task of dropping a large shopping mall in front of the Royal Hawaiian Hotel has been solved masterfully, but in the long term it was not possible to convince corporate capitalist consumerism to buy into it. Previously occupied by the 1960s one-story tectonic wood shopping arcade by Pete Wimberly, this replacement from two decades later was powerful: a bush-hammered vulcrete monolith as the boldest of (under)statements. Set back from Kalakaua Avenue to camouflage itself further with lush foliage, its few openings lead like a treasure chest to the surprise of the courtyards inside, which are connected by sun- and rain-covered shopping streets. In some ways the building could be understood

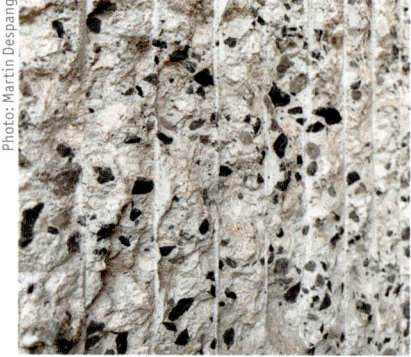

Photo: Ulivier Koning

Photo: DeSoto Brown

renaturalizing its only recently redone center landscape of tourist fauna astro turf, because after all, this of all buildings in Waikiki respects Waikiki's once giant royal palm grove the most. Is this retrofitting at all possible? The Hermes Store renovation, included near the end of this book, very much proves it. *MD*

Princess Ruth Keelikolani Building ↓

129 B

830 Punchbowl St
Honolulu, HI 96813
Architects Hawaii
1986

Long and low, this three-story government office building offers a sedate and comfortable example of tropical brutalism at its finest. Its bold lines, raw ribbed concrete walls, and sculptural forms merge with the tropical environment thanks to its wrap-around arcade, thin, irregularly spaced brise-soleil, and verdant interior courtyards that exude an airy sense of openness. It presents a comfortable and inviting atmosphere despite the metal detectors and security guards at the entry, which are ubiquitous at far too many federal-, state-,and county-operated facilities in Hawaii. It is one of several Joe Farrell-designed tropical brutalist buildings to utilize a broken rib concrete finish. Others included the neighboring federal building (1974), the Poinciana (now Sand Villa) Hotel (1970), and the 30-story Pacific Trade Center (1972), the tallest building in Hawaii upon its completion. Farrell, who cut his architectural teeth under Paul Rudolph, joined Architects Hawaii in 1961, becoming a partner in 1969. *DH, DHa*

as conceptualized as a modern abstract analogy of a volcano with lava tubes by the goddess Pele. The crater courtyard cones open to the sky with bold beams carrying the chandeliered lighting. The recent partial covering of one of them with glass should be undone, as it is counterproductive to the natural theme of the courtyards, with one having been built around a preexisting large tree. This hidden gem project deserves to be reoriginated by stripping it of all of the added cheesecaking pastiche shopfronts and

Photo: DeSoto Brown

9

Ward Warehouse

1240 Ala Moana Blvd
Honolulu, HI 96814
Au, Cutting and Smith
1974

130 B

Originally comprised of land owned by the Ward family since the 1800s, Victoria Ward Ltd. began developing its property in central Honolulu to a higher standard beginning in the early 1960s. Its first large project was the IBM Building (also in this book), then going bigger with

Ward Warehouse in 1974–1975. Replacing various commercial and industrial structures – mostly rundown – along with used car lots, this complex included both retail and wholesale tenants. It straddled parcels with different urban zoning, which required some juggling of types of businesses. Initial plans called for 87 tenants, potentially, depending on what individual space needs would be. Ward Warehouse was composed of six buildings, two of which were one story. The others offered ground floor units with 19-foot

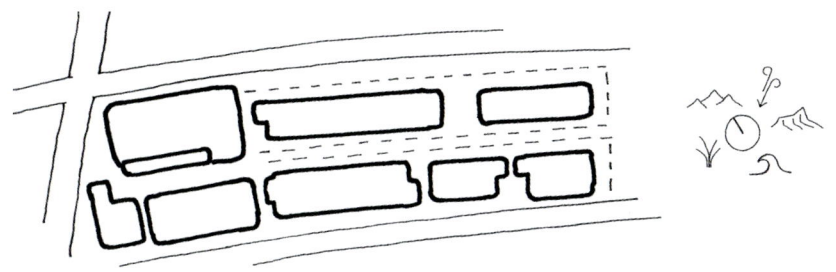

ceilings that could accommodate mezzanines. Second floor spaces were smaller. The usual niceties of shopping centers were not present; conduits and pipes were left exposed, and industrial-style light fixtures were standard. Overall the Ward Warehouse was a product of its time, being built of stained or dark-painted wood, including massive square beams held together by large iron brackets. This was in keeping with the hippie goal (well-known in popular culture by this time) of being 'real' and honest, not dressed up or overly ornamented. The only decorative elements on the exterior were some bold painted 'supergraphics' of geometric patterns in bright colors. This architectural style had been pioneered in the 1960s in a planned oceanside community in Sonoma, California, called Sea Ranch. Similar to Ward Warehouse, the homes there were plain, boxy structures without roof eaves, and built of unpainted, weathered wood. The Ward Estate land was eventually sold, coming into the hands of the Howard Hughes Corporation. Ward Warehouse was demolished for the construction of more large high-end residential towers, as part of the overall development of the district. *DB*

Photo: DeSoto Brown, 1975

9

Art Department Building
2535 McCarthy Mall Rm 144
Honolulu, HI 96822
Group 70 Lab
1975

131 C

In the early 1970s, the University of Hawaii's various art departments were scattered around through 14 different locations, including some that were not even on the campus. To remedy this dispersal, a new central Art Building was constructed. While all of these varying endeavors were categorized together as 'art', they encompassed greatly differing needs. Art History was academically-oriented, while glass blowing required furnaces that reached extremely high temperatures to literally melt glass. Sculpture might entail forging and hammering metals while photography needed light-proof darkrooms to process and print photos. The overall diversity of these fields, along with drawing and painting, textiles and weaving, printmaking, and graphics meant that the Art Building had to be as utilitarian as possible. Dropped ceilings and other comforts were eliminated in favor of exposed pipes and electrical conduits, along with plain concrete and cement walls and floors. Muffling sound and venting smoke and heat were among the required concerns.

A large multi-use auditorium was included in the structure. Overall, this 1970s building is typical of the brutalist years. Textured cement blocks are contrasted with smooth poured-concrete surfaces. Some of the ground floor footprint is left open, with large X-form supports between vertical beams. Another 1970s touch is the respect for the natural environment where an existing baobab tree was left in place on the site, with the building positioned around it. The University of Hawaii's Manoa campus has numerous such unusual tropical trees, many planted by staff botanists decades ago. Non-students will be familiar with the central courtyard of the Art Building, where a bamboo grove has been growing since the 1970s This is also the site of the Art Gallery, which was designed with a minimum of interior walls so that it could be staged with maximum creativity to allow temporary display panels to be installed as desired for each new showing. *DB*

Treehouse ↓

212A Luika Place
Kailua, HI 96734
Steve Au
1977

Clinging to the side of what seems to be an impossibly steep, heavily vegetated cliff above the Lanikai seaside neighborhood, architect Steve Au's personal residence looks over the windward Oahu coastline towards the two small offshore islands, Moku Nui and Moku Iki. Like Au's previous project, Ward Warehouse of three years earlier, the Treehouse incorporates elements of the 1970s movement toward natural materials and stripped-down, unadorned surfaces. In turn, this aesthetic was inspired by the Sea Ranch development in California, particularly in the unpainted raw wood exterior that was allowed to weather naturally. The extreme grade of the site required the structure to be skinny, incorporating multiple levels

[Image of kitchen interior with people]

with large windows and small lookout-like balconies. Glass louvers were used to allow the normal trade wind air flow to ventilate the house without air conditioning. Indoors, light-colored wood surfaces were varnished to retain the original colors and patterns, contrasted with white walls and some darker wood square

structural beams. Overall the feeling is of rectangular, squared-off corners, along with flat roofs with others at 45-degree angles. As time passes and architectural styles change, unique buildings like the Treehouse gain the appreciation of those who recognize the best of history and work to preserve it. *DB*

Aloha Stadium

99–500 Salt Lake Blvd
Aiea, HI 96701
Luckman Partnership, Inc
1975

133 A

When the original Honolulu Stadium, which was located on King Street, was deemed too old and small in the boom of the 1970s, it was replaced in the periphery of the city in Aiea with a stadium with a capacity of 50,000-plus people. It has captivated audiences with sports to music events, hosting everyone from Frank Sinatra to the Rolling Stones. In some of the last concerts before its closing in 2019, your author saw the Eagles perform. One of the last shows was local boy Bruno Mars, who sold out consecutive nights. Out in the wide openness all by itself, the stadium has a stark appearance through its pretty crazily cantilevering bleachers structure. Its architect Charles Luckman has showcased expertise of iconography before with the Theme Building at Los Angeles LAX Airport with his former business partner William Pereira. He was similarly ambitious with this projects' materialization in Corten Steel, which principally builds up a rust patina protecting further corrosion. In the humid tropics of Hawaii and in this proximity to Pearl Harbor's Pacific Ocean, this did not hold quite so true and the lack of dryer periods allowed the steel to further rust. Preventive protective measures with rust protecting sealants had not been taken to begin with and the outcomes were used as the arguments and excuses to demolish the stadium and replace it with a ninth-island-like (Las Vegas) entertainment complex around a new stadium decorated with housing. Demolition by pseudo neglect is a sad tradition on the island, particularly with a building like this from the mid-1970s that just turned 50 (and therefore making it eligible for preservation). Unlike other related arts such as cars or bell bottom pants, we have not seen regained appreciation of architecture. In the Aloha Stadium's case, as demonstrated by this rusty Alfa automobile,

9

Photo: Martin Despang

it is possible to keep steel architecture running here by cutting out parts, welding in new ones, and finally adding a rust-protecting coat in a rust color. It would also be possible to reinforce the structure with tensile cables tied back into the grounds, weaving agroforestry landscapes into its center and creating a neo-indigenous, cliff-dweller-inspired habitation in its peripheral ring of bleachers around the stratosphered center made of self-sufficing gardens. The cables could be made of basalt cord quarried nearby. Imagine, instead of a paradise centered around gambling, an open system for juvenile youth and rejuvenated elderly living together again in synergy and harmony, as projected by Jay Fidell. With a balanced live-work setup, they could run the swap meet/market on the ground floor, shaded by the multifunctional tensile scapes hovering above. *MD*

9

Photo: State of Hawaii

10

Tamarind Square

1001 Bishop St
Honolulu, HI 96813
James Hubbard
1981

Bernice Pauahi Bishop, a member of Hawaiian royalty, is famous for the large amount of land she owned in the Hawaiian Islands, which was turned into the endowment for the Kamehameha Schools. It was her husband Charles Reed Bishop who carried out the goals of her will after her death in 1885, founding the schools that still thrive today. When Pauahi was born at her parents' home in what is now downtown Honolulu, a tree was planted following Hawaiian tradition. This tamarind tree stood on the grounds of the home until about 1900 when the house was demolished and the first block of Bishop Street was constructed, which, of course, was named for this renowned couple. Built facing onto this section of Bishop Street was the imposing Alexander Young Hotel: five stories of classical architecture and modern conveniences. It opened in 1903 and gradually evolved into a pure commercial building by 1970, containing many doctors' offices. Meanwhile, downtown Honolulu continued to grow. In 1972 the 30-story Pacific Trade Center tower and its attached parking structure was built to occupy the other half of the Alexander Young's block, and in 1981 the former hotel itself was demolished, against the wishes of a great many community members. In its place the Pauahi Tower was constructed, along with one acre of open park space known as Tamarind Square. This name honored Bernice Pauahi Bishop's tree that once grew there. Diagonally across the crowded intersection of King Street and Bishop Street is the 1968 Financial Plaza of the Pacific, a complex of three business structures. It had broken tradition in its design by not filling the entire block with buildings out to the curb, as had stood there before, but in leaving open public spaces. The largest of these was across from Tamarind Square and undoubtedly inspired its creation. The owner and developer of the entire block, which was named Bishop Square when completed, was the Northwestern Mutual Life Insurance Company. It deserved praise for the construction of this asset of open space, grass, trees, and innovative water features. Most notable of the latter is in the narrow space starting at Hotel Street, which contains a long water pool that uses the 9-foot drop in elevation to allow the water to actually flow. Varying platforms of pavement cross the different pools and add interest to what could have been a flat expanse. Grassy lawns are interspersed, and low raised walls form lengthy benches that are popular for downtown workers to sit on while eating lunch. The largest pool contains a metal Henry Moore sculpture titled *Upright Motive No. 9*. Created in 1979 and measuring 11 feet in height, it was selected for this location to tie in with the two high-rise towers that bracket the square. The sculpture's unveiling in 1983 served as the official completion of Tamarind Square, which continues to successfully fulfill the ideal of providing an appealing space for pedestrians and park-goers in an otherwise urban location. *DB*

Halekulani Hotel

2199 Kālia Rd
Honolulu, HI 96815
Killingsworth, Stricker,
Lindgren, Wilson & Associates
1983

135 C

At the time of writing this entry, our dear friend architect Ron Lindgren, a postmodern marvel master, had given everything to the world and just left it. Ron Lindgren told us that of all the numerous projects he designed all over the world, this one was his favorite. A previous design by another architect was luckily rejected by the client. Ron's subsequent design more than met the client's wish to have a serene tropical oasis camouflage the sheer mass of a building with close to 500 rooms. Having gracefully integrated W. C. Dickey's Lewers building as a centerpiece, the arrangement of the program rises around two courtyards, allowing one to wander around never realizing the larger hotel above it, which Ron softened by having it step down toward the ocean. The separation of the vehicular and pedestrian porte-cochères makes both these thresholds transition from the public streets to the private grounds powerfully processional. The friendliest security and valet staff, many having worked here since the hotel opened, keep it discreetly inclusive despite the exclusivity of it being the most starred hotel

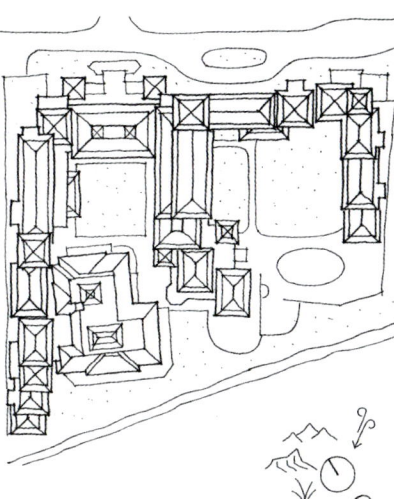

in Waikiki. Given its bioclimatically optimized orientation – with mostly single-loaded corridors and fenestration with self-shading lanais, wooden sliding shutters with adjustable blades, and perforated roll down tarps that provide efficient and effective low-tech climate control – an energy assessment of the structure would likely see it achieve LEED Platinum certification in a testament to Ron's mid-century modern master intuition. The hotel's management is to be commended for the recent renovation having not altered but only refreshed its originality. The only suggestion was to restore one hotel room back to its original condition and reimagine the blank exteriors in the signature style of Killingsworth's planter boxes with lush vegetation. Ron, always the youngest at heart, said that it (see Outrigger Hotels illustration) would be a lovely enhancement, so he should have thought of it himself. So, check out Ron in the three TTH h(e)a episodes and the 60-plus follow ups explaining everything much better than we ever could. *MD*

Liliuokalani Gardens ↓→ 136 C

300 Wai Nani Way
Honolulu, HI 96815
Architects Hawaii
1984

Bringing back old, palm-groved Waikiki with high-rises that look like trees? This development, designed by lead architect Fred White, surprisingly makes that happen in a convincing way. Conducting a case study of the 1976 zoning ordinance for Waikiki, which prevents the entire block from being covered with build mass, mandates 70 per cent of the site to be preserved as lush, park-like grounds, into which the two towers were placed. The unit's tinted glass sliding windows were inserted between plastered pilaster strips inspired by banyan trees, providing shade for the openings on the south side, which is the most vulnerable, and to a significant extent on the other orientations as well. A truly 1980s building, yet it courageously resists the zeitgeisty feistiness of the pomo-fossil Ronald Reagan era. *MD*

Photo: Martin Despang

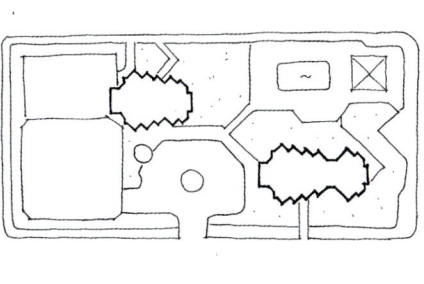
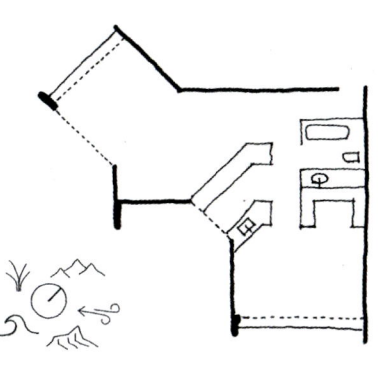

10

Kaiser Permanente

137 B

1010 Pensacola St
Honolulu, HI 96814
Architects Hawaii
1986

Kaiser Permanente's six-story Honolulu Clinic offered Honolulu in 1986 a glimpse of architecture's emerging late modern sensibility with its raked concrete walls and the vivid contrast of its discontiguous, modular front wall and the serrated syncopation of its east wall. The design's distinctive light shelves extend out from the exterior windows, shading the lower two thirds of the windows while reflecting natural light onto the ceiling of the offices. At least two decades before LEED became a buzzword, this innovation was producing at least 30 per cent energy savings. The lobby, with its pastel colored walls and circular reception desk rising from a retro glass block base, further contributed to the move away from modernism and its perceived machine aesthetic. *DH*

Photo: Olivier Koning

10

11

Uraku Tower
1341 Kapiolani Blvd,
Honolulu, HI 96814
Kajima Associates
1990

This slick, 29-story, ultra-luxury condominium with its eye-catching, brilliantly white walls and pale blue-green windows rises from a lushly-planted front plaza featuring a black granite fountain and a postmodern semicircle of six free-standing columns, each terminating with a planter as a capital. Fronting the plaza is a segmental arched, floor-to-ceiling glass entry, which is surmounted by a stately, glass-block cylindrical dome that sparks further visual intrigue while illuminating the lobby and its Italian marble floor. Generous, curvilinear lanai

Photo: Martin Despang

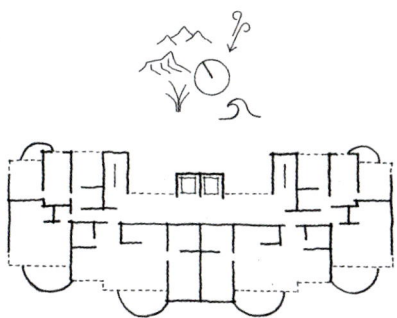

run up the front and rear of the building to add a futuristic appearance to the façade with their tube-like dynamic. The lanai open the 92 two- and three-bedroom apartments to Hawaii's inviting climate, while also augmenting their already generous floor space, with two-bedroom units ranging from 1,136 to 1,652 square feet and three-bedrooms offering 2,255 to 2,841 square feet. *DH, RK*

11

Imperial Plaza
725 Kapiolani Blvd
Honolulu, HI 96813
DMJM
1991

139 B

A soaring explosion of smooth-skinned, angular pink glass and pointed lanai, this eye-catching mixed-use complex helped usher in the postmodern luxury condominium to Honolulu. It occupies a full block, bounded by Kawaiahao, Cooke, and Drier Streets and Kapiolani Boulevard, and includes 174 residential condominium units situated in a 40-story tower as well as another 33 units at its makai end in a terraced, eight-story aggregation of townhouse-like units. Sleek entry lobbies of marble, granite, and chrome welcome the residents and their guests, and all units have 10-foot-high ceilings, while the townhouse units, as well as the tower's penthouse, feature two-story living. The 55 commercial condominiums include offices and shops, a number of which are situated in the historic, four-story, former Royal Brewery

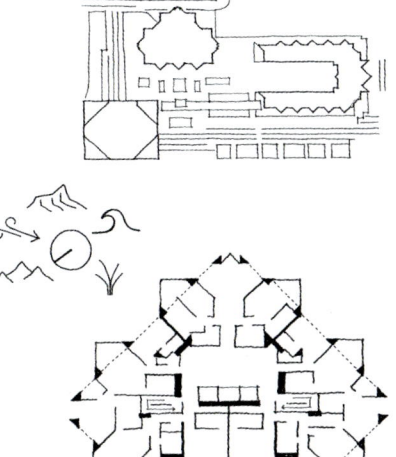

building that the Hawaii Community Development Authority required the developer, Colin de Silva, to retain. In addition, the agency conditioned its approval upon DeSilva's development of a 10,000-square-foot pocket park at Cooke and Kawaiahao Streets just makai of the building. The cascading, precast concrete planter box sunscreens flowing down Cooke Street soften the parking podium and provide a rhythmic, street-level tropical allure with an almost 60-foot setback from the street. The sidewalk servicing the Cooke Street shops flows into an open-air shopping arcade that also functions as an entry to the former brewery building. Postmodern columns, capped with planter boxes, adorn this indoor-outdoor transition space. The building was one of the earliest high-rise residential condominiums to be constructed in Kakaako, and the first in the district to be considered a luxury development, raising fears at the time concerning the direction of the district's redevelopment, which have proven to be all too true. *DH, RL*

11

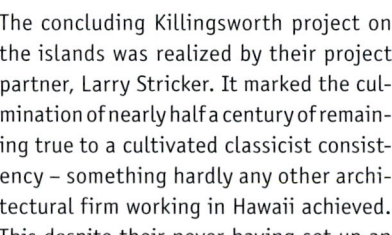

Ihilani
92–1001 Olani St
Kapolei, HI 96707
Killingsworth, Stricker, Lindgren,
Wilson & Associates
1993

140 A

The concluding Killingsworth project on the islands was realized by their project partner, Larry Stricker. It marked the culmination of nearly half a century of remaining true to a cultivated classicist consistency – something hardly any other architectural firm working in Hawaii achieved. This despite their never having set up an office in Hawaii, but rather remaining in Long Beach, California, and returning only when asked to design another project. Here, Larry introduced John Portman's atrium lobby concept to the firm's oeuvre, using it as a trick to make mostly single-loaded corridors. Theatrical front and back porte-cochères guide guests through the lobby along with the trade winds. This project in many ways represents the cumulation of several Killingsworth themes, such as structural expressionism through the quadrupling of columns and maximization of lanai that front glass sliding doors. Hear it better from Larry himself. *MD*

11

Harbor Court

141 B

55 Merchant St
Honolulu, HI 96813
Norman Lacayo
1994

With this final firework of a building, Norman Lacayo fully embraced the flamboyant pitfalls of the Clinton era. The complex has a Jekyll and Hyde dynamic. Here, however, the second is the taller one – a boxy commercial tower with fixed glazing facing southeast and southwest, brutally exposed to the sun throughout the day. The first is the residential wing facing northwest and is much different. Designed from the inside out, both socially and in response to solar orientation, its staggered massing provides single-family-quality visual privacy for the units, while also producing

significant shade for each other until sunset. It is only toward their crowns that the dwellings become Hyde-ish with their glazed-in lanais. The layouts of the dwelling floors are florally swooping, the curviness continuing down to the lobby, which is comprised of an open pathway plaza and an elevator lobby. Despite its stylistic eclectic mix of Gothic, Egyptian, and art deco revival styles, supported by lots of waterways and fountains, the private and public processional areas of the composition have a fantastical, exotically tropical atmosphere. The architect's affectionate attention to exuberant excellence at every scale of the building reportedly did not pay off financially, leading him to retire in exile in Mexico. Within Lacayo's own vocabulary of the parking garage's golden grills lies the potential of perfectioning. Because of the grill's intuitive proportions, they provide superb sun shading and adding them externally to the glazed areas as sun protection in the next renovation would make this entire postmodern powerhouse bioclimatically fully Jekyll-ish. *MD*

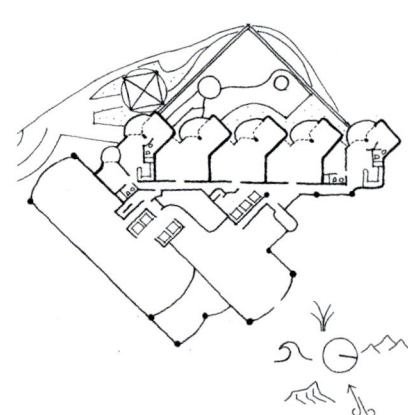

HMSA Building

818 Ke'eaumoku St
Honolulu, HI 96814
CJS
1995

The Hawaii Medical Service Association is a large private health insurance company, providing health cost coverage for thousands of residents. Its headquarters building in Honolulu covers an entire city block. It is not a tall tower, but rather a relatively low and squat structure. However, it avoids a monolithic and blocky appearance by the use of multiple patterns and surfaces, including some projecting out at 45 degree angles. Windows of varying sizes and shapes add to the variety. The overall effect is not disjointed or disorganized, but instead is appealingly eye-catching, particularly in comparison to the great majority of large Honolulu buildings whose façades are very rigidly ordered and symmetrical. The HMSA Building could be likened to a group of different structures that have been almost randomly stacked next to and on top of each other, particularly with the variations in heights. This almost playful disparity should be explored more frequently, especially in the dense and increasing urbanization of the city of Honolulu. *DB*

Photo: Martin Despang

Photo: DeSoto Brown

Contemporary

12

HoMA Parking Booth

1111 Victoria St
Honolulu, HI 96814
Tadpole Studio/Studio Kiowao
2012/2021

All indigenous cultures have embraced DIY: Do IT Yourself. In Hawaii, it is kept even more alive through the visitor industry's depictions, such as hula dance performances in grass skirts and the Polynesian Center's hale replicas. While these are often staged fantasies of the past performed in the modern city, this project revisits the DIY tradition of making from scratch in an evolved way. The domination of tourism and its facilitation of a Western lifestyle centered on hotels with air conditioned bedrooms that get periodic makeovers leaves the islands with tons of discarded beds ending up in landfills. Tadpole Studio used 48 of these bed frames – as found and collected materials – to upcycle into a new parking booth for the Honolulu Museum of Art, replacing the old 'hot hermit' booth in their parking lot. The bed frame material as well as the design service

and construction labor were donated pro bono as a design build demonstration that reactivated the tradition of reciprocal thinking – making a structure open to the elements yet providing shelter from the sun and rain. The project was nominated for a topDwell (Magazine) Vision Award. In keeping with its tradition of empowering the emerging generation of architects, Tadpole Studio passed the project in 2021 to STUDIO KI`OWAO – recent graduates of the University of Hawai'i School of Architecture and now emerging professionals – to adapt and evolve it in response to the museum's and maintenance team's evolving needs ... just as pre-contact Hawaiians periodically rethatched their hales. *DH*

Elevate ↓

Nathan and Tiffany Toothman
2015

Continuing the island's tradition of structures that are more engineered than designed, the freshest evolution of this tradition of building the most with the least comes from naval nuclear engineers Tiffany and Nathan Toothman. Their brainchild, Elevate, was a long-held dream plan made possible by a $10,000 'child support' gift from Tiffany's family, which funded the prototype built in Kailua's industrial quarry. Elevate makes only light contact with the ground, using a single central trunk that branches out above for habitation space. The

Principal 'Shrek-like' Elevate

Elevate's initial interior

Shrek-like prototype, to use Nathan's words, originally had living, vegetated fenestration. In a true Da Vinci spirit, the design has continuously further developed through several iterations, transforming its structure from wood to steel, with kinetic user participation by urban nomads (conventionally called homeless) coming back here after a day out and actively participating by pulling down their individual segments. When all neighbors do this, it naturally creates an open central communal core where they can gather around a fire and share stories of their day. After a good night's sleep in their individual segments, they pop their segments back up to restore the tree-like form – as prototypically performed by Tiffany's and Nathan's children. *MD*

Elevate evolved

Rainbow Drive-In Roof

145 C

3308 Kanaina Ave
Honolulu, HI 96815
Jim Gusukuma
2015

After all, architecture in Hawaii is about roof versus wall, and this structure does just that and does it right. Since the mid-twentieth century, Rainbow Drive-In has always fed people with good, affordable, simple local food. Jim carried that business identity into architecture with a simple, spot-on solution: one large asymmetrically cantilevering roof on three posts, all in steel. Underneath, people having parked wait in line for their loco moco and eat it at their tables, while birds and plants find shade in harmony with each other. The greatest operational damage and disruption to this idyll was caused by the Covid-19 pandemic, when all these functions had to be suspended. The new management is urged to bring back the entire idyll. Initially, the structure carried photovoltaic panels –powering the kitchen – as its primary water membrane, with open gaps like those the hale pili structures had. Replacing the panels due to aging could be seen as neo-indiginously reminiscent of the periodic replacement of the thatching of the indigenous hales after storms. Although the recent removal of the photovoltaic thatching and its replacement with cinq cladding might seem disappointing, it might just be a logical shift toward low-tech reindigenizing. Hear from Jim himself for the original. *MD*

12

Photo: Martin Despang

Hale Nohona

146 B

630 Cooke St
Honolulu, HI 96813
Bronx Pro, EAH Housing,
WCIT/Arup
2019

Since the mid-century, small studios have set a smart standard, but more recently, these rebranded microunits have largely failed in the era of the supersized. This project principally stands out as a sign of hope. Illustrations circulated early suggested a prefab, plug-in, neo-metabolist structure proposed from as far away as the Bronx in New York City, linked to philanthropist Peter Magistro. When your author came back to Honolulu after the pandemic, the project under construction had been value-engineered to use poured-in-place concrete. The building's layout features doubled up single-loaded corridor units directing southeast and northwest, arranged around an open, easy-breezy circulation core. It continued to be strikingly promising as it went up, including its detailing with arrayed photovoltaics integrated into concrete cast indents in the southern façade. Given the building's climate engineering by Arup, achieving LEED Gold is no surprise. When it undergoes its first renovation, achieving LEED Platinum in Hawaii style would be wonderful – for example, by retrofitting the conventional cushy yellow lobby to its original green by fully integrating aqua, hydro, and aeroponic systems inside and out. The current planter boxes on the second-floor terrace offer a promising start. It would be equally beneficial to optimize the building's easy breeziness by substituting the unfortunate last-minute addition of single-wall AC units. *MD*

Photo: Olivier Koning

Hau'oli Lofts
917 Hau'oli St
Honolulu, HI 96826
Tadpole Studio
2018

147 C

The small Tadpole Studio worked carefully to create this apartment building, keeping many considerations in mind. Located in a residential neighborhood consisting of a mix of private homes and low-rise walk-up apartments, the Hau'oli Lofts were specifically kept to a minimum height to fit in with the existing scale.

Just one block from King Street, a major Honolulu thoroughfare, numerous businesses, restaurants and bars are a convenient walk away for residents. Although the building is seven stories in height, it appears to be less since each of the nine units consists of two stories. This allows the luxury of 19-foot ceilings in the common living/dining space – a rarity in Honolulu apartments. The structure is intentionally situated for the tall windows of the two-story spaces to face north, which catches the prevailing trade winds that usually provide natural ventilation.

Photo: Olivier Koning

917 HAUOLI

12

Photo: Olivier Koning

This also shields these larger windows from direct sunlight, avoiding excessive interior heating. On the sunny side, less-expansive openings are shaded by small sunshades projecting out just above them. The building's roof is mostly covered by a framework holding photovoltaic panels that generate electricity and also shade this surface, again reducing interior sun-generated heat. Hau'oli Lofts was constructed using precast concrete panels that were made on the island of Oahu and trucked to the site to be assembled – another notable innovation. *DB*

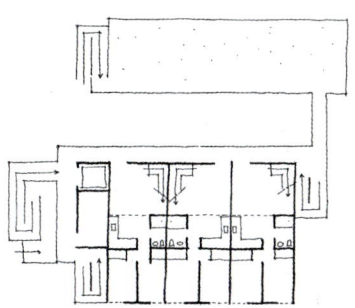

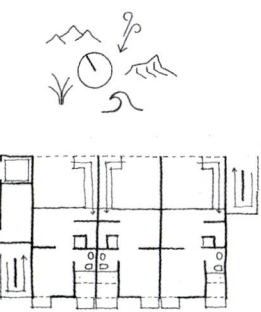

Photo: Olivier Koning

12

Hermes Royal Hawaiian Center

148 C

2201 Kalākaua Ave A204
Honolulu, HI 96815
Montes Laudano Architects
2019

It seems that a fresh, foreign perspective – in this case provided by fellow tropical Argentinian architects – was needed to appreciate and rejuvenate the forgotten jewel of the Royal Hawaiian Center (see the previous discussion of the origin of this building earlier in this book). Whenever the center is remodeled and its tenants strip away the previous makeover, there's a sense of sentimentality as its original volcrete structure is revealed. This time, there was a moment of awe when the construction scaffolding and screens came down. Freed from its former coverings, the real beauty of the bush-hammered vulcrete was recovered and celebrated, with carefully contrasting new elements inside and out. An airy yet solid timber stairway reanimates indigenous Hawaiian woodworking traditions on the inside behind a glass shopfront. Vines climbing up on cables have been added in front of the glazing and adjacent thermal-mass concrete to moderate solar gain to the southeast elevation, while horizontal slatted bronzed screens serve the same purpose on the northeast façade along Kalakaua Avenue. When dusk comes, the store is illuminated from the inside, making it shine like a lantern. The rear entrance side contextually compliments the center's interior original wood slat theme. Imagine if this approach spread to all other tenant renovations; the dream of rejuvenating the original Royal Hawaiian Centerpiece would come true. In a zeitgeist-like twist, the Cheesecake Factory façade was imposed onto the original tropical brutalist volcrete as abruptly as Ronald Reagan's handshake marking his takeover from Jimmy Carter. This retrofit feels like when Jimmy had just turned 100 and voted for Kamala Harris, extending a hand as she walks toward Donald Trump. The only optimization for this rejuvenation would be to take advantage of all the tropical exotic vegetative and Venetian-style screening and open up to the air outside in order to replace the current chilly air-conditioned atmosphere inside with the full essence of Hawaii – something Jane Birkin would like for her bags. *MD*

Photo: Martin Despang

Photo: Martin Despang

Photo: Martin Despang

Single-wall Construction Homes with Shaded, Edible, Tree-filled Front Yards

149

Everywhere
Everyone
Everytime

With Honolulu squeezed between the Ko'olau and Waianae mountain ranges and the ocean, building tall is really the only option. However, the legacy of sprawling single dwellings remains part of the city. Within that paradigm, everyone should follow Jon and Eileen's example: after buying and retaining an old single-wall construction house, they planted mango and avocado seeds from their neighbor and nurtured them over the years into a full, fruit-bearing canopy that provides natural shade. Your author initially got to know them by walking past their house. So, stop by and say hello in their inviting outdoor living room. They might as well treat you to a homemade mango drink from their outdoor kitchen – a refreshment you will never forget. Here's a lesson for city planners: require the planting of fruit-bearing shade trees by code, so our beloved urban Honolulu becomes a paradise once again. *MD*

Hales

150

Anywhere
Urban and Suburban Nomads
Anytime

Coming full circle from the first buildings in this book – a pre-contact shelter made to protect from sun and rain – today we find temporary housing popping up to accommodate those most in need as part of Hawaii's effort to address its housing challenges. From contact through annexation to statehood, the more recent the times, the less care seems to be given to sheltering/housing people – despite all the increasing talk. As Jimmy Carter himself said and demonstrated by building homes for those in need with Habitat for Humanity on the neighboring Big Island, there's often too much talking and not enough action. As a result, many people have to take matters into their own hands, creating informal settlements using whatever materials are available, reclaiming and repurposing objects in a neo-indiginous way. Although looked down on by society, through their practice these communities have become the true stewards of the land in a paradigm shift away from commercialization. Most well-intended, so-called 'transitional housing' has, however, been developed in a mostly missionary style using hermetically sealed metal containers, plastic igloos, cardboard boxes, or A-frame-like structures. These designs miss the key

understanding that here in Hawaii, buildings primarily just need a roof. Without romanticizing homelessness, the ways urban and suburban nomads build are not only more ethically and environmentally responsible, but in many ways are more creative than the means and methods by the affluent. The linear informal tent settlement pictured below is in Waimenalo along Kalanianaole Highway, near where Tom Selleck as Magnum, P.I. drove his borrowed Ferrari out of the adjacent Robin Masters Nest estate, which was razed and replaced by the beach pavilion-style mansion rebuilt by Barack Obama and friends. After processing his Vietnam PTSD, Magnum lived like an underdog in the guest house near the gate – a building preserved during the Obama construction, raising hope that it might be kept and transformed into a live-work Magnum Museum operated by the nearby suburban nomads. So, Mr. President, yes, you are cool, and in that way, reunited with your buddy Magnum, you are super cool. *MD*

Philipp and Martin, P.I. patrolling past Magnum's/Obama's nests

Reparadising

Martin Despang / DeSoto Brown

Let's look at Honolulu in connection with existing architectural discussions and criticism from the archives of ThinkTech Hawaii, with links referenced here for further learning. If your initial introduction to the built environment of Hawaii is through the authors' insights in this book, we hope our words will make you want to come to see it first hand, as that is the only true way to experience it. If you happen to be familiar with Hawaii's built environment or have helped create a part of it and feel that what you might have contributed is missing here, we hope this book might motivate and even inspire you to explore different perspectives on tropical gestalt, both now and for the future. If your inaugural work appears in this book, we hope you may be encouraged to reconnect with your professional roots – just like this encouraging example of an emerging talent from the Midwest: — 01 Here, like everywhere in the world, there is a huge amount of emerging talent to tap into: — 02

While the perception may be that the natural environment of Hawaii, including Honolulu, is protected, this is partly the result of the tourism industry being the islands' main economic force, seeking to preserve its image. But climate change is taking its toll in the form of rising sea levels, making it now impossible to walk the entire shoreline of Waikiki, with one significant break being the damaged oceanfront concrete walkway at the Halekulani Hotel. The contemporary built environment seems to have abandoned harmony with the natural environment, as the number of buildings the authors decided to share in this book has decreased in recent years. The ThinkTech Hawaii series 'Human(e) Architecture' has been broadcasting weekly for over a decade and

has had to critique current new developments in Honolulu's Kakaako district. Led by major developers Howard Hughes and Kamehameha Schools as well as others currently working in the so-called Midtown Ala Moana area and surrounding neighborhoods, these developments often fail to comply with responsible architectural principles. Most of these new towers follow a fossil formalism style, relying on oil-based, electrically-generated systems for human thermal comfort. If that power was interrupted, residents would feel as if they were being microwaved inside. This is sadly ironic given that Hawaii has such an abundance of renewable natural energy resources, and the fact that fossil fuel supplies cannot be taken for granted forever. Two of Honolulu's architecture critics, Curt Sanburn and DeSoto Brown (both contributors to this book), recall Kalakaua Avenue in mid-century Waikiki as the coolest street in the world during their childhood. This has since changed; now, it is quite the opposite. On a Lufthansa flight from Hanover to Honolulu, a flight attendant recognized author Martin's destination and asked where in Hawaii he calls home . After being told it was the island of Oahu, she was less excited, but probably hoped he would say the North Shore. When he said the South Shore, meaning the city of Honolulu and specifically the Waikiki district, she gave up on him, saying she would prefer Los Angeles. For many years, Honolulu ranked fourth among American cities in the number of skyscrapers. While other cities have since caught up, Honolulu is still the US city with the highest per capita density of skyscrapers measuring 328 feet or 30 floors. Although these structures may rise high in size, they fall

— 01

— 02

— 03

— 04

short socially, as their concentration of capital increasingly excludes many people, particularly those who used to only live here: the Hawaiians. Too many people continue to have to move away, especially to what is ironically called the 'ninth island', Las Vegas. Contemporary efforts at 'affordable' housing often feel almost cynical when compared to projects like Frank Slavsky's social senior housing or I. M. Pei's Hale Manoa for the University of Hawaii, both included in this book. Given the strong architectural heritage described here – the unique 'only in Hawaii' style – the goal should be to reconnect with both pre- and post-contact virtues, following author DeSoto Brown's 'evolution of tradition of innovation' in Hawaiian history: — 03.

King Kalakaua, the first monarch to travel the entire world, installed Thomas Edison's light bulb in his Iolani Palace before it was installed in the White House by the President of the United States. The first shipping containers to cross the Pacific Ocean in the 1950s traveled from LA to Honolulu; many decades later we now see these containers as a potential neo-indigenous building material made of cargo steel. This is because we continue to irresponsibly ship everything in – including up to 90 per cent of our food – while shipping little of significance back. Can we make use of the containers that are no longer in service? Prof. Han Slawik of the Technical University of Hanover kicked off shipping container architecture some time ago, and his teaching is relevant for Hawaii today as demonstrated by Hawaii's emerging architectural generation: — 04, 05.

'Tropiceering' is an initiative for a new way of thinking and constructing for the tropics: — 06.

This promotes promising proposals that the ThinkTech Hawaii's 'Human(e) Architecture' series concludes on in an optimistic note. Here in endless-summer Honolulu, everything could/should be easier, including ending the global crisis of the human right to shelter in one simple step: replacing all individual combustion vehicles with electric transportation in a multimodal system of tropical exotic mobility. Imagine bringing back the electric streetcars that ran for 40 years from 1901 to 1941 and adding a ski lift-style system cruising through the treetops up to the University of Hawaii at Manoa, with students finishing their homework at the last minute on the lifts: — 07.

Currently, there is not even a dedicated bicycle lane to the University of Hawaii … Speaking of bicycling, efforts to make Honolulu the pedaling capital of the world – pioneered by Jay Fidell, Ben Takayesu, and others – should continue to include perfecting it with bike cruising under a widespread shady tree canopy as bringing back the pedicabs that once cruised Waikiki. Perhaps even adding a zipline between the high-rises! The end result could be a heaven for housing: eliminating cars from the parking garages that dominate every high-rise's lower floors would free up these spaces for habitation. These spaces would provide shelter from rain and sun from above and they are even already equipped with various forms of wall screening (installed to hide the shameful view of parked cars). These screens will then protect our fellow humans from wind and sun from the side while also providing visual privacy: — 08. These stacked lanai structures could be inhabited in a nomadic way, much like the many aging, air-cooled VWs still present in Hawaii: — 09.

12

— 05   — 06   — 07   — 08   — 09

These Volkswagen Vanagon campers could be seen as James Vine's version of high-rises – made of mobile homes. Here is an 'only in Hawaii' housing trend that hopes to revive the mass planting of Hawaiian coconut palm groves to reintroduce this tropical wood for use in building, as prototyped by Keli'i Keanu and Rainer Kiessling: — 10, 11.

On a small scale, Tropiceering's 'White House' is providing promising personal shelter utilizing commercial two-by-four lumber to replace the round pole of the indigenous Hawaiian hale: — 12.

Imagining re-naturalized ways of building tall on this small mountainous island leads to a vision of a sequence of 'Primitiva' high-rise towers: — 13, 14.

Jay Fidell of ThinkTech Hawaii worries that the hundreds of artificially-clad glass high-rises in Honolulu are going to be around for centuries as social and solar-overheating eyesores. In response, the concept of 'freescaping' hopes to reintroduce the islands' tectonics of tensegrity – building through weaving, as Native Hawaiians did with their hale pili (grass houses) – rather than relying on gravity (by pouring concrete). This could be done via transcontinental technology transfer – bringing from Germany the processes and skills of making cords from basalt à la Frei Otto and his collaborator Conrad Roland, who spent his final years on Hawaii Island, home to vast landscapes of volcanic basalt. Honolulu's hermetic high-rise invasion – resembling the invasive imperialist 'Bridgehead' setting depicted by James Cameron in *Avatar: The Way of Water* – can be cured through those 'freescapes'. Larry Medlin, Otto's collaborator on the tent-like German Pavilion at Montreal's Expo '67 World's Fair, makes you imagine high-tech cables stretched between the now-stripped down high-rise scapes with food-producing hanging gardens, fishponds made of rolled-out ETFE membranes, and the easy, breezy circulation of residents within. The porous, multilayered design of this new city would result in self-shading agricultural forest stratospheres. The existing high-rises would serve as the anchors of the new cable-strung urban area. Their increased structural capacity would be activated by removing the extraneous deadloads, revealing their natural vulcrete core. Aside from the invasive cement, the other three of the four ingredients of concrete are local: water, fine sand-like gravel (from pulverized and ground basalt), and aggregate from the same basalt. Left exposed in its original form and polished to a shine, it could be contrasted with the harvested wood of locally-grown introduced or invasive species, creating a rich appearance that would be nicer than any of the imported pastiche finishes we now see on modern high-rises. This would turn those high-rises back into stacked lanai's with a primary function of sun and rain protection. The former glass curtain walls – once applied in the same way the missionaries forced Hawaiian women to wear all-covering muumuus to hide their bare skin – will be replaced by the emerging generation by water curtain walls: — 15. These will encompass functions from food-producing vegetative buffers to fish-friendly fenestrations: — 16.

The massive renovation and reuse of the former Davies Pacific Center in downtown Honolulu, designed by Steve Au, could be re-imagined by the emerging generation of students from the University of Hawaii School of Architecture and the Technical University of Munich's School of Engineering and Design's SHIFT. This could serve as a collaborative case study with owner Christine Camp, University of Hawaii 's President Wendy Hensel, and University of Hawaii's Dean of Architecture Mo Zell: — 17.

'Building as the beach, beach as the building' – sees the Travel Industry Management department educating visitors upon arrival to leave their clothing in their suitcases. Coached by the Outrigger Reef Hotel's A'O initiative, guests are

— 10

— 11

— 12

— 13

— 14

encouraged to reduce their clothing during their stay — 18.

On a visit to the freescaped urban fabric in an idealized Honolulu, with its cooperative connecting tissue, you can become a short-term inhabitant, volunteering in harmony and synergy with local residents. This non-territorialized nomadic open system sees privacy as temporary and public as permanent. As per Daniel A. Barber's *After Comfort:* 'Comfort , like capital, is unevenly distributed. Comfort however, is in short supply ... in the face of the climate crisis, we have to collectively adjust to its going away ... Architects are on the front lines – finally the avant-garde! Express and build non-carbon possibilities, to explore life after comfort.' Think of achieving the maximum in human comfort in Hawaii's incomparable climate with a dress code/address code: buildings taken back to the traditional Hawaiian attire – a pau skirt for women and a malo (loincloth) for men – offering only the essential protection. Coming full circle to the introductory Curt Sanburn as portrayed by him a decade ago in the timelessly topical: 'Rethinking Waikiki – A Model'. A perfect paradise once again, a twenty-first century version of the Eden that Hawaii has always been. A team of third-year studio students from the University of Hawaii School of Architecture, provoked by their Professor Martin Despang, became depressed when they looked too closely at Waikiki's Kuhio Avenue during a survey walk and concluded that paradise no longer existed there. So, they swam out into the waters off Waikiki to look anew at twentieth-century Waikiki and begin to re-imagine the resort district. 'How can you convert that concrete artifact into a bioclimatically natural environment that harmonizes with the elements and the lush Koolau backdrop?' Despang asked his charges. They pondered the place and spent the spring semester of 2015 reinventing Waikiki's hermetic concrete forest as a skeletal framework made of chipboard. Stripped of all walls, windows, ducts, and other accretions, the district was left with its columns and floor slabs – vernacular lanai-stacks in concrete, hotels and apartments replicated ad infinitum; the primal, easy-breezy template for Hawaiian life: shade and shelter. Green textile ribbons run up the southwest faces of the stacks, representing living plant matrices that feed and purify the air, produce food, and provide privacy. Streets with reintroduced clean streetcars are shaded by tree canopies filled with edible fruit trees. A dream [re]envisioned: Paradise, as it can be.

White House II

White House III

Rainer's Lahaina reimagined

12

Cargo courtyard cyclooned – habitated

Cargo courtyard cyclooned – cored

Cargo courtyard cyclooned Felipe-d

Cargo courtyard clustered – circulation

Cargo courtyard cyclooned – kukuied

Cargo courtyard clustered composition

Cargo courtyard cyclooned choreograped

Bamboo stacked lanai groveing

Bamboo stacked lanai testing

Primitiva I, slice of paradise

Primitiva I, Ala Moana

Primitiva I, farmers market

Primitiva I, publicized

Primitiva I, mobilized

Primitiva II, nomadic

Dustin's water curtain wall

12

Primitiva II, logic

Primitiva III, sprouting

Primitiva II, grounds

Primitivas

Tropiceering assemblage

Primitiva III, environment

Primitiva III, woven

Kendal's fishy fenestration

Freescaping connecting tissued

Freescaping contemplated

Freescaping bottom-uped

Freescaping rewildered

Freescaping labed

Water curtain walls performing

Waikiki Reparadised

Photo: Ren Shiroma

Waikiki stacked lanai-ing

Rethinking Waikiki – A Model

Beach as Building/Building as Beach

A Oahu

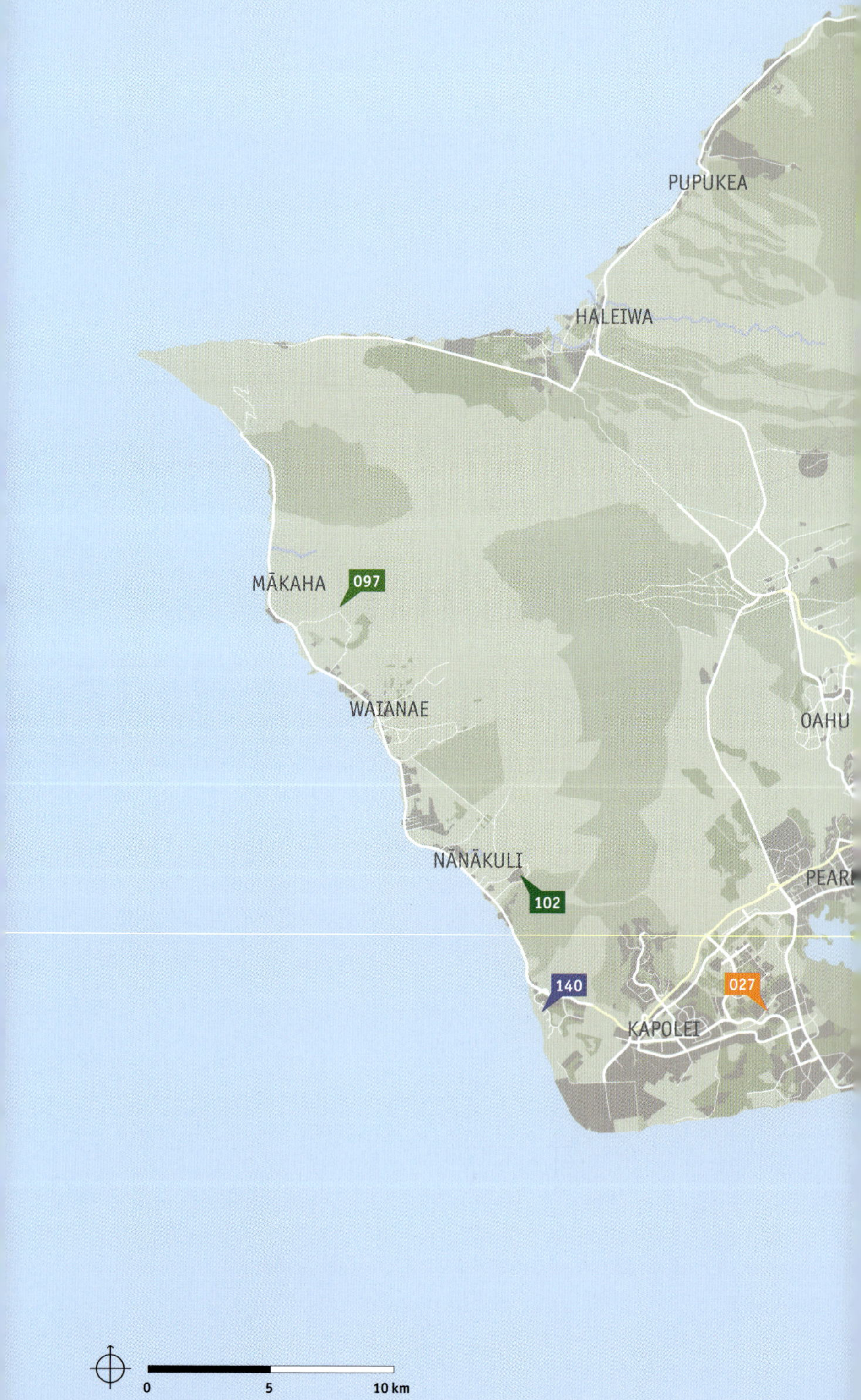

PUPUKEA

HALEIWA

MĀKAHA 097

WAIANAE

OAHU

NĀNĀKULI

PEAR

102

140

027

KAPOLEI

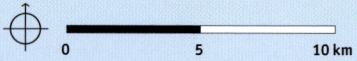

0   5   10 km

AHUKU

LAIE

KAAAWA

K a n e o h e   B a y

072

101

054

KANEOHE

049

KAILUA

132

055

071

133

117

119

iel K. Inouye
ernational
Airport

045

B

HONOLULU

C

WAIMANALO

M ā m a l a   B a y

B

008
065
Lunalilo Fwy
Kam Hwy
N King St
Kalihi St
N Nimitz Hwy
120
Kapālama Canal
Dillingham Blvd
KALIHI-
PALAMA
043
Sand Island Pkwy
SAND ISLAND

0   0.5   1 km

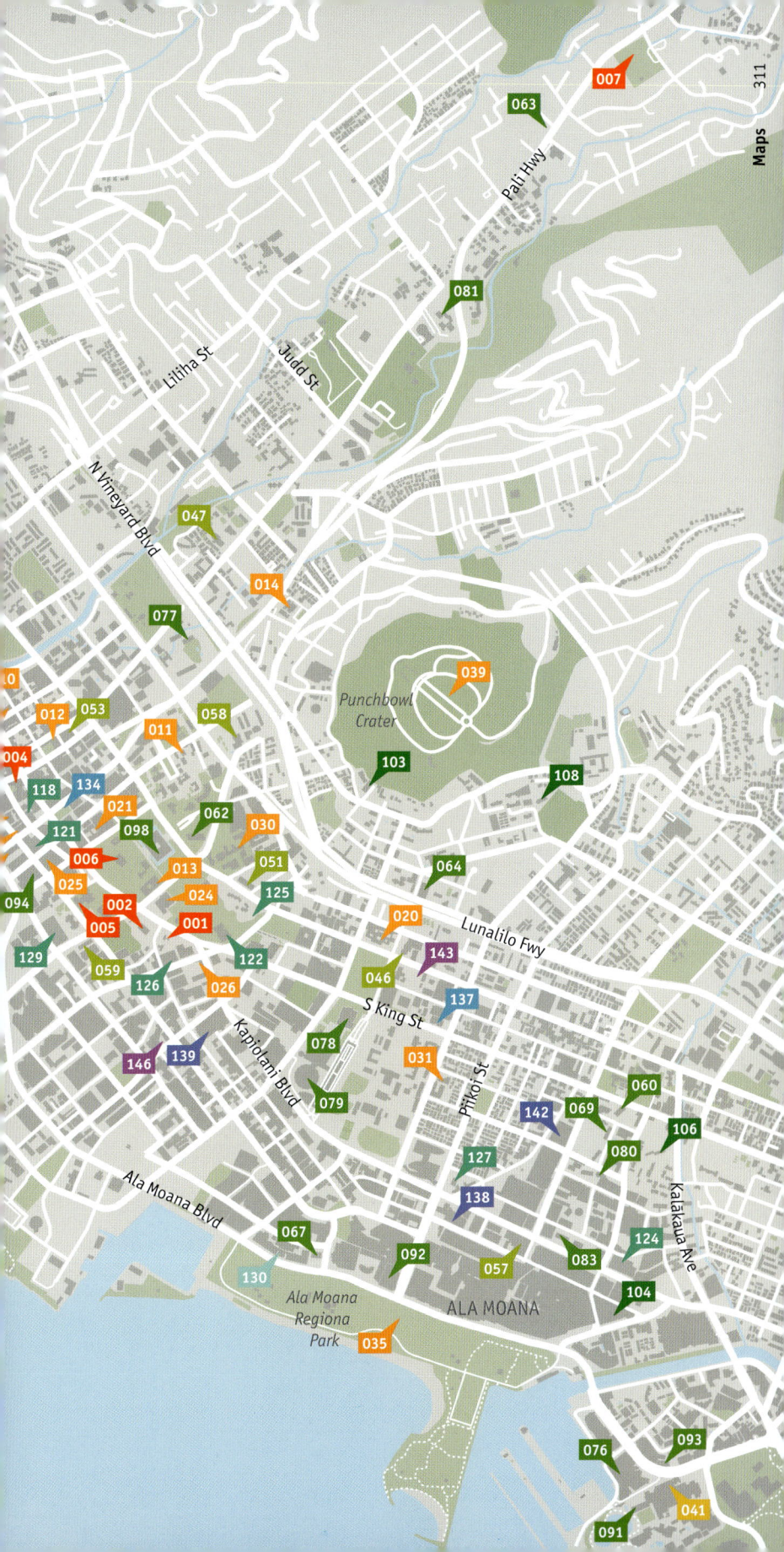

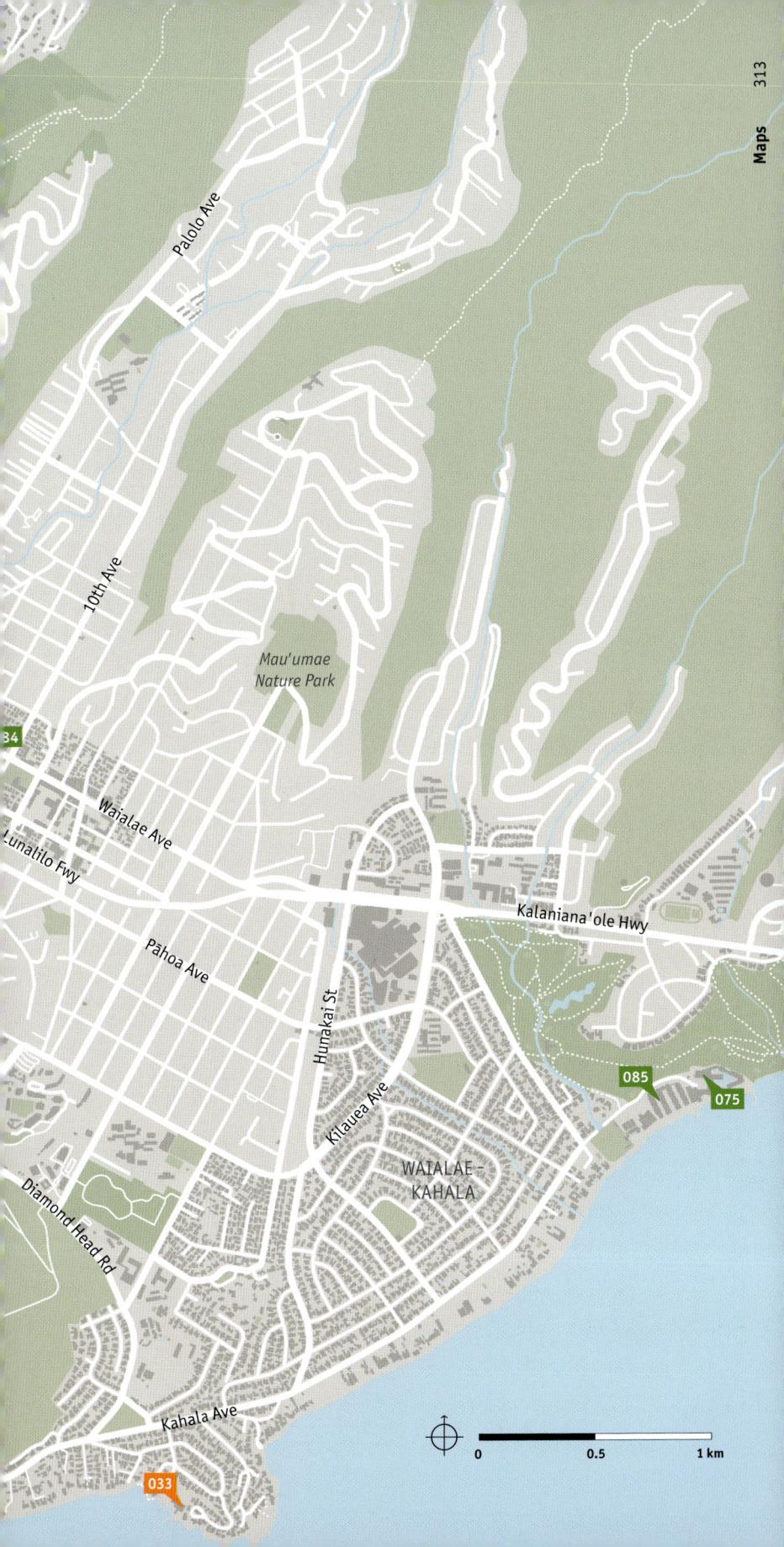

Video Archive

**Bishop Museum &
Bishop Hall**
Page 34

**Aloha
Tower**
Page 50

**Aloha
Tower**
Page 50

**Halekulani
Hotel**
Page 56

**War Memorial
Natatorium**
Page 62

**Canlis
Restaurant**
Page 84

**Waikikian
Hotel**
Page 85

**International
Market Place**
Page 86

**La Mariana
Sailing Club**
Page 88

**Honolulu Zoo
Entry**
Page 89

**Liljestrand
Residence**
Page 98

**First United
Methodist**
Page 100

Breakers Hotel
Page 102

Breakers Hotel
Page 102

Breakers Hotel
Page 102

Breakers Hotel
Page 102

Princess Kaiulani Hotel
Page 108

Board of Water Supply
Page 110

Ala Moana Building
Page 116

Ala Moana Building
Page 116

**Aliiaimoku Hale, the
Territorial Highways
Department Building**
Page 122

**King
Center**
Page 128

**Waikiki Shore
Condominiums**
Page 129

**Hawaii State
Department of Health**
Page 130

**Hawaii State
Department of Health**
Page 130

**Bishop Museum Kilolani
Plaentarium**
Page 134

**Waikiki Grand
Hotel**
Page 134

**Waikiki Grand
Hotel**
Page 134

IBM Building
Page 136

Hale Manoa
Page 146

**Liona
Apartments**
Page 148

**Waikiki Circle
Hotel**
Page 150

**USS Arizona Memorial
of the Pacific**
Page 151

Varsity Building
Page 156

Kahala Hilton
Page 157

Kahala Hilton
Page 157

Kahala Hilton
Page 157

Kahala Hilton
Page 157

Ilikai Hotel
Page 159

Queen Emma Gardens
Page 160

Queen Emma Gardens
Page 160

Queen Emma Gardens
Page 160

**Blaisdell Concert Hall,
Exhibition Hall**
Page 163

**Blaisdell Center
Arena**
Page 164

**Pagoda
Restaurant**
Page 168

**Punahou Circle
Apartments**
Page 170

**C. S. Wo
Building**
Page 172

**Kaimuki
Jade**
Page 172

**Kahala Beach
Apartments**
Page 178

**Kahala Beach
Apartments**
Page 178

**Seaside
Hotel**
Page 181

Bank of Hawaii
Page 182

Lagoon Tower
Page 189

1350 Ala Moana
Page 193

Harbor Square
Page 195

Harbor Square
Page 195

Outrigger Hotels
Page 197

Outrigger Hotels
Page 197

Outrigger Hotels
Page 197

Makaha Valley Towers
Page 201

Hawaii State Capitol
Page 203

Ka Hale Moi
Page 212

Makua Alii
Page 216

**Hotel
La Croix**
Page 222

**Hyatt Regency Waikiki
Beach Resort and Spa**
Page 225

**Hyatt Regency Waikiki
Beach Resort and Spa**
Page 225

Island Colony Hotel
Page 226

Waikiki Townhouse
Page 227

Franklin Towers
Page 228

**Financial Plaza of
the Pacific**
Page 232

**Financial Plaza of
the Pacific**
Page 232

Honolulu Airport
Page 234

Honolulu Airport
Page 234

Pacific Davies Center
Page 236

Pacific Davies Center
Page 236

**Frank Fasi
Municipal Building**
Page 238

**Hale Koa
Hotel**
Page 246

**Pan Am
Building**
Page 247

Honolulu Municipal Parking
Page 248

Kawaiahao Plaza
Page 250

615 Piikoi
Page 251

Royal Hawaiian Center
Page 252

Ward Warehouse
Page 256

Ward Warehouse
Page 256

Art Department Building
Page 258

Treehouse
Page 259

Treehouse
Page 259

Tamarind Square
Page 266

Halekulani Hotel
Page 267

Halekulani Hotel
Page 267

Halekulani Hotel
Page 267

Halekulani Hotel
Page 267

Halekulani Hotel
Page 267

Halekulani Hotel
Page 267

Halekulani Hotel
Page 267

Halekulani Hotel
Page 267

Uraku Tower
Page 274

Ihilani
Page 278

Ihilani
Page 278

Elevate
Page 285

Elevate
Page 285

Elevate
Page 285

Rainbow Drive-In Roof
Page 287

Hale Nohona
Page 288

**Hau'oli
Lofts**
Page 289

**Hermes Royal
Hawaiian Center**
Page 293

**Single-wall
Construction Homes
with Shaded, Edible,
Tree-filled Front Yards**
Page 294

Hales
Page 295

... and hundreds more:
Human(e) Architecture

Ala Wai Canal with Waikiki in its background

Index of Architects

Sorted by project number

Index of Buildings

Sorted by project number

Contributors (Authors)

Martin Despang *MD*

Climate and culture became the basis for Martin's co-coaching (SoA architecture and TIM hospitality) at the University of Hawaii at Manoa in Honolulu, based on critical practice (with his family firm Despang Architekten in Germany) and practical critique (as a weekly video journalist with ThinkTech Hawaii). He was born and raised in moderately-tempered Hanover, Germany, where he first studied architecture, followed by the more extreme-tempered prairie of the USA at the University of Nebraska, which then invited him back to teach. After this he continued to the hot arid desert at the University of Arizona and finally to the tropics at the University of Hawaii. He dedicates his parts of this book to his family in Germany for allowing him to spend so much time halfway around the world, particularly his wife Susanne. Ultimately, Martin thanks fellow author Don Hibbard for the lingual levelling assistance and censorial civilizing of his writings here in English (except this sentence :)).

DeSoto Brown *DB*

A lifetime resident of Honolulu since his birth there, DeSoto's lifetime has covered the city's growth from containing only two structures of almost 10 stories in height to today's total of over 400 high-rise towers. Always fascinated by history and feeling a need to preserve objects of the past, he's assembled a large collection of Hawaii-related paper ephemera mostly connected to advertising and promotion for tourism. He's worked at the Bernice P. Bishop Museum in Honolulu for over 40 years in its Archives and Library. Among his publications as a sole author or contributor are *Hawaii Recalls* (1982), *Aloha Waikiki* (1985), *Hawaii Goes To War* (1989), *Finding Paradise* (2002), *The Art of the Aloha Shirt* (2002), *Hawaii At Play* (2003), *Surfing: Images from Bishop Museum Archives* (2006), and *Art Deco in Hawaii* (2014).

Photo: Olay's Thai Lao Cuisine

Publisher Philipp Meuser with some of your contributors

William Chapman *WC*

William Chapman is the former Dean of the School of Architecture at the University of Hawaii at Manoa (UHM). Educated at Columbia (M. S. in Historic Preservation) and at Oxford University (D. Phil. in Anthropology), Chapman is a frequent contributor to UNESCO and ICOMOS projects as well as serving as reviewer for numerous World Heritage nominations. He is a member of the ICOMOS History and Theory Committee, the Historic Town Committee, and the Vernacular Architecture Committee. His latest publication is *Architectural Conservation in Australia, New Zealand and the Pacific Islands* (Routledge 2024). A four-time Fulbright scholar (Italy, Cambodia, and twice in Thailand), Chapman previously served as the Chair of the Department of American Studies and is the Director of the Graduate Certificate Program in Historic Preservation at UHM.

Don Hibbard *DH*

After toiling for 24 years in the Hawaii State Historic Preservation Office, first as an architectural historian and then as division administrator, he entered the private sector and for the past 20-plus years has provided heritage specialist services to various architectural firms, governmental agencies, and individuals in Hawaii. In addition, he has taught courses in historic preservation and architectural history at the University of Hawaii and Hawaii Pacific University. Two of his books, *The View from Diamond Head* (Honolulu: Editions Limited, 1986) and *Designing Paradise* (New York: Princeton Architectural Press, 2006), consider the development of Hawaii's visitor industry and architecture as a conveyor of history and a sense of place. Other books include *Hart Wood, Architectural Regionalism in Hawaii* (2010) and *Buildings of Hawaii* (2011).

Bundit Kanisthakhon *BK*

Bundit Kanisthakhon is an architect, educator, and founder of Tadpole Studio, a multidisciplinary design firm based in Honolulu, Hawaii, and Bangkok, Thailand. He serves as an Associate Professor at the University of Hawaii at Manoa's School of Architecture, where he brings real-world experience into the academic setting. Kanisthakhon's work emphasizes simplicity, climate responsiveness, and community integration. His ongoing research focuses on how architects can collaborate effectively with other disciplines to create more holistic and responsive designs. His design philosophy embraces continuous learning and adaptability, traits he associates with a 'tadpole' mindset – always curious and open to growth.

Richard Lowe

Richard Lowe (1928–2024) was a distinguished urban planner and real estate professional whose career bridged practice and education. He earned his Masters in City Planning from the Massachusetts Institute of Technology, studying under the influential urban theorist Kevin Lynch. In the 1960s, Lowe moved to Hawaii to contribute to Honolulu's Civic Center Plan with John Carl Warnecke and Associates, later serving as a lead planner for the Victoria Ward Estate (shown below). In his later years, Lowe volunteered at the University of Hawaii at Manoa's School of Architecture, where his mentorship and encouragement were valued by students and colleagues alike. Even in his elder years, Richard's magnificent skill on the piano added another dimension to his interactions with both friends and strangers.

Ronald Lindgren

Ronald Lindgren (1941–2024), with a Masters in Architecture from the Massachusetts Institute of Technology, served as a partner in the California architectural firm of Killingsworth, Stricker, Lindgren, Wilson & Associates. This company's first Hawaii commission was the famous Kahala Hilton Hotel (described in this book), which led to their eventual specialization in the field of resort design. Ron was the lead architect for the redevelopment of Waikiki's Halekulani Hotel (also covered in this volume), where he skillfully retained the complex's original 1930s main building while surrounding it with complimentary modern structures. His success with this project has made the Halekulani a continued favorite for both visitors and local residents who recognize its beauty. In his retirement, Ron elegantly and eloquently shared his explanations and critiques of a variety of Hawaii buildings in ThinkTech Hawaii shows as well as coaching Hawaii's emerging architectural generation from his modest duplex home in Long Beach, California. Always both humble and honest in his self-assessments, Ron gave personal insight into how various projects had been designed, along with astonishing descriptions of his experiences in the US Army during the Vietnam War in the 1960s. The 30-plus hours of Think Tech Hawaii's 'human(e) architecture' program continue to make it possible to listen to and learn from Ron and those who use that resource know they are fortunate to do so.

Jay Fidell

Through his online platform ThinkTech Hawaii, Jay Fidell has provided the 30-minute architectural YouTube programs that can be accessed by clicking the QR codes found throughout this book. Jay came to Honolulu in the mid-1960s as a US Coast Guard lawyer, depositing his first paycheck at the Bank of Hawaii branch located in the Ala Moana Building (reviewed in this book) where he fell in love with the teller who helped him, Sharon. Soon, together with Jay's lawyer colleague Carol Mon Lee, they felt that Hawaii needed more critical media discourse, so Jay began a radio broadcast from his law firm's office in the Davies Pacific Center (also reviewed in this book). This evolved into online video programming, which were aired from downtown Honolulu tropical brutalist buildings. ThinkTech is today the most uncompromisable media source in Hawaii. Jay believes that a well urban planned and built environment is indispensable for a happy and healthy Hawaii, which has led to him facilitating programs with several of the authors of this book for the last decade.

Curt Sanburn *CS*
Raised in Honolulu, Curt attended Iolani School and graduated from Yale University. Being the son of a real estate developer led to his awareness of the need to protect the beauty of his home islands, and then in turn to his distinguished standing as Hawaii's most activist journalist. Living in San Francisco for some years, the distance from his hometown of Honolulu sharpened his view, tongue, and pen to bravely report on the good and bad in Hawaii, consistently recommending turning the bad back to good. His media outlets include *Honolulu Weekly* and *Civil Beat,* along with *LIFE, Gentlemen's Quarterly, Harper's Bazaar,* and *Hana Hou* magazines.

Olivier Koning
Freelance photographer Olivier Koning is a long-time Hawaii resident and a graduate of the University of Hawaii. He spent 10 years with the Hawaii-based architectural firm Wimberly Allison Tong & Goo as in-house photographer, which enabled him to provide the photos in this book that are credited 'WATG', in addition to the numerous photos he took for this book.

Andrea Brezzi
Andrea Brizzi was born in Firenze, Italy, where he studied architecture. (Only he says) he did not learn much. Andrea has been working as an architectural photographer since the days of large-format film. He is passionate about his craft; the best job in the world. He traveled plenty and lived in a few places. After over two decades in Hawaii, he now lives in Brooklyn and the Hudson Valley. When not taking pictures, he tends to his bees.

Kikuyo Hibbard, Philipp Meuser, Rima Soueid and Lenny Despang
Drone operators and photo scavenger hunters who created and shared the aerial views printed in this book.

Rainer Kiessling *RK*
Rainer graduated from the University of Hawaii at Manoa School of Architecture with a Doctor of Architecture degree. His dissertation explored utilizing locally-grown timber as a sustainable building material here in Hawaii and utilized several projects in this book as inspiring case studies. After his graduation, Rainer – besides working full time in an architectural firm – took on the complex responsibility of creating the layout of this book with its multiple authors and diverse sources of illustrations, for which he has earned the gratitude of all involved.

Helena Kuntz Moura

Helena Kuntz Moura, architect and UH SoA graduate student, practices and resides on Oahu, Hawaii, but is originally from Brazil. Passionate about tropical architecture, she has hand-drawn her explorations and designs from around the world. Her contributions to this guide are the plan illustrations through which the essence of each building is revealed. It's hoped that these will show readers the intention, functionality, and creativity behind each project, created by retracing and reconstructing from imagination to aspiration.

Martin Anzellini Garcia-Reyes

Martin's work in architecture is at the crossroads between critical practice, applied research, and urban management. As a native of Colombia, Martin served as an architectural consultant for the Oscar-winning 2021 Disney animated film *Encanto,* which was set in his home country. He advised regarding the family's home whose magical qualities enhance the plot, and which was recreated as a toy for children internationally. Martin appears on many TTH H(e)A shows, teaches in UH's Travel Industry Management program, and works at the Hawaii Community Development Authority.

Ulf Meyer

Ulf selflessly encouraged the creation of this guidebook with his expert raw modeling.

Susanne Despang

With a German diploma and Masters Degree equivalent in Tourism – Management, Susanne is the ThinkTech Hawaii human(e) architecture show's 'exotic escapism expert'. With her

information and inspiration, she inspired the hospitality episodes particularly about the places she has called home since her youth: her native Bavaria (Germany), Portugal, and Hawaii; and based upon case studies covered in this book.

'Treetecture Arch 692' classes

This graduate elective class at the University of Hawaii continually explored ways to reconnect/return to the climate and culture compatibility of the built environment, which resulted in the Tropiceering initiative, this book somewhat being it's manifesto and foundation/orientation for past and future classes. The spring sessions of 2023 and 2023 were dedicated to assistance with the research, photography, and graphics for this book. Unlike the DOM Hanover guide, for which students served as final authors, in this case your authors were informed, inspired, and motivated by this intergenerational academic discourse around this professional publication. We sincerely thank each and everyone listed here.

2024 participants:

Jessica Aellen (*JA*), Jacob Boles (*JB*), Nicole Gdula (*NG*), Drew Harris (*DHa*) Karolyn Jones (*KJ*), Bhargav Kaiushik (*BK*), Rainer Kiessling (*RK*), Raymond Lei (*RL*), Daniel Luna (*DL*), Hana Matsunaga (*HM*), Thanh Nguyen (*TN*), Janice Sonson (*JS*), Austin Torralba (*AT*), Hanna Angelica Valencia (*HV*) Valencia, Chunya Wu (*CW*), Melissa Yoo (*MY*), Lijin Zhao (*LZ*).

2023 participants:

Nicole Bowman (*NB*), Aidan Brown (*AB*), Mickey Chacon (*MC*), Jannah Lyn Dela Cruz (*JD*), Tyler Dinnocenti (*TD*), Felix Gottdiener (*FG*), Riza Lara (*RL*), Yin-Shan Lin (*YI*), Helena Moura (*HM*), Diana Rogava (*DR*).

The Publisher's Participation:

At Pagoda with Don's book

At Tropiceering

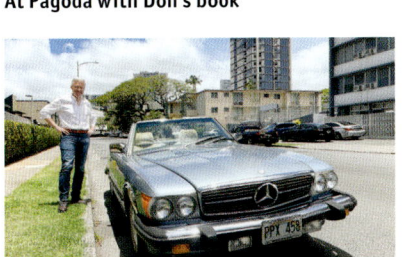

At The Rock's roots

At the White House I

At Obama's Magnum's

At indiginous

At Ossipoff's IBM

At 'whats new'

At work at Bishop Museum

Makai with artificial and natural mauka

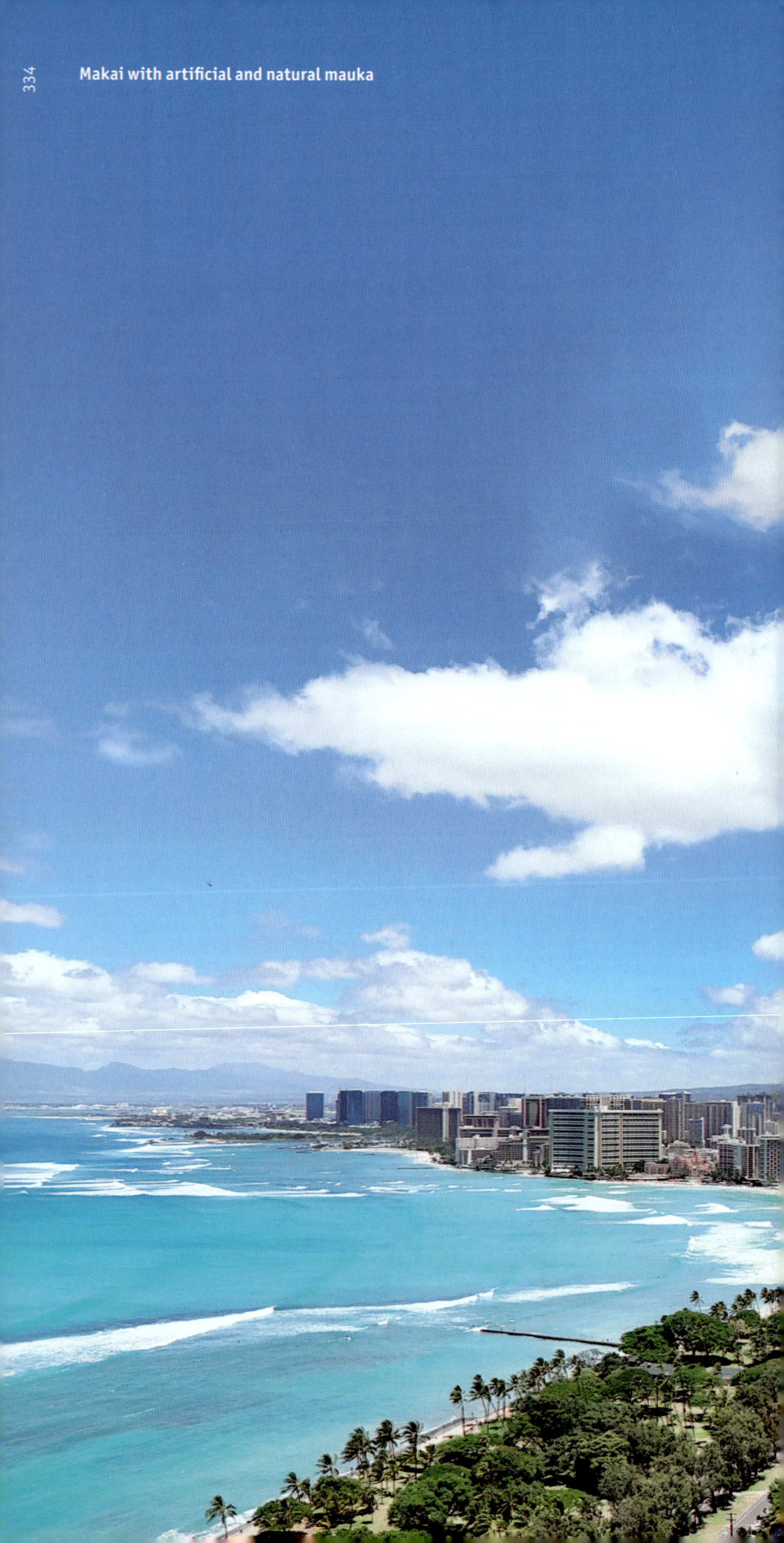

The *Deutsche Nationalbibliothek* lists this publication in the *Deutsche National-bibliografie*; detailed bibliographic data are available at *http://dnb.d-nb.de*

ISBN 978-3-86922-845-7

DOM publishers

© 2026 by DOM publishers, Berlin/Germany
www.dom-publishers.com

In preparing this volume, the authors have prioritized clarity and consistency in the presentation of place names. To enhance readability and navigability, especially for an international audience, the use of diacritics and fully localized spellings has been limited. This decision does not reflect a disregard for local linguistic conventions. The authors and the publishers acknowledge the significance of native orthographies and welcome corrections and suggestions from readers familiar with local forms.

Proofreading
Sandie Kestell

Maps
Ee Dong Chen

Design
Rainer Kiessling

Final Artwork
Masako Tomokiyo

Printing
Tiger Printing (Hong Kong) Co., Ltd.
www.tigerprinting.hk

Institutions/Inspirations your authors associated with: